The
World's
Greatest
Idea

John Farndon is the author of many books on contemporary issues, including *China Rises* and *India Booms* (Virgin), and *Bird Flu* and *Iran* in the *Everything You Need to Know* series (Icon). He also writes widely for children, including the best-selling *Do Not Open* (Dorling Kindersley), and has been shortlisted four times for the Junior Science Book Prize.

He is also the author of *Do You Think You're Clever? The Oxford and Cambridge Questions*, also published by Icon Books.

www.john-farndon-books.co.uk

The
World's
Greatest
Idea

THE FIFTY GREATEST
IDEAS THAT HAVE
CHANGED
HUMANITY

JOHN FARNDON

ICON BOOKS

First published in the UK in 2010 by Icon Books

This edition published in the UK in 2011 by
Icon Books Ltd, Omnibus Business Centre,
39–41 North Road, London N7 9DP
email: info@iconbooks.com
www.iconbooks.com

Sold in the UK, Europe and Asia
by Faber & Faber Ltd, Bloomsbury House,
74–77 Great Russell Street, London WC1B 3DA
or their agents

Distributed in the UK, Europe and Asia
by Grantham Book Services,
Trent Road, Grantham NG31 7XQ

Distributed in Australia and New Zealand
by Allen & Unwin Pty Ltd,
PO Box 8500, 83 Alexander Street,
Crows Nest, NSW 2065

Distributed in Canada
by Publishers Group Canada,
76 Stafford Street, Unit 300
Toronto, Ontario M6J 2S1

ISBN: 978-184831-245-6

Typesetting in Plantin Light by Marie Doherty

Printed and bound by the UK by Clays Ltd, St Ives plc

Introduction

When the notion of writing a book entitled *The World's Greatest Idea* was first suggested to me, my first reaction was that it was absurd. How can ideas as profound and complex as justice or logic or Marxism be reduced to a simple popularity contest? And what's meant by greatest, anyway? Is the greatest idea the one that brought humanity the most benefit or the one that had the most impact? How can you say which is better – coffee or capitalism, marriage or monotheism? The whole concept is of course nonsensical – and so fatally flawed with contradictions that it is doomed to failure. And yet …

There's something rather beguiling about the notion of *The World's Greatest Idea*, something that slyly seduces you into thinking about it before you can stop yourself and say, 'Hold on; this is ridiculous!' So this book is about yielding to that temptation. And if you do yield, I hope you will find, as I did, that it is actually a thoroughly fascinating game.

Ideas matter. They shape our experience of the world. They bring us good things and bad. They alter our lives for better or worse. They change our beliefs and our hopes for the future. Ideas such as fire, metals and pottery dramatically changed how we live. Democracy and capitalism established fundamental principles underpinning the way society is run. Ideas such as the abolition of slavery and feminism are vital attempts to right a wrong. Each one of these ideas is important and has had a huge impact on humanity, whether good or ill.

That makes them worth thinking about, and that's at the heart of my aim in writing this book – to provoke thought. In writing each of the entries, I haven't simply argued the case for it being a great idea. Indeed, it won't always be obvious whether I personally think it's a great idea or not. Instead, what I've done, I hope, is provide food for thought, with some of the background to the idea and its impact on the world as well as some of the arguments for and against.

There are lots of footnotes (some quite long), not because this an academic treatise in which every statement needs careful qualification or reference, but because often it can be a little aside, an extra snippet of information, that actually triggers ideas. This is not a book full of answers, nor even opinions; it is simply intended to spark ideas and give readers enough material to get them thinking about what really matters – which ideas we really need and which we can do without.

There is another purpose, too, which is to simply revel in humanity's ingenuity – to appreciate the wealth of brilliant ideas that people have had through the ages. There are so many things we take for granted – from tea and refrigeration to logic and romance – that someone, somewhere actually introduced to the world. And it's worth raising a glass to them – and therein lies another great idea.

For similar reasons, the range of ideas in this book is entirely arbitrary. There is no attempt to rigidly define what is meant by a 'great' idea or even an 'idea'. It was compiled entirely on the basis of a straw poll among a panel of experts, each of whom had their own reasons for their choice. The result is extraordinarily eclectic, and we have ideas both as basic as sewerage and as high-flown as quantum theory.

My own initial view when writing this book was that a great idea would be one that changed the world for the better. But as I came to explore the ideas, I realised that very few ideas are unmixed blessings, and even ideas I think are damaging are often worth giving some time to.

After the list compiled by the panel and myself was finalised, we set up a website and invited visitors to the site to vote for which idea they thought was greatest. The entries in this book are ordered to reflect the results of that poll. The online voters put the Internet top which is quite extraordinary. The Internet is indeed an amazing an idea, and has had a huge impact on the way we communicate in the brief time it's been around. But is it really the greatest idea ever? Is it really greater than logic or democracy or the abolition of slavery? Or does it rather reflect the demographic of the voters who put contraception third and marriage bottom?

What do you think?

To get you thinking, here's a selection of comments from contributors to the website:

> *'To pick an easy target, monotheism is listed as one of the top fifty. For all their noble beliefs and ideals, it is easy to argue that different monotheistic beliefs' inability to accept one another have caused more grief and suffering than any other single thing in history and, quite possibly, still do. Somehow we would like to feel a great idea should be positive, but quite a number are very double-edged. Ironically, however much suffering it has caused, it would be hard to find an idea that has had a greater impact than monotheism, so if impact is a measure of greatness then it deserves a far better vote, even though many could argue that the impact has far greater negative value than positive.'* David Macdonald

'*Just because an idea hasn't yet become reality, it doesn't mean it can't be great. Time travel and teleportation seem great ideas – which if ever realized would seem sensational. And how about ideas for a better world? Thomas More's* Utopia, *Einstein's vision of a world government, Martin Luther King's dream? And maybe even Marxism, since it has never been realized in the way Marx envisaged. No, they've never happened, and may never do, but they remind us that great ideas can give us a vision of a better world, better things, and give us goals to aim for, whether it's how to make a self-cleaning house or how to bring world peace.*' John

'*Surely the invention of anaesthetic would have to be one of the greatest ideas ever? Can you imagine life beforehand, when even the most minor surgery or dental procedure could be agonising?*' Susan

'*It's so obvious to me what the world's greatest idea was. It's amazing that nobody has put it forward yet. If you're look-ing at ideas that completely changed the world and that we couldn't live without and which everyone uses every day, then it's got to be.....Mathematics.*' Geoff H

'*Psychoanalysis should definitely be on the list. Think of how much it's changed the way we perceive ourselves!*' Helena H

'*Hope isn't remotely wishy-washy. You could argue that it's not exactly an idea, but the conceptualisation of it is. And where would we be without aspiration and vision? None of these other things would be possible if we didn't have the possibility of imagining change. We'd still be fighting each other for the best cave.'* Sarah W

'I think the greatest idea was time telling, or time measurement. Humans evolved a "time consciousness" that is far superior to that of other mammals. We have superior memories, and we also have superior foresight. Somewhere along the line, a human must have decided that dividing time into intervals, and measuring or marking these intervals in some way, would be useful. Indeed, if you combine time measurement with foresight (which is influenced by memory), you get planning.' Anon.

'Most definitely the Holodeck. Depending upon your relationship with the space/time continuum, it may be that the Holodeck has yet to BE invented. However so, placing this virtual technicality aside I'd say this magnificent potentiality is by far the greatest idea. In fact, I had tea with Philip Ball on the Holodeck just this morning!' Amy

'As much as it pains me to say this, my vote went to mass production. It completely changed the shape of society and how we function in our day to day lives. I wouldn't say it's been entirely positive idea, but does the greatest idea of all time have to be?' Currie

'Mass production? But surely the greatest idea has to be something that has facilitated humanity's progression? Mass production is responsible for making and continuing

to keep over half the world's population below the poverty line. Also why did monotheism make it, but Hinduism didn't? Surely it should just be religion?' NK

The Ideas

#50 Marriage

'Marriage is a great institution,' said Groucho Marx, 'But who wants to live in an institution?' Groucho was wrong, of course. Nearly 100 million people around the world volunteer to be incarcerated into the marital asylum every year. In some countries, the popularity of marriage is dropping slightly. In the UK, for instance, the number of single adults exceeded the number of married adults for the first time in 2007, but more than a third of singles had been married previously (divorcees and widows). But for most people, everywhere in the world, marriage is still the normal experience.

A hundred years or so ago, many anthropologists believed that marriage was quite a new thing. They believed that in prehistoric times sexual relations were a free-for-all, and some even argued that this was the 'natural' way for men and women to behave. Who knows if this was some kind of wish-fulfilment, but there is actually no evidence to suggest that this was so at all. Marriage is the norm in all recorded history, and so it seems to be in most 'primitive' tribes around the world. Of course, marriage takes different forms, but it always involves a publicly recognised union between a couple who undertake to live together for life.

Anthropologists have various explanations as to why people would marry even in the simplest of societies, but there are several powerful benefits. First of all, it's good for the stability of society if people get married. If people remain unattached, there's potential for at least a lot of stress, if not conflict, as people continually compete for sexual partners. Once two people are married, it's clear they have made their choice and other single people must look elsewhere. That doesn't prevent married couples 'having a fling', of course, but at least it sends a clear message. It also makes it clear who is responsible for looking after any children and, in theory, assures women that the burden is going to be shared.

Then there are also powerful personal reasons. People want to make a choice and demonstrate their commitment to one person. Lifelong pair bonding is common in many animal species and it seems that this is how we humans like it, too. We want to have the kind of emotional bond that marriage provides and also the close companionship through life. Of course we can survive by ourselves, but the boon of a constant partner to share both troubles and joys is something few people would want to miss out on. The statistics in modern society are telling. Single people suffer far more from illness, far more from depression, and die younger than married people. Marriage is not a guarantee against loneliness but it certainly helps.

Of course, our perception of what marriage means has been hugely coloured by history. As soon as people began to live in settled societies, it became entangled in legalities. To avoid disputes over property ownership, for instance, it was vital that it was clear who the legitimate offspring were. Marriage provided a simple framework for legitimacy. For the same reason, adultery, especially by a woman, became deeply problematic, and often criminalised. Gradually, as society became more and more complex, marriage gathered an increasing burden of problems, tied mostly to the protection of property. Among the upper classes in particular, the high stakes involved in property meant that in many cases couples couldn't be free to make their own romantic choice, but marriages had to be arranged for them, along with very elaborate financial agreements. The result is that marriage, for many people, became a business deal rather than a personal and emotional choice.[1]

People used to modern Western attitudes to marriage as, essentially, a romantic union would be surprised by how pragmatic couples were about this. For a woman, marriage provided security and the reassurance that she and her children were going to be recognised and provided for. For a man, it was a reassurance that any children were his own, and also offered the comfort of a companion and helpmeet to look after the house. It didn't necessarily matter that your spouse wasn't the target of your romantic dreams. Countless men had mistresses and concubines to satisfy that side of their nature, without necessarily leading to the divorce courts. It was more of a problem for women, of course, because extra-marital relations could muddy the inheritance waters. Women became increasingly disadvantaged as the need to preserve legitimacy

---

[1] In Christian society, the whole pattern of marriage is very particular. In the early Christian era, marriage was of surprisingly little interest to the Church. St Paul's writings show that it was all thought rather pointless anyway, since the end of the world was nigh and it was better to spend the time preparing for the end than bringing children into the world. That changed in the Middle Ages when the Church began to become legally involved in the marriage process. In the thirteenth century, too, marriage became a sacrament, a holy bond equivalent to committing yourself to Christ. Instead of just agreeing to live with your spouse and raise a family together, you were committing your souls. This dovetailed very neatly into the romantic ideal of marriage, which is perhaps why many people today, whether they are believers or not, still choose a Church wedding.

placed more and more control in the man's hands, eventually often making even the woman herself his property.

All of this, though, was essentially a problem for the moneyed classes. Among poorer people in the West, property wasn't such an issue. Men and women married, or had their marriages arranged for them, and generally lived well together. The husband husbanded the land and their meagre resources outside the house; the housewife looked after things in the house, and brought up the children. It was, on the whole, companionable and practical.[2] There were surely many problems and times of stress, but people rarely divorced over romantic difficulties; couples were too dependent on each other and the stakes were far too high.

The Enlightenment, however, saw attitudes and circumstances beginning to change. Among the upper classes in England, for instance, young people began to want to make their own choices in marriage and to look at it more as a romantic attachment than a business partnership. This, ironically, was what made the actual wedding a far more formal, legalistic event. In former times, a word and exchange of hands before witnesses was enough to make a marriage. But in 1753, Lord Hardwicke was persuaded to bring in a marriage law because increasing numbers of couples were running off by themselves to get married without their families knowing.

---

[2] Just how 'pragmatic' this could be is indicated by the surprisingly common practice in some countries of leasing out or selling your spouse. The very idea seems shocking today, but wife sales, such as that portrayed in Thomas Hardy's *The Mayor of Casterbridge*, were not that uncommon. It was a simple way of moving on, since marriages were often business arrangements. But by Hardy's time, the practice was rare.

Hardwicke's law meant that for the first time, people were obliged to get married in church.[3] If they were old enough, they did not need parental consent – but the announcement of banns and all the arrangements for the wedding meant that the parents had plenty of time to intervene. So the romantic church wedding is actually something quite new.

The romantic idea of marriage now so dominates the Western mindset that it is hard to think of it in any other way. Contact with other cultures is making people more aware of arranged marriages and even forced marriages, but for most people in the West it is all about love. Amazingly, the majority of people do manage to find 'the one' and make their own choice freely and lovingly.[4] The downside of this, of course, is that when love goes, most people feel that the marriage must go, with distressing consequences not just for the couple but for any children involved.

---

[3] From 1836, civic marriages were permitted as an alternative.

[4] Perhaps one of the most touchingly humane arguments for marriage was put by Robert Louis Stevenson in *Virginibus Puerisque*: 'A man expects an angel for a wife; [yet] he knows that she is like himself – erring, thoughtless and untrue; but like himself also, filled with a struggling radiancy of better things … You may safely go to school with hope; but ere you marry, should have learned the mingled lesson of the world: that hope and love address themselves to a perfection never realized, and yet, firmly held, become the salt and staff of life; that you yourself are compacted of infirmities … and yet you have a something in you lovable and worth preserving; and that, while the mass of mankind lies under this scurvy condemnation, you will scarce find one but, by some generous reading, will become to you a lesson, a model and a noble spouse through life. So thinking, you will constantly support your own unworthiness and easily forgive the failings of your friend. Nay, you will be wisely glad that you retain the … blemishes; for the faults of married people continually spur up each of them, hour by hour, to do better and to meet and love upon a higher ground.'

Most romantic marriages are actually successful. Considering how easy it is to get divorced, it is remarkable how many not just survive but thrive. Banner headlines may alarm you with the statistic that 45 per cent of marriages in the UK end in divorce. That means, of course, that 55 per cent last a lifetime. For 1 in 10, marriage lasts for more than 60 years. Couples who stay together a lifetime mostly confirm that their spouse is the best and most important thing in their life by far. Most of those marriages that fail, fail quite quickly, but the failure does not put the divorcees off marriage. In the USA, three out of every four divorcees remarry within four years, and one in three within a year.

So marriage brings immense happiness to many millions of people, even though it has been the butt of countless jokes.[5] Yet it has come in for a great deal of criticism beyond the jokes, which are essentially affectionate and almost always come from men who love to make a meal out of how henpecked they are. Feminists have been particularly strident in their condemnation of marriage. 'The institution of marriage is the chief vehicle for the perpetuation of the oppression of

---

[5] 'Bigamy is having one husband or wife too many. Monogamy is the same.' – Oscar Wilde

'I have great hopes that we shall love each other all our lives as much as if we had never married at all.' – Lord Byron

'God created sex. Priests created marriage.' – Voltaire

'Courtship to marriage is as a very witty prologue to a very dull play.' – William Congreve, *The Old Bachelor* (1693)

'Marriage is the only war in which you sleep with the enemy.' – François, Duc de La Rochefoucauld

'The Wedding March always reminds me of the music played when soldiers go into battle.' – Heinrich Heine

'Marriage is the chief cause of divorce.' – Groucho Marx

women,' Marlene Dixon wrote. 'It is through the role of wife that the subjugation of women is maintained.'

It wasn't just that many wives were made to suffer a life of drudgery and isolation by their husbands; they were legally at a disadvantage in many ways. In the UK, for instance, a wife used not to be allowed to own property; any property she had at the wedding immediately became not jointly held but solely her husband's. This finally changed with the Married Woman's Property Act of 1882. Much more distressingly, it was a husband's legal right to rape his wife until shockingly recently. Indeed, Andrea Dworkin scathingly asserted that: 'Marriage as an institution developed from rape as a practice.' In most countries, spousal rape, as it is called, wasn't made illegal until the 1980s and 1990s; and in many countries, such as Pakistan and Sudan, it is still permitted.

Fortunately, the weight of the law in Western countries has been gradually putting right some of these wrongs, and the pressure of feminist arguments has dramatically changed the way many husbands behave in the home.[6] Since the middle of the last century, though, the stigma of 'living in sin' has gradually weakened, and numerous couples are choosing to cohabit rather than get married. As a result, the number of marriages

---

[6] This has opened up another area of contention, though. In divorce settlements, the court usually awards custody of children to the mother, often along with the family home, and the husband is obliged to pay maintenance. It's not easy to see a solution to this, since most children prefer to stay with their mothers and they need a home and support. But the ex-husband may be left with no home, no access to his children and crippling debts. So there has been a lot of media coverage about men who are going on 'marriage strike' – refusing to get married because the cost of a failed marriage would be too high.

has declined steadily. Yet it has not declined nearly as dramatically as some people predicted in the 1970s, when it seemed that all young couples were simply living together. In fact, the number of marriages in the UK is little more than 20 per cent down on its highpoint in the 1960s.

It seems that for all its drawbacks, for all the ease of simply living together, most people still want the bigger commitment of a formal marriage. Just how important it remains is borne out by the expenditure on the wedding itself. A survey in 2007 showed that the average cost of a wedding in the UK has soared to £25,000 and although many people try unusual ceremonies and locations, such as scuba diving weddings and camel-mounted weddings, millions still opt for a full-blown 'traditional' wedding. The Victorian novelist, George Eliot, explains it all very simply in *Silas Marner*: 'That quiet mutual gaze of a trusting husband and wife is like the first moment of rest or refuge from a great weariness or a great danger.'

#49 Weaving and Spinning

There is not a task more humble, yet more lastingly valuable than making cloth through spinning and weaving. For tens of thousands of years, this time-consuming labour absorbed almost every waking moment of the lives of countless women and girls.[7] Women spun while they walked to market. They

---

[7] It wasn't always women, of course, but it generally was. In 1381 the preacher John Ball famously opened his sermon to the Kentish peasant rebels with the words, 'When Adam delved and Eve span', as if the man digging and the woman spinning was the most ancient arrangement for honest toil. Spinning, though, was so time-consuming that quite often only young

spun as they fetched water. They spun as they watched the flocks. They spun as they tended the cooking or looked after the children. And when they had finished the spinning, they started weaving. Indeed, spinning and weaving took up more time than all other activities put together. This stopped only when the business of making cloth was automated with coming of the Industrial Revolution, with its power looms and spinning jennies. Today, cloth-making is bigger than ever, a gigantic global industry worth over a quarter of a trillion pounds.

We naked apes cannot really survive without clothes, except in the very warmest climates. Although a few primitive tribes in remote tropical areas go pretty much naked, most of us have to dress for warmth and protection from the elements, not to mention social reasons. Furs and leathers just aren't practical or comfortable to wear for long either. A few remote peoples in the cold parts of the world were prepared until quite recently to put up with the discomfort of furs for their warmth, such as the Inuit with their caribou skin clothes and the Chukchi with their reindeer and seal skins. But they were the exception. For most people, through most of history, woven clothes have been essential.

The idea of spinning and weaving is incredibly ancient. Indeed, it may be almost as old as humanity itself. Recently, German anthropologists Ralf Kittler, Manfred Kayser and Mark Stoneking used molecular dating to establish that human body lice, lice that live in clothing, first appeared at

---

girls and unmarried women had the time to do it properly – hence the term 'spinster' for an unmarried woman.

least 107,000 years ago, not so long after the emergence of *Homo sapiens*. Archaeologists have found objects that may be sewing needles dating back 40,000 years ago and, in a cave in Georgia, dyed fibres dating back 36,000 years. Imprints of woven cloth have been found on clay figurines dating back up to 27,000 years ago at Dolní Věstonice in the Czech Republic.

The oldest actual cloth is a fragment from Çayönü in southern Turkey. Here a 9,000-year-old piece of linen was found in 1988 wrapped around the handle of a tool made from antler bone. To make the linen, the people of Çayönü would have had to strip fibres from the flax plant and soak them in a river or pond, leaving them supple and golden blonde (the origin of the poetic 'flaxen' for a girl's blonde hair). Then the fibres can be spun and woven into cloth, but it is a long and elaborate process.

Natural fibres, either from plants such as cotton or flax, or from animals such as sheep and goats, tend to be far too thin, weak and short for using to make clothes. But they can be twisted together to make much longer, stronger threads. When twisted like this, the fibres are bound together by friction. The fibres can be twisted in the hand or rubbed together on the thighs. But someone in the forgotten past had the simple but brilliant idea of 'spinning' them. That meant rather than twisting them by hand, you let a stick called a spindle and a weight called a whorl do the work. You just wrap the fibres around the spindle, drop it and start it spinning like a top, or rather a yoyo with the momentum of the whorl. Then you keep feeding in fibres to build up the growing thread which gradually wraps around the spindle.[8]

It's a task that requires considerable skill. You can't afford a lapse in concentration. You have to keep stretching the fibres, for instance, to keep the thread an even thickness – the origin, maybe, of the phrase 'spinning a yarn' to describe someone who was stretching the truth a little in a story. Yet despite the problems, countless women became adept enough at it to carry on spinning while doing other activities. It was too time-consuming not to, but it certainly confirms women's reputation for multi-tasking.[9]

However marvellous, though, by itself a spun thread is of only limited use. Where it really comes into its own is when it is woven into cloth. Nobody can be sure how it was first done, but Ancient Egyptian tomb models and Ancient Greek vase painting show a loom in use many thousands of years ago. The loom's not the only way to weave, but it is an invention of genius. Remarkably, it was in use both in the Americas and Eurasia at least 3,000 years ago, so its invention may just possibly date back far enough to be carried to the Americas by the first migrants from Asia.

---

[8] The unspun thread was usually stored on a stick called the distaff. In the past, the female side of a family was often referred to as the distaff side, maybe because of the way women were ever there supplying the family with its basic needs, or maybe because holding the distaff was women's work. The term is still sometimes used in horse-breeding.

[9] Of course the classic image of home spinning is with the spinning wheel, not the simple spindle. Spinning wheels were known in both China and Baghdad, as well as in Europe, in the thirteenth century, and it's likely they were invented in China some time earlier. The first spinning wheels were hand-turned, but in the sixteenth century a treadle was added so the spinner had both hands free to spin.

Whatever the truth, there are always two sets of thread at right angles to each other in woven cloth, the warp and the weft (or woof). The warp threads are the threads that are held in place during weaving; the weft, which may be one long thread, is woven over and underneath them alternately to bind them together. In a loom, a series of parallel warp threads is stretched between two pieces of wood. Alternate threads are separated, so that first all the odd threads can be lifted or warped together, then all the evens can be.

As one section of warp is lifted one way, the weft ('woven') thread can be fed through the space or 'shed' between them, so that it passes with all the odd warp threads on one side and the evens on the other. When it reaches the other end, the lifted section is dropped, and the other section is pulled up, so that when the warp is fed back through it passes with the odds and evens on the opposite sides to the first pass. In this simple way, the weft is woven under and over the warp so that it alternates in both directions.

There are many different varieties of loom, of course, and various technical improvements were made, even early in its history. One was the heddle, which is a simple bar that allows the weaver to lift selected warps into the shed. This enabled the weaver to create complex patterns. Another innovation was the treadle loom, which allowed the weaver to lift the warps with a foot bar, freeing the hands to work better.

A third ancient innovation is very intriguing indeed. This is the warp-weighted loom, which uses weights hung from the warps to stretch them, rather than a fixed frame. What makes it intriguing is that not only is there archaeological evidence for it right across Europe dating from around 6,000 BC, but an astonishingly similar loom was also used by the native people of the coast of north-west America long before any Europeans apparently crossed the Atlantic.

For tens of thousands of years, hand-spun thread and hand-woven clothes provided people around the world with all their clothes. Whether the threads were vegetable fibres such as cotton and flax, or animal fibres such as sheep and goat's wool and silk, they were all made in essentially the same way. Poor people had neither the time nor the resources to make anything but simple, coarse clothes. But the rich could have the best spinners and weavers make them incredibly elaborate clothes from the most delicate silk and the softest wool. Fine clothes were not only functional as well as valuable status symbols, but could also be things of extraordinary beauty. Indeed, the very finest hand-made clothes are among the most beautiful of all human creations.

Beyond clothes, though, woven cloth found a host of other uses, from tents to curtains – and perhaps most importantly in sails. Sails can be made from other materials. But there is none that has the lightness and strength of woven material – and in particular canvas, made from the spun and woven fibres of hemp.

The automation of spinning and weaving in the Industrial Revolution took away the livelihood of many skilled hand weavers and spinners, but it also saved many women from a labour they did not necessarily relish, however much we may romanticise it now. Automated weaving and spinning were the industries that kick-started the Industrial Revolution, the first global manufacturing industries, and in some ways they are what gave us our modern world. The manufacture of textiles was a key factor in the growth of the first big industrial cities – and of course, it provided the cheap clothes that all the rapidly growing population needed.

Weaving and spinning has none of the technological wizardry of a computer, nor the intellectual weight of logic, nor the magic of aerofoils. Yet this incredibly simple yet absolutely ingenious idea has endured almost as long as humanity and continues to bring us more comfort from day to day than all of them put together. Mahatma Ghandi regarded hand-spinning as the most wonderful and worthwhile of all activities: 'If there is one activity in which it is all gain and no loss, it is hand spinning.' Maybe he was right.

#48 The Stirrup

The stirrup is included in this book not because it is a great idea, though it may be that, but because of the power of a good story, and a bit of provocation.

Just under half a century ago, Stanford medieval history professor Lynn Townsend White wrote a groundbreaking book entitled *Medieval Technology and Social Change*. In it, he contended that technology played a key role in medieval society, and ever since then, no one seriously seeking to understand the Middle Ages has been able to ignore its technology.

The most attention-grabbing bit of White's book, though, was the idea that it was the introduction of the stirrup that led to the development of the feudal system. Never one to understate his case, White asserted that: 'Few inventions have been so simple as the stirrup, but few have had so catalytic an influence on history. The requirements of the new mode of warfare which it made possible found expression in a new form of western European society dominated by an aristocracy of warriors endowed with land so that they might fight in a new and highly specialized way.'

About a century ago, historians such as Heinrich Brunner had asserted that the key to the success of Frankish and Gothic invaders over the fading power of Rome in the fourth and fifth centuries was its individualism. While the once legendary discipline and cohesion of the Roman infantry was breaking down, the individualism of the Franks and Goths spurred them on to become heroes, and what better way to become a hero than mounted on a horse? The hero horsemen of the Franks and Goths, the theory goes, developed into the famous knights of the Middle Ages. It was these horsemen that gave the Carolingian kingdom of the Franks in France – the kingdom of Charles Martel and Charlemagne – its strength and stability.

The Franks, it seemed, weren't able to put great ranks of disciplined infantry into the field like the Romans. But what they could do was send out elite cavalry. Cavalry had been used on the battlefield for thousands of years before the Carolingian knights. But their role was fairly minor; simply harrying and chasing, while the victory centred on the ranks of infantry. There was something so new and so frightening about the new breed of Carolingian horsemen that they had the power to turn battles. These powerful horsemen were so firmly mounted on their big steeds that they could wear heavy armour and ride full tilt at the enemy with lances and swords in shock assaults so overwhelming that ranks of infantry crumbled before them. Heavy cavalry became like the tanks of the world wars.

White's contention was that it was only the introduction of the stirrup that gave horsemen the firm platform to fight this way. Stirrups, he argued, gave horsemen the stability to fight from horseback with swords. They gave the support the rider needed to wear heavy armour. Above all, stirrups allowed the rider to channel the power of the horse into a lance thrust out in front like a deadly missile. Shock assault by heavy cavalry introduced a third phase for the horse in warfare, after chariots and then mounted horsemen.

Training knights, equipping them with horses and armour, swords, lances and shields and giving them a proper support team must have been an expensive business, however. Each one was a costly, specialist unit. This is why, White contends, the Carolingians in the eighth century and subsequently other Western European countries adopted the feudal system. The kings seized land and gave it to overlords who would have serfs to work it. Only such a system, in which serfs were obliged to provide the support for their lord, would provide the financial support for such elite fighters. The deal was that while the peasants were obliged to labour, the knight was obliged to provide protection. So, White contends, we owe class society, the aristocracy and the working class, to the stirrup.

It's a fascinating thesis, and one so potent that it's sunk into popular consciousness. Unfortunately, the evidence is not on White's side, as many scholars have since pointed out. One of the problems is that White dates the arrival of the stirrup in France to about 700 AD. Yet there is plenty of evidence that heavy cavalry were in use without stirrups in other places long before this time. Indeed, heavy cavalry called cataphracts[10] were seen in battles against the Romans 1,000 years earlier. It's the shape of the saddle that is the key to stability, it seems, and not the stirrup.

Another problem is that there is no evidence that the Carolingian kings won any of their key battles with shock assaults by heavy cavalry. A third is that stirrups aren't mentioned in any of the documents or military manuals of the time, nor do they turn up in any eighth-century warriors' graves. Finally, it seems the evolution of the feudal system and the seizure of land was far more complex and gradual than White's theory implies.

The Great Stirrup Controversy as it became known has now been laid to rest by most scholars. So what is the history of stirrups? It seems that horsemen in India may have had a leather loop for the big toe of the barefoot rider as long ago as 500 BC. And Buddhist carvings from the first or second centuries BC show riders with their feet tucked into the saddle girth. Recognisable pairs of stirrups, though, seem to have

---

[10] The cataphracts of Eurasia predate the medieval knights by a thousand years, yet they too were heavily armoured warriors on horseback. Like the knights, they rode big horses, with both horse and rider draped from head to foot in heavy scale and chain armour. Like the knights too, they rode into battle bearing a lance. Indeed, when the Roman general and historian Ammianus Marcellinus describes cataphracts riding against them in the fourth century, he could have been describing knights: 'But no sooner had the first light of day appeared, than the glittering coats of mail, girt with bands of steel, and the gleaming cuirasses, seen from afar, showed that the king's forces were at hand.' Their origins lie in Persia, in the time of the Medes, perhaps 2,500 years ago, but they reached their apogee with the Parthians in the third century BC and the Sassanid Persians in the third and fourth centuries AD. They managed entirely without stirrups, though.

first appeared in China as late as the fourth century AD. From there they spread east into Japan by the fifth century and west to Europe by the seventh century, particularly with horse-riding invaders from Central Asia such as the Avars. Over a hundred seventh-century cast-iron Avar stirrups have been found at various sites in Hungary.

There is no doubt that stirrups greatly aid a rider's stability, and they have been almost universally adopted for leisure riding long after the days of the knights. They make riding much, much easier, not only helping the rider stay in the saddle, but increasing control. Indeed, they make riding so much easier that most people can learn to ride in a fairly short time. Without them, the balance required is beyond all but the most agile and dedicated.

So the greatness of the stirrup as an idea lies not in something as grand and world-changing as the creation of the knight and feudal society, but something far more down-to-earth. It was the stirrup, perhaps, that turned the horse from the mount of the soldier or specialist to everyday personal transport for millions of ordinary (well-enough off) people down through the ages until the coming of the automobile.

The impact of the horse as personal transport was huge, and is the reason why the horse looms so large in personal and social histories. It not only gave countless people the kind of personal freedom that we often associate with the coming of the car – but it did so many, many centuries earlier. It also gave many a personal relationship with an animal that is quite unique, special and thrilling. Listen to the Dauphin in Shakespeare's *Henry V*:

When I sit astride him, I soar, I am a hawk. He trots on air. The earth sings when he touches it. The lowest part of his hoof is more musical than Pan's pipe.

And many riders through the ages, most of who would never have ridden without the stirrup, would echo his words. Even today, it gives to many people a magical, transcendental experience. 'A man on a horse,' wrote John Steinbeck, 'is spiritually as well as physically bigger than a man on foot.' That's, of course, a tribute to the horse but maybe, without the stirrup, very few would ever have got to know.

#47 The Aerofoil

There is perhaps no simpler nor more elegant idea in our list than the aerofoil. And what an idea! Just a little gentle curvature, a curvature that makes a wing – and on those wings we can soar into the sky far above the ground, we can glide over high mountains, we can cross the world's widest oceans in hours. Even for those used to flying, the moment when your accelerating plane finally gains the speed to lift off with a kick beneath you is still exhilarating. How can such a vast weight, something so heavy that it would take a crane to lift, suddenly become so feather-light, so fantastically defiant of gravity that it can bear not only its own weight but yours and your fellow passengers' rapidly up into the air? It seems like magic.

The magic, of course, is in the physical interaction between the wings and the air. If the shape of the wing – the aerofoil – is right and the plane is moving fast enough, the wing is pushed into the air as it slices through it. It seems like magic because our all-too-literal brains tell us that because air is invisible it must be insubstantial too. But air is not nothing; air is a substance, chock-full of gas. Think of a wing slicing through water rather than air and you can begin to imagine how air might provide the upward push that aeronautical scientists call 'lift'.

The key to the aerofoil's lift is the flow of air around it. Of course, still air is neither moving nor flowing; air flows around an aerofoil because the aerofoil is moving, just as the bow of a boat creates a flow in still water. What matters is the way the curved shape of the aerofoil diverts the flow around it. To really see why, it's worth playing about with knives and spoons under a running tap.

Hold a knife flat under the stream and the water flows straight and undisturbed past the blade. Twist the blade slightly at an angle to the stream and you can see how it begins to block and split the flow, breaking it into turbulent eddies – and you may see the turbulence increase as you increase the angle of the knife. Hold a spoon under the stream instead, however, and something different happens. Unlike the flat knife, the spoon diverts the water, but does not disrupt it. You have to twist the spoon at a much steeper angle before it disrupts the flow. Like the curvature of the spoon, the curvature of the aerofoil ensures the flow of the air around it is diverted but not broken up.

It is the way that the flow is made to curve like the aerofoil that is crucial. Far above or below the aerofoil, the airflow is undisturbed, but the closer it is to the aerofoil the more its flow is bent to follow the aerofoil's shape. As the flow changes direction it begins to push in a different direction too, and the more it bends the greater the change. Right on top and underneath the aerofoil the pressure of the airflow turns effectively at right angles, pushing the aerofoil upwards and creating lift.

Since it is the way that the airflow is distorted that creates lift, it is clear that the pattern of the airflow distortion is important. This depends on the angle that the aerofoil moves through the air – its 'angle of attack'. The steeper the angle of attack, the greater the lift, up to the 'stall' point where the angle is so steep that the airflow is broken up altogether and all lift is lost.

The shape of the aerofoil is also crucial. A gentle, thin, flat curve provides the best lift, and this is the shape of bird wings and the shape that the flexible wings of hang-gliders and microlights bow into. But it is hard to make a large wing strong enough in this shape. So the wings of most large aircraft are a narrow teardrop shape in profile. This doesn't give us much lift, which is why the wings have to be huge, but is easier to make strong, and the hollow inside the wing provides room for fuel storage. Elevator flaps on the rear of the wings swing up or down to alter the aerofoil curvature and its effective angle of attack and so allow the pilot to vary the lift to climb or descend.

Of course, the wings of birds were the original inspiration for the aerofoil. Countless thinkers in the distant past must have marvelled at birds gliding through the sky and guessed that they were held aloft by their outstretched wings. And maybe some even guessed it was the shape of the wings that mattered, such as the fifth-century Greek philosopher Archytas who is said to have built a mechanical bird that flew. Brave pioneers like the ninth-century Cordoban, Abbas ibn-Firnas, were bold (or foolish) enough to strap artificial wings to their arms and leap from high places. Ibn-Firnas was successful (or lucky) enough to glide through the air for ten minutes before crash-landing and almost breaking his neck.

Yet the first person who really began to explore the shape of wings methodically was the British engineer Sir George Cayley (1773–1857), and it is to Cayley that we owe the idea of the curved aerofoil. Yorkshire-born Cayley was an extraordinary and inventive man, and he is credited with developing self-righting lifeboats, wire-spoked wheels, seatbelts and even an internal combustion engine. But it is mostly as the 'father of aviation' that he is remembered, and it is he who pioneered much of the theory of flight. He carried out many experiments with wings on whirling arms to discover the forces acting on them, and what shapes and angles produced the greatest lift. In his analyses, he developed the names for the four key forces involved in flight – weight, lift, drag and thrust – still used by scientists today. Flight itself involves a balance between these four forces.

Cayley wasn't just a theorist, though. In the early 1800s, he began to build model gliders to try out his ideas. Then in 1849, he built a miniature biplane in which a ten-year-old boy is said to have flown a short distance, using 'flappers' to propel himself along. Most famously, however, in 1853 the by then 80-year-old Cayley built a full-size glider in which his terrified coachman or butler is said to have been launched out across Brompton Dale near Scarborough on Cayley's estate. The butler survived and thus made the world's first aeroplane flight. Cayley had clearly mastered lift, but for a successful aeroplane you need both power and control, which is why it took another half-century before the Wright brothers made their historic flight at Kittyhawk on 17 December 1903.

The development of air travel since that pioneering day has been astonishing. According to the travel organisation IATA, 2.3 billion people flew on 35 million flights in 2009 alone. It is a remarkably safe way to travel. Of those 35 million flights, only nineteen came to grief in accidents, and fewer than 700 of those 2.3 billion passengers were killed in air accidents – in other words 1 in 30 million.

Flight has transformed the way we experience the world. It seems a smaller, more connected place and many of us now frequently visit on brief holidays and business trips places that before air travel we may have travelled to only once in a lifetime. Millions of Britons, for instance, hop on a plane for weekend breaks in European cities, or travel right the way around the world for a short holiday in Thailand. Many ordinary people know about many foreign places and cultures not just because they have looked them up on the internet or watched a TV documentary, but because they have actually travelled there by plane.

Air travel is not essential. Indeed, there are plenty of critics who argue that it is a wasteful luxury, and the global warming debate has focused attention on just how much we should be flying. The high energy cost of getting a plane into the air means that air travel is a major contributor to the greenhouse gases that are triggering global warming. Aeroplanes are very noisy, too, as anyone who lives under the flight-path near an airport will no doubt testify.

Yet whatever level of flying ultimately proves sustainable, there is no doubt that the simple shape of the aerofoil has introduced something remarkable into our lives. It has given us all the chance of a magical experience. According to Plato, writing long before the aerofoil became a reality: 'The natural function of the wing is to soar upwards and carry that which is heavy up to the place where dwells the race of gods. More than any other thing that pertains to the body it partakes of the nature of the divine.'

For the pioneering aviator Charles Lindbergh, that divine quality was perhaps even too much: 'Sometimes, flying feels too godlike to be attained by man. Sometimes, the world from above seems too beautiful, too wonderful, too distant for human eyes to see.' (*Spirit of St Louis*, 1953)

#46 Monotheism

Back in 2005, conservative American Supreme Court Justice Antonio Scalia ruffled quite a few feathers when he said that monotheistic religions were the only ones the US government could endorse under the Constitution. The remarks certainly stirred up debate, but whatever the American legal position, Scalia certainly had numbers on his side.

Well over 3.5 billion people around the world belong to the three great Abrahamic religions that are essentially mono-theistic – Christianity (about 2 billion), Islam (1.5 billion) and Judaism (14 million) – and a further billion belong to the Hindu (950 million) and Sikh (23.8 million) faiths, which some people consider to be monotheistic at heart. So in purely democratic terms, monotheism gets the world's vote as the best way to look at the world, with pretty much 75 per cent of the vote.

It wasn't always this way. Up until 2,000–3,000 years ago, the world's religious beliefs were hugely varied and, as far as anyone can tell with such scant evidence, every small group of people had its own spirits or family of gods. Some worshipped tree spirits, some sky gods and moon gods. Some believed in the Great Goddess. Others followed the Bull. Many paid homage to stones. There wasn't so much of a moral or social dimension or any personal insights in this cornucopia of beliefs; it was more a matter of keeping the gods happy to make sure that they were on your side, whether it was in the hunt or in the harvest, or in the field of battle. And then, it seems, it all changed.

All across Eurasia, people began to look at the world in a different way. Sixty years ago, German philosopher Karl Jaspers talked of an Axial Age, a remarkable time when in just four centuries from 750–350 BC, 'we meet with the most deep dividing line in history. Man, as we know him today, came into being.' And he points out how, almost simultaneously, thinkers such as Confucius and Laozi in China, Prince Siddhartha (Buddha) in India, and Socrates in Greece all began to question the meaning of life in an extraordinarily new and profound way. 'What is new about this age,' Jaspers wrote, '… is that man becomes conscious of Being as a whole, of himself and his limitations.'

For the first time, almost simultaneously, Chinese, Indians, Persians, Jews, Greeks and many others began to emerge as individuals seeking an 'inner' truth rather than looking outside to the landscape and the sky and a host of spirits and minor gods. It's as if there was a new kind of consciousness. Although by no means all of the new faiths and philosophies were monotheistic, they all focused on a single being, whether human or divine. According to author Karen Armstrong, it was a reaction to the growing prevalence of war and conflict in early civilisations: 'In every single case, the spiritualities that emerged during the Axial Age – Taoism and Confucianism in China, monotheism in Israel, Hinduism, Buddhism, and Jainism in India, and Greek rationalism in Europe – began with a recoil from violence, with looking into the heart to find the sources of violence in the human psyche.'

Many historians question the idea of an Axial Age and trace the development of monotheism differently. They are sceptical of any connection between these developments, although there is no need to invoke some mass psychological sea-change as Jaspers did; a simple 'viral' word of mouth sharing of ideas might have been quite enough. Most Jewish theologians, for instance, believe that Judaism was the original monotheistic religion, and that the other main Abrahamic faiths, Christianity and Islam, followed suit. The Jewish tradition tells how Abraham banished the false gods and idols of his ancestors and made a covenant with Yahweh, the one true god. Christianity and Islam follow this tradition, which is why they are all known as Abrahamic religions. Sigmund Freud in his last book controversially suggested that Moses, the prophet who led the Jews from their exile in Egypt and gave them the Ten Commandments, was actually Egyptian. Few people agree with him, but Egypt is the setting, nevertheless, for what is the first known example of monotheism.

In 1824, one of the first British Egyptologists, the redoubtable John Gardner Wilkinson, stumbled upon traces of an ancient city in the middle of nowhere on the banks of the Nile at Amarna. Strangely, the ruins looked as if they had been systematically destroyed, with every decoration obliterated. Since then, the mystery of Amarna has been partly revealed.

Amarna is the story of the pharaoh Akhenaten, the father of Tutankhamun, who founded the lost city in the fourteenth century BC as the site of a religious revolution. In the pictures and texts uncovered by archaeologist Flinders Petrie in the 1890s, Akhenaten is shown addressing his prayers to one god and one god only, Aten, the disk of the sun, rather than the Egyptians' multitude of deities.[11]

Akhenaten's monotheistic revolution was brief, and rubbed from history by his successors the moment he died, but his vision of a different world and his motto, 'Living in truth', inspired Petrie to comment in awe: 'No King of Egypt, nor of any other part of the world, has ever carried out his honesty of expression so openly. Thus in every line Akhenaten stands out as perhaps the most original thinker that ever lived in Egypt, and one of the greatest idealists in the world.'

Other historians trace the origins of monotheism back through another route to the Zoroastrian religion. No one knows exactly who Zoroaster was, or when he lived. The

---

[11] Akhenaten's experiment wasn't just a change from many gods to one; it was a revolution in thought too. Petrie found art in Amarna that had a freshness, a love of nature and informality unique in Egypt – painted floors with birds flying over marshes, walls with animals gambolling in fields, and, most extraordinary of all, intimate, tender portraits of the deformed pharaoh and his wife, cradling their children on the lap or kissing affectionately. It was as if he had stumbled upon a pharaoh's family snapshot album.

traditional view is that he lived around the tenth century BC, but it may have been up to 1,000 years earlier. In his famous *Also Sprach Zarathustra* (*Thus Spake Zarathustra*), Nietzsche identified Zoroaster as the first to divide the world into good and evil – it is this division that Nietzsche wished to end by killing God. Zoroaster's vision was of a world shaped by the battle between light and dark, good and evil. This is not just a cosmic battle between the supreme god Ahura-Mazda, who may be the first example of a single and supreme deity, and his evil opponent Ahriman; it's a battle in which every human is free to play his part. According to Zoroaster, we are all 'angels' descended to join the fight against evil and save the world. Yet we are not compelled to join the fight; we have free will. The drawback is that if we don't live well, we will come to grief at the Final Judgement and may be sent to hell.

Zoroastrianism is now an almost forgotten religion, practised by people such as the Parsees in India, but it was the root of many key Christian and Islamic ideas. Christians, of course, believe in the God of the Old Testament, the same God worshipped by Jews, but they temper their monotheism by the idea of the Trinity – the Father, Son and Holy Ghost. Most Christians believe that the division of God into three parts doesn't diminish his complete transcendence. Some critics argue that this makes Christianity a tritheistic religion, and a few insist that the inclusion of the Virgin Mary, Satan and the angels makes Christianity a polytheistic religion, but they are very much in a minority. Islam, however, is uncompromisingly monotheistic. The Islamic concept of *Tawhid* holds that God (Allah) is one and unique. Indeed, this is the central belief of Islam. This has very profound implications, which Islamic scholars have debated ever since the time of Mohammed.

The term 'monotheism' was coined in 1660 by Henry More[12] to show how it was the most advanced form of religion, following on from primitive animism and slightly less primitive polytheism. And many before and since have argued that monotheism is the most rational religious belief. It was felt to be rational because monotheism allowed the world to be a completely logical place. Because God was both internal to people and external to the reality of the universe, there was no need for superstition and irrationality in the real world. God could simply inhabit the inner man and be behind everything.[13]

The tenth-century Islamic polymath Abu ibn Sina (Avicenna) argued that it was illogical to imagine that existence popped out of nothing, so a belief in God was rational. Many Ancient Greek thinkers used logic to argue that the

---

[12] Henry More was writing at a time when the notion of monotheism was receiving particular attention from philosophers and rational theologians. The poet John Milton, a contemporary of More, had considerable problems with writing his great epic *Paradise Lost* in the style of a Greek epic – with its polytheistic conventions, divine councils and cosmic scope – and yet presenting a monotheistic God who is all-knowing and all-powerful and who has no physical image. The result was a unique and powerful creation.

[13] One argument for monotheism is that if there were more than one God, the universe would be in chaos because of competing deities, and it couldn't be studied logically. Another is that since God is perfect, there can be no other, since any other would have to be different, so not perfect, so not God. A third is that since God is infinite and everywhere, there is no room for any other. All this shows the danger of arguing for or against God on a rational basis. The arguments sound like clutching at straws, pursuing the kind of logic that goes round in circles rather than convinces with its truth. Very few people have been persuaded to believe in a single God through rational argument.

existence of a single divine principle was essential for the cosmos not to be utter chaos. Aristotle talked in terms of a Prime Mover. Otherwise how did it all start? Why does anything happen? Why does logic work at all?

All seem to be arguing, in their different ways, that without the presence of a God, things make no sense and seem almost irredeemably chaotic and meaningless. A whole panoply of divinities doesn't offer this reassurance; a single omniscient, omnipotent, omnipresent being does. It is this powerful reassurance that has drawn millions of people to the monotheistic religions over the centuries, providing an answer on both a profound intellectual and a simple personal level.[14]

On the other hand, monotheism has been accused of fomenting conflict in a way that polytheism never could. It has been argued that one key factor in the success of the Roman empire was the way it allowed conquered people to keep their local gods, because they presented no threat to the panoply of Roman gods. If you believe there is just one God, however, then you must believe that people who don't believe in the same God are wrong. You might even believe you were failing in your belief if you did not assert God's dominion over others. This is why, the argument goes, there have been so many catastrophic holy wars, and why there is still such

---

[14] Sigmund Freud in *Moses and Monotheism* argued that monotheism played a central role in human intellectual development. The prohibition of worshipping idols was particularly crucial: 'The compulsion to worship a God whom one cannot see,' wrote Freud, meant that 'a sensory perception was given a second place to what may be called an abstract idea – a triumph of intellectuality over sensuality.' In this way, monotheism taught people to reflect on the symbolic – which was the spur to the great achievements of Jews, Muslims and Christians in mathematics, science and the arts.

potential for conflict between, for instance, Islam and the West.[15]

In the same way that monotheism might provoke conflict like this, however, it can unite people and create a sense of brotherhood of shared beliefs in a way that is far beyond either polytheistic religion or atheism or agnosticism. Monotheism has a unique power to sweep people up in an evangelising wave because of the sense of belonging it creates – which is why Christianity and Islam have grown to encompass so many billions of people. Whether you think this shared experience is ultimately a good thing or not, there is no doubting monotheism's lasting power as an idea.

#45 Honour

Honour is not something people talk a great deal about these days, yet for much of human history it was considered the highest human virtue, a virtue so far above all others that it was worth dying for. 'Hold it the greatest sin,' wrote the Roman poet Juvenal two millennia ago, 'to prefer existence to honour, and for the sake of life to lose the reasons for living.' And 1,400 years later, Shakespeare put remarkably similar sentiments into the mouth of Thomas Mowbray in *Richard II*: 'Mine honour is my life, both grow in one. Take honour from

---

[15] It may be, though, that the link between monotheism and conflict is more subtle – because it relies on revelation, messages direct from God, it encourages a certainty that you have the answers and others don't. But this kind of delusion is not exclusive to monotheism; it could happen just as easily to polytheists and to atheists. Monotheists assert that God is behind them and them only; atheists and polytheists can be equally pigheaded.

me, and my life is done. Then, dear my liege, mine honour let me try; In that I live, and for that I will die.' Both Juvenal and Mowbray make it clear that even life is worth less than honour; without honour, life is meaningless. About 3,300 years ago, the visionary Egyptian pharaoh, Akhenaten, explained it thus: 'Honour is the inner garment of the Soul; the first thing put on by it with the flesh, and the last it lays down at its separation from it.'

What's extraordinary is just how pervasive the concept of honour was. Just as it is embedded in Ancient Egypt and Rome, so too it is there in Ancient Greece, where Socrates writes in high praise of honour; in Ancient China, where the philosopher Laozi, the founder of Taoism, writes of the importance of honour for a leader; and in Ancient Japan, where the Bushido code of the Samurai warrior insisted that if you lost your honour, the only way to save it was to commit *hara-kiri* or *seppuku* – ritual suicide by slicing your belly with a sword. And it's not just ancient history. When the Germans demanded that Belgium surrender at the start of the First World War, the Belgian Prime Minister, Charles de Broqueville, responded: 'Our submission would serve no end; if Germany is victorious, Belgium, whatever her attitude, will be annexed to the Reich. If die we must, better death with honour.' Honour has really mattered to many people, for a long time, in many places.

Of course, when people talked about their honour being lost or offended, they were often really talking about status. Status maintained your place in the world, so losing it could be calamitous. That's why honour was crucial for leaders. To lose their honour could mean losing their power to command (unless they resorted to sheer brute force or low cunning), and it was worth fighting for.

This didn't just apply to people, but to kingdoms and empires, who fought wars on the basis of offended honour. Sometimes, this was just a pretext to war for more basic reasons; sometimes it really was a matter of honour. Either way, honour was public justification enough. Similarly, those seeking to avoid war often looked for 'peace with honour'. But, of course, this can be tainted with the implication that it wasn't so honourable after all – an undertone of weakness or deviousness. Think of Neville Chamberlain returning from the 1938 Munich conference with Hitler, declaring that he had brought back 'peace with honour', or Richard Nixon broadcasting to the American people in 1973 that he had brought 'peace with honor in Vietnam and South Asia'. These instances stick in the mind rather than the countless times, perhaps, when peace with honour was genuine.

Too often, honour seems, with twenty-first-century hindsight, to be merely macho posturing. Too often, too, it is used to dress up violence and prejudice with respectable clothes. This is the kind of honour that the Mafia embraced as they embarked on bloody spates of revenge killings. It's the kind of honour that fuels teenage gang warfare today, inspires terrorists to commit atrocities in the name of righteous anger, and drives families to kill their own daughters in 'honour killings'. Again it's about status, and calling it 'honour' is just giving an ugly deed a pretty face.[16]

---

[16] And this deed is very ugly indeed. There are twelve so-called honour killings every year in the UK, most shockingly brutal. And the news that a sixteen-year-old Turkish girl was buried alive for talking to boys, or that

Yet honour has another side. To talk of honour simply as a status symbol or macho posturing is to forget its powerful allure to the wisest and best minds, and its ability to inspire the most wonderful human lives and deeds. Some of the most appealing heroes place honour above all, and so do many humble, decent people. Dr Johnson defined it as 'nobility of soul, magnanimity and a scorn of meanness'. Others would say it is the quiet determination to do what is right.

The concept of honour is so overlaid with cultural history that it's hard to pin down. Yet most of us can recognise what is an honourable act and what is not. And almost all of us want people to behave honourably. We want our politicians to be incorruptible, our friends to be trustworthy, the people who affect our careers to judge us fairly, our teachers not to show favouritism.

Karl Marx insisted that honour is an aristocratic value, handed down from the feudal age and helping to keep the working class in their place.[17] Yet some of the most recognisably

---

a Saudi Arabian woman was killed by her father for chatting to men on Facebook, are only the most publicised examples of a distressingly widespread tendency in some Islamic countries.

[17] In the Western world, many of our ideas about honour, and this aristocratic side, have come down from the age of chivalry. We may caricature the knight in shining armour, but the knight's honour code was a powerful creation that had enormous influence for half a millennium. By the end of the Middle Ages, though, pragmatic power politics was taking the place of the chivalric code, and a new sense of individual freedom made the honour code seem restrictive or obsessive, as Shakespeare brilliantly shows in the character of Hotspur in *Henry IV*. Those chivalric idealists who lamented its passing were increasingly portrayed as naive dreamers, such as Cervantes' Don Quixote, or heroic failures like Corneille's El Cid, or were swept away as reactionary throwbacks, like the cavaliers of the English Civil War.

honourable people of the last century have been those bucking the system, like the first Labour leader Keir Hardie, or Nelson Mandela. Perhaps it's the insistence on doing the right thing in the face of adversity that is the hallmark of the person of honour.

It's about 'integrity' and 'decency' and knowing right from wrong, but it's more than just morals; it's morals in action. It's what makes you hand in the cash-stuffed wallet you found on the train. It's what makes the most admired sportspeople play in the right spirit before playing to win.

The conflation of the two sides of honour – between the urge to do the right thing regardless of cost and the protection of status, between the personal and the public – comes together tellingly in the New Year's Honours List in the UK.

Yet as the world moved on, centuries later, the upheaval of the Industrial Revolution and the growth of massive, turbulent cities revived the feeling that something important had been lost. Was the cold, hard reason of the head really preferable to the warm truth of the heart? Walter Scott's *Ivanhoe* (1819) and other novels opened a deep vein of nostalgia for the bygone age of honour that ran through a Victorian age also fascinated by tales of the noble King Arthur and his knights. In his book, *The Broad-Stone of Honour* (1822), Kenelm Henry Digby insisted that: 'Chivalry is only a name for that general spirit or state of mind which disposes men to heroic actions, and keeps them conversant with all that is beautiful and sublime in the intellectual and moral world.' His book inspired a new generation of conservatives, and helped to ensure that the schools of the rich, from English public schools to the private schools of the USA, still celebrate a reactionary honour code and an obsession with heraldry.

In time, nostalgia for 'days of yore' seemed childish, lampooned in Mark Twain's *A Connecticut Yankee in King Arthur's Court*, and was treated as fodder for countless tongue-in-cheek Hollywood movies. And yet it just won't go away. Nearly every adventure movie, from *Star Wars* and *Lord of the Rings* to *The Matrix*, owes something to the chivalric code of honour.

In the list, many ordinary people are honoured for genuinely selfless works and their services to the community, alongside celebrities who have done little more than become famous.

The German philosopher Arthur Schopenhauer argued that honour is within reach of us all, while celebrity is not. 'Honour,' Schopenhauer wrote, 'means that a man is not exceptional; fame, that he is. Fame is something which must be won; honour, only something which must not be lost.'[18] He made a crucial distinction between a false idea of honour that is simply reputation, which when insulted can be restored only by inflicting a greater insult, and true honour, which is entirely internal and cannot be hurt by anyone else.

Some people associate honour with hot-blooded cultures, where people flare up at the slightest provocation. Others say honour arises in lawless tribal cultures, like the Bedouin and Scottish clans, where an honour code provides essential protection. Or that honour is essentially a martial code to instil discipline and loyalty.

All these things are true, yet only touch the surface. They don't explain why Akhenaten thought it so important, why Socrates and Aristotle did, and why so many other thinkers have done. And it's not simply in the distant past, either. Listen to the young American, Oliver Wendell Holmes, in 1866: '[T]he power of honor to bind men's lives is not less now than it was in the Middle Ages. Now as then it is the breath of our nostrils; it is that for which we live, for which, if need be, we are willing to die.' Or George Bernard Shaw:

---

[18] Here, interestingly, Schopenhauer is using even the word fame in a much more positive sense than we use it now. It is being well-known, not in our sense of being known by a lot of people, but known widely as admirable.

'The most tragic thing in the world is a man of genius who is not a man of honour.'[19] Even the acerbic Gore Vidal suggested in the 1970s that: 'perhaps our schools should train a proper civil service. Train people who prefer payment in honor rather than in money.'

Our heroes remain men and women of honour, people who do the right thing whatever the personal cost. In almost every story and movie, any hero who is truly admirable has this core of honour. As the writer Michael Novak says: 'Americans [and others today] love professionals, killers especially, ruthless investigators, determined secret agents, anybody who absolutely concentrates on proficiency, undistracted by human involvement.' Yet there is a sense that this single-mindedness is a sign of honour, a dedication to duty that is ultimately admirable. Dr House in the TV series *House* may be a curmudgeonly misanthrope but he appeals because at his core he seems an honourable man. Indeed, it is the very difficulty of being honourable that is heroic. As Hemingway writes in *Death in the Afternoon* (1932): 'Too much honor destroys a man quicker than too much of any other fine quality.'

---

[19] Of course, it is not coincidence that people often talk of 'men of honour' but rarely 'women of honour' (except in the telling title 'maids of honour'). A woman's honour, in many honour codes, lay solely in her ability to protect her virginity ready for its rightful owner, her husband-to-be. And it was the knight's (or her family's) duty to make sure that she received this protection. The chivalric code of honour is inherently chauvinistic and aristocratic, and this is why the whole idea of honour seems deeply suspicious and reactionary, especially when tied in with all its ugly sides, from gang warfare to honour killings.

#44 Epic Poetry

Everyone loves a hero, and heroes don't come bigger than the heroes of epic poetry. The heroes of epics didn't just save a cat from a tree, or even rescue an old lady from a burning building. Their heroics were on a grand scale, and on their great deeds turned the fate of cities and empires, and even of all humanity itself. That's what makes them so uplifting; they remind us that one man's actions and his moral as well as physical courage matter, even on such a big canvas.

Today, few people but scholars read the great epic poems of the past – such as Homer's *Iliad*, Virgil's *Aeneid* and Milton's *Paradise Lost* – but they inspired countless people through the ages, and they still have a certain resonance. Faint echoes of them are plain, too, in the adventure and fantasy films and stories of today. The *Star Wars* films and the *Lord of the Rings* trilogy may be childish next to Homer, but the deeds of Luke Skywalker, Frodo and Aragon clearly owe much to the epics of old, and can inspire some of the same thrill that people must have felt in ancient times when they listened to the bards recite their epic poems.

That's of course how epic poetry began. It was an oral tradition. None of the first epic poems were written down. Instead, they were learned and handed down orally from one bard to another for generation after generation. Occasionally, the bard learned the whole poem by heart. More often, it seems, he simply knew the basic storyline – the key events and characters, the meetings and partings, the victories and defeats, the settings and the images. Then, armed with a few stock phrases and a prodigious skill for improvisation, he made it up as he went along, blending old and new, never telling the story quite the same way twice, adapting it each time to suit his audience. All the same, memorable phrases must have stuck in the mind and been passed down through the ages, and the poem must have become more and more refined and distilled with each telling.

Of course, much of this ancient oral epic poetry has been lost. But in the last two centuries, academic researchers have collected a wealth of stories from remote peoples living in Siberia and Central Asia, with some great stories, for instance, coming from the Kara-Kirgiz people of the Tien Shan mountains and the Yakut of northern Siberia. This research confirmed that huge and elaborate epic poems could be composed and even remembered orally. In the 1930s, American scholar Milman Parry transcribed an epic poem of 12,000 lines, the length of Homer's *Odyssey*, from an illiterate Serbian bard.

The chances are that every culture in Europe and Eurasia had its own oral tradition of epic poetry.[20] Epic poems probably played a key role in defining and uniting each culture. They gave each their own special hero, their own unique bond and inspiration. Even today, so far into the modern age, the

---

[20] Scholars distinguish between primary epics, which come directly from the oral tradition, such as the *Iliad* and the *Odyssey*, *Beowulf* and *Gilgamesh*, and secondary epics, which are sophisticated literary creations in imitation of the original form, such as Virgil's *Aeneid*, Dante's *Divine Comedy* and Milton's *Paradise Lost*. Sometimes, only a vague memory of the story survived orally and the verse was lost. Sometimes, later poets have tried to recreate the epic from mythical fragments, like the eighteenth-century Scot James MacPherson with his tale of *Ossian*, the legendary Gaelic bard, which MacPherson notoriously tried to pass off as original.

heroes of ancient myth – from Hercules and Achilles to King Arthur and Robin Hood – have a rich resonance. How much more power they would have had in a time when there were few other ways in which a culture could express its aspirations, when there was nothing else to fill the dark nights by the fire but the sound of the poet's voice and nothing to distract the imagination from taking flight within the story. They had the power to ennoble a culture and create a sense of moral purpose and energy.

What is extraordinary about what we know of epic poetry is how high it aimed. Aristotle regarded epic poetry as the greatest form of literature except for tragedy. Renaissance scholars placed it even higher. Each poem was an astonishing feat of literary creation. The story had to be told on the grandest scale, using the most elaborate imagery, the most intricate and carefully crafted words, and embody the highest ideals and the most profound ideas. You could say it was pretentious, and anybody trying to imitate it today is in danger of being skewered for pseudery. But that was only because its intentions were so lofty. Artistically, intellectually, morally, spiritually, it was intended to give us something to aspire to – something to encourage each of us to be the best and fulfil our potential, to rise above the mundane.

The high aims and achievements of epic poetry are borne out magnificently in one of the first actually written down, Homer's *Iliad*. This great poem tells of the events during the tenth and final year of the Greek siege of the city of Troy and the quarrel between Achilles and King Agamemnon. It dates from the turn of the 8th and 9th centuries BC, and along with the *Odyssey*, also attributed to Homer, it is the oldest known work of European literature. And what a work it is. In 15,700 lines of stirring verse, Homer tells a tale that has been described as one of the greatest pieces of literature ever written, full of rich imagery, powerful storytelling and high drama.

Some scholars think Homer was the name of the writer and creator of the *Iliad*. Others think there was no such person as Homer, and the poems were handed down orally from bard to bard until they were finally written down. In the 1920s, the scholar Parry showed clearly how the *Iliad* and *Odyssey* both use stock phrases and verses and even storylines that place it in the same oral tradition as the ancient Sumerian epic *Gilgamesh*.

Whatever the origins of Homer's great poems, they set the benchmark for countless imitators since then. Sometimes, a poet even chooses the same subject matter, the siege of Troy, as did the Roman poet Virgil for his *Aeneid*, which is perhaps the greatest of all Roman literary works. Other poets create their own subject matter, picking up mythical stories as did Edmund Spenser for *The Faerie Queene*, or Biblical tales like Milton for his monumental *Paradise Lost*.

But the model is clear. Scholars have tried to pin down just what it is that makes an epic, and list a number of common features. An epic is a long narrative poem on a serious subject telling the tale of a larger-than-life hero. The setting is on a grand scale, with the hero often journeying the whole world. Typically, the hero is an outcast of some kind or a victim of the gods' ire. But the fate of a nation or a people depends on his heroic fortitude in responding to his lot.

In keeping with the oral tradition and the pyrotechnic displays of the performing bard, there are all kinds of literary devices. It's all on a grand scale, and there are no half measures, even in similes. In Homer's *Iliad*, Achilles doesn't just run after Hector like a hound, he chases him 'nonstop as a hound in the mountains starts a fawn from its lair, hunting him down the gorges, down the narrow glens where the fawn goes to ground, hiding deep in brush until the hound comes racing fast, nosing him out until he lands his kill'. Many of Milton's metaphors are equally high-flown and extended.

All this creates a sense of excitement as well as grandeur. Similarly, in another trick inherited from the oral performance tradition, epic poems tend to start *in media res* (in the middle of things), pitching right into the action. Virgil's *Aeneid*, for instance, doesn't begin neatly with Aeneas's childhood, or even the beginning of the siege of Troy, but with Aeneas already on a boat, fleeing the captured city:

Arms, and the man I sing, who, forc'd by fate,
And haughty Juno's unrelenting hate,
Expell'd and exil'd, left the Trojan shore.

It's a technique that's taken up by pretty much every adventure movie today. Just think of that fast-paced action sequence that kick-starts the movie even before the credits start to roll, before the background is filled in by flashbacks or by fast-forwarding.

The oral heritage is often evident, too, in the dramatic reportage style of the verse, a style that still influences our way of telling a story when we want to create a sense of excitement. There is a hypnotic repeated use of little phrases or epithets, like the 'wine-dark sea' in the *Odyssey*. And there's a literary technique, for instance, known as parataxis, which is widely used in epic poems. It's the way sentences are kept short and staccato – without any of the normal linking phrases of other styles of writing – keeping the audience/reader actively engaged, by leaving them to make the connections in their imaginations. Instead of writing, for example, 'The rain hammered down, making Robin curse under his breath', the epic might say: 'The rain hammered down. Robin cursed under his breath.' It's a breathless, pointedly dramatic style that's been so widely adopted for thrillers that it can be a cliché.

Poets rarely attempt epics these days. First of all, the technical challenge is too great for most poets, though Seamus Heaney made a great retelling of the Anglo-Saxon epic *Beowulf*. Secondly, the heightened literary style and high seriousness is something we now find hard to accept. But epic poetry has in the past given Western literature some of its greatest and most inspirational masterpieces, and its shadow lingers on in other forms of literature and art, in serious form in epic novels like Tolstoy's *War and Peace* and Melville's *Moby-Dick*, and through to the modern pastiche of fantasy and science fiction novels like *Lord of the Rings* and Arthur C. Clarke's *2001:A Space Odyssey* (which makes its debt clear in its title) and film adventures like *Gladiator*.

#43 Qi

Qi is either one of the greatest insights into the nature of our lives, or one of the greatest delusions. It is the idea that our lives are sustained by an intangible natural energy or life-force that flows through all things. The word is Chinese and comes originally from the steam wafting off freshly cooked rice. But the concept is linked to the Taoist religion, and similar concepts are found all over the world, such as in the Indian *prana* and the Western tradition of vitalism.

Chinese legend tells that ideas about *qi* were originally collected about 4,600 years ago by the Yellow Emperor Huang-di, who is credited with inventing the principles of Chinese medicine. But it emerges most strongly between the fourth and sixth centuries BC in the writings of three key Chinese thinkers: Kong Fuzi (Confucius), Mo Zi and, especially, Laozi.[21]

---

[21] The collapse of the western half of the Zhou dynasty in the seventh century BC left the remaining eastern half split between countless warring states. It was a period of constant strife and anxiety. Yet it was a time of intellectual ferment and technical innovation, and four great philosophical ideas emerged out of the turmoil, as thinkers tried to work out just why times were so troubled.

The most famous was Confucianism, named after Confucius, the Roman name given by the Jesuits in the seventeenth century to the man his disciples knew as Kong Fuzi ('Master Kong'). Confucius' ideas have come down mainly in the form of sayings compiled by his followers in a tract called the *Analects*. His central belief was that we should seek to live in a good way, always behaving with humanity and courtesy, work diligently and honour properly our family and our rulers. He thought of himself as a conservative in that he was always emphasising the 'Way of the Former Kings' in an earlier Golden Age, but in some ways he was quite revolutionary in that he insisted that status should be earned by moral behaviour, not by heredity. Politically, Confucianism championed a highly ordered society.

The second central philosopher of the age was Mo Zi. Mo Zi felt that Confucius' emphasis on the family could lead to nepotism and clan feuds. He argued in favour of 'universal love' – loving and honouring everyone, and looking after others as you would be looked after yourself. This was not, he felt, an idealistic dream, but the only practical way for society to function without strife.

The concept of *qi* comes from a fundamentally different way of looking at the world from that of the West. While in the West, everything can be seen as either matter or energy; in traditional Chinese philosophy, things are divided into *qi*, the life-force or energy, and *li*, which is pattern or form. The Chinese came to terms with things that had little vitality or form by talking about different levels or fractions of *qi*, from coarse, heavy solids, through lighter, smoother liquids to the life-breath of living things.

All animals are said to have the life-breath. Even the wind has life-breath. But it is at its most refined in humans. In Chinese thinking, the body consists of Essential Substances or energies, Organ Systems and Channels. *Qi* or 'breath' is one

---

The third philosophy was Taoism, with its central text, the *Tao Te Ching* (The Book of the Way). Legend has it that it was written someone called Laozi, but Laozi simply means 'Old Master' and it was probably written by several people. Laozi's solution to the troubles of the world is to do nothing. His belief is that strife arises because people are constantly striving, and so constantly coming up against opposition and obstacles. He didn't mean literally doing nothing, but going with the flow, like a stream running to the sea. 'The Way,' the *Tao Te Ching* says, 'never acts yet nothing is left undone.' Although nowadays people in the West associate the Way with a state of serenity that is totally apolitical, that is not how it was intended. The *Tao Te Ching* says that rulers should get on with ruling with no regard to their people, leaving them ignorant and treating them 'like straw dogs' – which may be one reason why many rulers took up Taoism. It implied no responsibility of care for the populace.

The fourth Zhou period philosophy was in many ways the flipside to this political Taoism. This was the idea of Legalism, which advocated creating such a complete and rigid framework of law that there was no room for anyone to err. But for this to work, of course, those initiating the laws would have to take over all of China. If both Taoism and Legalism came to colour the thinking of Chinese emperors through the ages, maybe it influenced the attitude of the country's communist rulers, too.

of the essential energies and takes various forms. *Yuan-qi* is the *qi* that we are born with, and is fixed throughout our lives. But there are various other *qi*s that vary according to how we live our lives, such as *xue-qi*, which is the *qi* of the blood.

We are conceived, apparently, when *qi* accumulates in the universe, and die when it dissipates. The point in thinking about *qi* is to learn how to maintain and develop our life-force to achieve long life and spiritual power. It's all about balance and harmony. Balance depends partly on how you breathe, your sex life and your diet. According to Confucius, this is how a man should manage his *xue-qi*:

> The [morally] noble man guards himself against three things. When he is young, his *xue-qi* has not yet stabilized, so he guards himself against sexual passion. When he reaches his prime, his *xue-qi* is not easily subdued, so he guards himself against combativeness. When he reaches old age, his *xue-qi* is already depleted, so he guards himself against acquisitiveness.

The idea behind acupuncture is that the body's health depends on the unobstructed flow of *qi* through the body. *Qi* flows through the body along twelve meridians, or pathways, each linked to a major organ such as the liver or kidney and also with a body system. The pathways get blocked when there is an imbalance in the body, and the purpose of acupuncture is to unblock the channels and get the *qi* flowing freely and harmoniously again. The art of *feng shui*, on the other hand, is about placing things, especially in your home or place of work, to control the flow of *qi* – using colours, shapes and location to slow it down, accelerate it or redirect it. Martial arts such as *qigong* are about mastering the flow of *qi* to achieve extraordinary feats of strength, endurance or agility.

Many Chinese people have followed these principles for thousands of years, and similar ideas have surfaced in the West, as well as in India. The idea of a life-force distinct from the biochemical body is known in the West as vitalism and goes back to the times of Ancient Egypt and beyond. In the classical notion of the four humours or elements, the vital force was linked to each. When the four humours were banished to the realm of fiction by the scientific revolution of the seventeenth and eighteenth centuries, many scientists began to look for a scientific basis for a life-force that they believed was essential to maintain living functions. When electricity was discovered in the late eighteenth century, many believed they had found the life-force. Famous chemist Carl Reichenbach (1788–1869) developed the idea of Odic force. In the 1930s, psychoanalyst Wilhelm Reich, originally part of Freud's circle in Vienna, spent an enormous amount of energy exploring the idea of *orgone*, a universal life-force linked to the libido.[22]

Vitalism is now thoroughly discredited in the West as, one by one, its possible functions in the body have been explained by more basic biochemical means. 'Dualism ... and Vitalism (the view that living things contain some special physical but equally mysterious stuff – *élan vital*),' writes philosopher

---

[22] Famously, Reich built extraordinary machines called 'cloudbusters'. Clouds, he believed, were accumulations of orgone energy, and the cloudbusters fired orgone at the clouds to make them swell and release their energy as rain.

Daniel Dennett in his book *Kinds of Minds*, 'have been relegated to the trash heap of history …'

Yet the concept of *qi* has been slightly harder to binbag. One reason, of course, is that even the most hardline rationalists in the West are wary of trashing oriental tradition for fear of, perhaps entirely valid, accusations of cultural aggression. A second may be the interest in and moderate success of acupuncture.

Many mainstream Western medical practices now include acupuncture in their range of treatment. This is partly because of demand for it from patients and partly because there are signs that it does have some effect. There are now more than 10 million adults in the US who have used acupuncture at some time in the past, or are using it currently, according to the National Institute of Health. Scientific studies have shown that it actually works for many ailments. They have not shown why, and many still argue that its effectiveness is mainly a placebo. However, some recent scientific studies have indicated that acupuncture may unblock the twisting and knotting of body fibres that effect mechanotransduction, which is the way body cells convert mechanical stimulus into chemical activity. If that's true, then it might validate acupuncture but undermine the idea of *qi*.

The idea of *qi* is rooted in people's belief that there is something else to life beyond the material and obvious. Over the centuries, the areas that belief can reside in have been eroded by the advance of science, and rigid logicians already insist there is no place for such ideas in the rational mind. Yet there is a logical problem with writing it off entirely. Science is essentially empirical and inductive, and the idea of *qi* has the empirical 'evidence' of thousands of years of testimony on its side. It is, however, essentially un-testable – or at least, no one's thought of a way to test it yet – so in that sense it has no scientific basis. It is simply a belief. And yet there are many examples of the extraordinary feats of martial artists, for instance, to suggest that the jury can't quite leave the building yet. And even if it has no physical reality, it may be a priceless metaphor for a way of looking at the world that has, at least, some wisdom.

#42 Capitalism

According to an article in July 2007 in the *Economist*, 'The fall of the Berlin Wall in 1989 ... proved once and for all that capitalism is better than communism.' That same month, the first warning shocks were rumbling out in capitalism's worst crisis for almost a century as the banking system threatened to slide into chaos on a collapsing mountain of debt. Of course, swift and desperate intervention by governments around the world to pump money into the failing banks forestalled the crisis – and so the world's arch-capitalists, some said with grim glee, had been rescued by state intervention. Now those arch-capitalists are apparently having the last laugh as governments across Europe scramble to cut expenditure to avoid a crisis in their credit rating.

Capitalism is, it seems, a survivor. It has been around for a long time. Indeed, while the theory of communism was worked out well before it became a reality, capitalism was practised many centuries before it gained its first theoretical justification in Adam Smith's seminal *The Wealth of Nations* (1776).

In some ways, capitalism is as old as history, for there have always been sellers and buyers, markets and traders. But it is the large-scale emergence of merchants from the 1500s on, as the medieval feudal system of barons and serfs broke down, that is commonly identified as the first stirrings of capitalism. National governments such as the British and Dutch encouraged merchants' efforts in accordance with what became known as the mercantilist doctrine. This argued that the world drew from a limited pot and so the wealth of each nation depended on ensuring a 'favourable balance of trade' in which more gold flowed in than out.

Smith believed that this was short-sighted. What mattered is not the wealth of individual nations but the wealth of all nations. Nor is the pot fixed; it can grow over time – but only if there is unrestricted trade between nations. If left free, Smith insisted, the market will always grow to produce the right amount of goods because it is guided by the invisible hand of self-interest. 'It is not from the benevolence of the butcher, the brewer, or the baker that we expect our dinner,' Smith contended, 'but from their regard to their own self-interest.' Any artificial restriction on trade such as taxation or regulations would, he believed, interfere with the smooth operation of this market of self-interest.

Over the next century, Smith's free trade ideas were taken up enthusiastically by British business and characterised as *laissez-faire*, from the French 'leave to do'. It became a mantra for governments, reminding them to leave the markets entirely alone to get on with trade without regulations or restraint.[23] Smith's book also launched a whole new science known as political economy, and eventually just economy. One of its leading lights was David Ricardo (1772–1823) who, more than anyone, brought the term capitalist into popular usage.

The guiding idea of capitalism, articulated not just by Adam Smith but many other political and economic theorists, is that businesses are privately owned and operated for profit in a free market. Private property is central because the desire to own and increase your property is what drives the market. In order to trade in the free market, you must have capital, which means everything that is needed to run a business, from buildings and machinery to money. If you don't have capital, you work for wages – but even labour is a commodity to be traded.

Open markets are seen as crucial to capitalism, because they allow the 'invisible hand' to operate, determining prices for goods and services through the balance between supply and demand. So capitalists invest time and money in ensuring that governments do not restrain their trade in any way. Indeed, in many capitalist countries, election campaigns are

---

[23] Some of the hottest debates centred on the Corn Laws, the import tariffs designed to protect British farmers from having their prices for grain undercut by cheap American and Russian imports. The turning point was the Irish potato famine, which persuaded Prime Minister Robert Peel to abolish the Corn Laws in 1846, to give the Irish the chance of cheaper bread. While most European countries kept their import tariffs, Britain and Belgium alone kept their borders duty-free, with the result that British dependence on imported grain rose from 2 per cent in the 1830s to over 65 per cent in the 1880s.

often won by those backed by the most capital, so that even politics operates like the marketplace.

For many supporters of capitalism, the freedom of the market is a freedom more fundamental than simply economic. Only under capitalism, they argue, are people free to choose what they want to do with their lives without interference from the state. In even the best socialist states, your choices are restricted because only the government can run certain operations. Under capitalism, in theory, you can choose to run a bus company or open a flower shop or work as a doctor or follow any career path you choose. In other words, you are free, in classic American parlance, to pursue your dream. You are also free to dispose of your money as you wish, frittering it away on alcohol or saving it for something worthwhile.

This inherent link between capitalism and liberty is, some would argue, its greatest moral strength. The drive for free markets also drives demands for personal and political freedom. Some might even argue that capitalism is liberty's greatest champion. There is certainly some truth in the view that it was the lack of liberty that led, ultimately, to the downfall of the Soviet regime, not its economic failure, or even its failure to provide adequately for people's well-being. China at the moment seems to be walking a fine tightrope between free markets and political freedoms.

Not everyone would agree with capitalism's version of freedom, however. 'Advocates of capitalism,' Bertrand Russell lamented sardonically, 'are very apt to appeal to the sacred principles of liberty, which are embodied in one maxim: The fortunate must not be restrained in the exercise of tyranny over the unfortunate.'

In the aftermath of the First World War, the faltering world economy in the Depression years caused the great Cambridge economist John Maynard Keynes to question the effectiveness of the 'invisible hand' in responding to crises. In particular, he focused on the problem of mass unemployment. The market, he argued, had no way to deal with this problem, at least in the short term. The classical maxim, known as Say's Law, that supply creates demand, breaks down in times of recession, because people are too worried to spend – thus accelerating the downward spiral.

Keynes argued that the only way to break this vicious circle was for governments to stimulate the economy. First, the central banks need to boost the supply of money by making lending easier and reducing interest rates. Then, if that doesn't prove enough, they must spend massively on public works to get the cashflow going. After the striking success of Keynes's ideas in Roosevelt's New Deal, when massive public works projects seemed to lift America out of the Depression, Keynes's ideas quickly became the standard for Western governments – so much so that President Nixon declared in 1967: 'We are all Keynesian now.'

But the oil shortage and economic downturn of the 1970s persuaded some economists to question whether throwing extra money into the economy without the market to back it up simply caused inflation. A new generation of 'monetarists' emerged, arguing that the supply and demand for money should be kept in balance. This seemed like plain old good housekeeping, and the idea of keeping a tight rein on the money supply soon became firmly entrenched in central bank policies, especially in the USA under Alan Greenspan, Chairman of the Federal Reserve.

American monetarist Milton Friedman pushed the argument further and argued for a stripped-back capitalism in which all regulation was removed and the market was allowed to let rip without control. Only that way could the invisible hand really work. It might be messy, but ultimately it was for the good of all to let capitalism out of its chains. 'What kind of society isn't structured on greed?' Friedman declared. 'The problem of social organization is how to set up an arrangement under which greed will do the least harm; capitalism is that kind of a system.'

Friedman's arguments were persuasive for right-wing governments like Reagan's in America and Thatcher's in Britain, which stripped back government spending, initiated a wave of privatisations and let loose the financial markets from regulations. For a while, after a few hiccoughs, it seemed to deliver the globalisation bonanza of Adam Smith's dreams.

There was a flaw, though. Capitalists had always argued that the inequalities inherent in the system were not a problem, because as overall wealth grew it would always 'trickle down' to the less fortunate.[24] But this globalisation bonanza seemed to widen the gap between rich and poor, and while the rich got richer, the poor saw very little improvement in

---

[24] The ever-shrewd Keynes was quick to nail the hypocrisy inherent in this line of argument: 'Capitalism is the astounding belief that the most wickedest of men will do the most wickedest of things for the greatest good of everyone.' Noam Chomsky believes that Adam Smith has been misrepresented by contemporary ideologists. Smith, Chomsky claims, supported markets not because they thrived on inequality but because he believed they would lead to equality.

their fortunes. And then, in 2008, it all went horribly wrong, as first the super-rich Lehman Brothers investment bank collapsed and then the whole world banking system threatened to implode. With striking irony, this crisis in capitalism was averted by concerted government support for the banks initiated by UK's Labour Prime Minister Gordon Brown.

With the banks seemingly on the road to recovery, capitalism has slipped quietly out of the spotlight,[25] and the attention has focused on just how governments are going to deal with the mountain of debts incurred and avoid deep recession. Some argue that Keynesian-style public spending is the right road. The nervous public, though, in countries like the USA, the UK and Germany have been persuaded that belt-tightening is the answer, a response that has Keynesians throwing their arms up in despair, fearing that this may bring a 'double-dip recession' as the vicious circle of collapsing demand kicks in.

Capitalism itself, though, has neatly evaded the attacks aimed either at greedy bankers or profligate governments. Indeed, capitalism, despite some shaky times, seems more firmly established than ever, and the body blows aimed at it by Karl Marx 150 years ago, and by the rise of communist countries in the mid-twentieth century, now seem well and truly in the past. It is not a good system. How can any system be said to be good if it leaves so many people around the world dying

---

[25] In a recent book, Anatole Kaletsky, an editor at *The Times*, suggests that the banking crisis will force a revision of the whole basis of capitalism and that in future a new version of capitalism will emerge, which he dubs, in software style, Capitalism 4.0. The previous versions are the classic *laissez-faire* capitalism of the nineteenth century (Capitalism 1.0), government-heavy Keynesian capitalism of the mid-twentieth century (Capitalism 2.0) and the free-market Friedman-style capitalism of the last 30 years (Capitalism 3.0).

from lack of food, living grim poverty-filled lives, or simply working in jobs they hate just to get by? It's a terrible system indeed that creates such inequalities and such suffering. Yet maybe it's a *great idea* for it to survive for so long and convince so many people that, for all its manifold shortcomings, it's the only viable way of running the world.

#41 Welfare State

In 1942, as war raged across Europe and much of the world, British MP William Beveridge released a historic report outlining his dramatic proposals for the creation of a welfare state in Britain. The plan was bold and far-reaching, and was received with tremendous excitement. Beveridge's plan was, many felt, just what the war-torn country needed. Its stirring vision of a nation in which everyone would be looked after, 'from the cradle to the grave', was something worth fighting for, 'a home fit for heroes'.[26]

Beveridge's aim, he said, was to slay the five evil giants that stalked the land: Want (by which he meant poverty), Disease, Ignorance, Squalor and Idleness (unemployment). Just how cruel these giants could be was still raw in the memory from the terrible years of the Great Depression of the 1930s.

There had been some kind of support for the poor in Britain dating back to the sixteenth century, provided by a

---

[26] It was also part of the campaign to, in modern parlance, win hearts and minds. Summaries of the report were issued to troops to boost morale. They were also dropped into Germany to let German people know of this promise of a golden future for all if the Allies won. A copy of the Beveridge paper, with a report acknowledging its strengths, was later found in Hitler's bunker.

hotchpotch of poor laws, friendly societies and charities. Since 1911, there had even been limited state welfare.[27] Indeed, the idea of state welfare goes back to the newly unified Germany of the 1880s, when Chancellor Otto von Bismarck introduced the first old age pension and a national insurance scheme to compensate workers who were unable to work through sickness or accident. Following the German example, Sweden developed a welfare system in the inter-war years.

What was revolutionary about Beveridge's plan, however, was its universal scope. Beveridge planned to take the responsibility of the public welfare entirely into government hands. The UK was to be a 'welfare state' in which everyone was looked after by the state when they were in trouble.

At the heart of Beveridge's plan was a compulsory insurance scheme under which every worker would contribute out of their pay-packets to a national pot that would pay out benefits to anyone who was unemployed or unable to work through sickness. There were family allowances including child benefits, maternity payments and training grants, too. And for those

---

[27] The first elements of the British welfare state date back to the early twentieth century. One spur was the research of Seebohm Rowntree, which showed just how difficult life was for the urban poor in York in 1899. A second was the shock that 25 per cent of volunteers trying to enlist for the Boer War that year were unfit for service, and in cities such as Manchester that figure rose to 80 per cent. Determined to put things right, Liberal governments under Herbert Asquith and David Lloyd George introduced free school meals in 1906, a means-tested pension in 1908, labour exchanges in 1909, and the National Insurance Act of 1911 to provide a basic level of health insurance and unemployment benefit. Interestingly, when Rowntree repeated his investigations in 1936, he found that poverty had more than halved, but whereas the main factor in poverty in 1899 was low wages, in 1936 it was unemployment.

who hadn't paid enough in insurance contributions, there was a second tier of benefits, known as national assistance (later renamed supplementary benefit and then income support). Beyond that, the plan would extend the government pension, and create cheap housing, universal secondary education and, most famous of all, an entirely free National Health Service.

It was a grand vision for a country where people would always be looked after if they were sick, old or vulnerable, where no one would lack the basic needs of life, and where everyone would live in decent houses and get a good education so that they would have the chance to fulfil their potential in life. Although it emerged from the wartime coalition, it was the Labour party who won the right to put the plan into action with their landslide election victory at the end of the war. They did so with an astonishing rapidity that spread an almost missionary zeal across the country, as people tried to create a better future from the ruins of the war. All the main measures were in place within four years. The crowning achievement was Health Minister Nye Bevan's establishment of the National Health Service in 1948.

Britain was not alone in creating a welfare society after the war. Appalled by the cataclysmic impact of fascism and communism, Winston Churchill and Franklin D. Roosevelt had already agreed in 1941 under the Atlantic Charter that there was to be global cooperation to improve social welfare and an international commitment to stop people living in want and fear. When the war was finally over, the Atlantic Charter became the inspiration for the United Nations, and in 1946, the UN General Assembly adopted the Universal Declaration of Human Rights, whose Article 22 recognised that: 'Everyone, as a member of society, has the right to social security'.

The western European nations, at least, were as good as their word. In the aftermath of the Second World War, every major western European state introduced its own welfare system. Each country started to provide a high level of social support, ranging from universal payments for those out of work to health insurance for all.[28] Other nations, such as Japan, South Korea and Saudi Arabia, would soon follow suit. The idea that the state should look after its poor, sick and vulnerable is now widely accepted around the world.

There is an argument that Western leaders embraced welfare not through benevolence but fear of what could happen if the problems of the poor were left unaddressed. Welfare, it

---

[28] There are three basic kinds of welfare system. Scandinavian countries have a social democratic system that provides universal support based on taxation. Continental European countries have a work-centred system based on insurance contributions. The UK and US systems target only the poorest using means tests. Beveridge's original intention was that the UK welfare system should be a universal system, with the national insurance payments ensuring that everyone has a stake in the system. It was never put into place as he intended and in the 1980s the Conservative government reduced the insurance element and shifted the system towards targeted, means-tested supplementary benefits. Many experts argue that this is why poverty in Britain has remained stubbornly high. 'The more universal nature of the continental system,' Professors Pat Thane and Noel Whiteside say, 'has ensured that it has deep support across all sections of society: all citizens can be part of the same system, and payments out are at a level that makes it genuinely attractive to the middle-classes.' The same professors also posit a reason why Britain's welfare system is like it is: 'The dominance of the Treasury has played a significant part in differentiating Britain from other European nations in the general course that the evolution of the welfare state has taken.'

is suggested, was simply a sop to keep a lid on problems. That was the accusation of many socialists who felt the Labour party had betrayed its cause by setting up the welfare state, helping to prolong capitalism. But for all those motivated by fear, there were many more who were deeply committed to creating a more caring state and many millions of ordinary people who embraced the idea enthusiastically.

The impact of the welfare state was immediate, and played a huge part in reducing the suffering of the poor. In the 1930s, many people in Europe still suffered the deprivation now associated with India. But within a decade of the introduction of the welfare state that kind of extreme hardship was all but forgotten. Even the very poorest people in Europe had at least a basic level of support that kept them fed, warm and well. No children in welfare state Europe were ever forced to wear rags and go barefoot, or die from malnutrition as they had before.[29]

The welfare state now seems such a part of the fabric of everyday life in many countries that it is hard to imagine life without it. Yet it still has many critics. Some object on principle. The imposition of taxes on everyone to pay for others' needs, they assert, is an infringement of individual liberty. The welfare state is a system based on compulsion because it needs everyone to contribute for it to work. This argument

---

[29] Poverty has not been eliminated by the welfare state. Indeed, a fifth of the UK's population is today defined as poor, which means their income is less than 60 per cent of the national average. That's not so much lower than the 1930s, when 30 per cent of people were poor. But what it means to be poor has changed out of all recognition. In the 1930s, it was still defined as someone who could not afford to buy a shopping bag of a few basic items. Now even those considered poor may own their own homes and have items such as TVs and dishwashers.

neatly forgets that the welfare systems in Sweden, Finland and Denmark were, until recently, entirely voluntary.

In recent years, though, critics have focused on the idea that welfare is bad for the country. The arguments are not new, but they seem to have been given a new impetus by opposition to US President Barack Obama's controversial healthcare reforms.

Welfare systems, the critics say, encourage fraud, as people claim benefits that they are not entitled to.[30] Generous benefits, too, encourage people to sponge off the state rather than work, and so fuel resentment among those working hard for meagre wages.

Worse, the welfare state is said to be psychologically damaging. It not only becomes a 'nanny state', in which the government patronisingly interferes in every aspect of people's lives, from child-rearing to basic safety; it can also create a 'dependency culture' in which successive generations of families become incapable of looking after themselves. The use of the word 'dependency' is deliberate; it's a casually insidious way of associating living on welfare benefits with drug addiction.

The recession has added extra fuel to the critics' attacks on the welfare state. Now the argument is that with countries deep in debt to pay for the banking crisis, the developed

---

[30] Interestingly, headlines in the UK proclaim that a massive £1.5 billion is claimed fraudulently, inspiring government ministers to announce a crackdown while fuelling the public perception that the welfare system is badly flawed. What the headlines often omit is that this £1.5 billion is much less than 1 per cent of the welfare budget, which is about the same percentage as the unidentified loss in any private business.

world simply cannot afford its generous welfare provisions. Spending on welfare is not only unaffordable, they say; it is a drag on the economy, discouraging people from seeking work. Remarkably, this argument seems to have won the day in many countries, with media polls of public opinion seemingly in agreement with politicians on the need to cut back.

And yet this 'common sense' argument has no actual foundation in reality. Welfare systems have rarely acted as a brake on a country's economy. It's not just that rich countries can afford welfare. In nearly all cases, countries that have introduced a welfare system have experienced dramatic economic growth. After Germany introduced its welfare system in the 1880s, its economy grew rapidly – so rapidly that Britain was shocked to find it had an economic rival for the first time, and right on its doorstep. And in the post-war years, western Europe has experienced a time of unparalleled prosperity. Moreover, the most prosperous countries, such as Sweden and Germany, are those with some of the most generous welfare provision.

The nervousness of people facing recession makes it clear why this might be. A society in which the poor and the sick and the old are looked after feels at ease with itself. It feels confident and outward-looking. Young people can enter further education with a sense of security about the future, a sense that they will not be left high and dry if it doesn't work out as they hoped. People can buy houses with the reassurance that the state will be there to catch them if they fall. They can spend money on improving their circumstances confident that if they fall sick they will receive proper medical care. More significantly, perhaps, entrepreneurs can start or expand a business, knowing that if it goes wrong, neither they nor the people they have employed will be out on the street. Without that cushion, many of these decisions – the decisions that are essential for the economic as well as social well-being of society – might seem risky if not reckless.

The lessons of the 1930s – the lessons of fascism and the worst aspects of communism – taught that a country cannot afford to ignore its poor and disadvantaged. Common humanity means that we should not. In our own personal interest, we want that safety net to be there to catch us should we fall, however comfortable our circumstances are now. That's what a welfare state should do when it's working at its best.

#40 The Sail

The sail is the perhaps the most beautiful of all human technologies. There is no finer way of moving around the world than slipping through the water, wafted along by the wind, using no more energy than is given freely by the atmosphere. Even in rough weather, when one is buffeted by the elements, there is a grandeur about it matched by no other way of travelling.

For 5,000 years, the sail provided the principal way of getting around the world. It was the driving force of exploration, trade and communications. Without the sail, Columbus could never have crossed the Atlantic, Cook would never have found Australia and Ibn Battuta would never have explored Africa. Without the sail, countless goods from overseas would never have reached us. Without the sail, Europeans would never have colonised America. Maybe all of these things have a downside, but it was the voyagers, not the sail, who were responsible for the damage of colonialism. The day-to-day food of countless millions through the ages was supplied by fishing boats driven by the wind towards the best shoals and back.

It's impossible to tell just how long ago sails were first used. Prehistoric boats were made from perishable materials such as wood and reeds. The sails themselves are even more perishable. The oldest fragment of sail is a scrap of linen with a wooden ring from second-century BC Egypt. But there are Minoan pictures of sailing boats dating from 2000 BC, and one on a vase from Naqada in Egypt that dates back to 3100 BC. It seems likely that the Chinese had sails around the same time. It is quite possible, though, that sails date back much further. Cloths such as linen, and later canvas, make the perfect sail material, but native Americans simply used bushes.

The first sails were probably square rigs – that is, square sails hung from a beam or yard from the mast, across the boat at right angles. These were simple and effective. It's easy to appreciate how the wind drives the boat along when the boat is travelling 'downwind' – that is with the wind behind. The wind simply pushes against the sail and the boat 'runs' before it. Because the wind is behind the boat, the boat remains stable, despite the area of sail and the mast on top.

Although the yard can pivot up to 45° to catch the wind from different angles, the wind still has to be behind the boat. By tacking – taking a zig-zag course – a simple square-rigged boat can make some headway against an oncoming wind – but no closer to the direction of the wind than about 70 degrees.

That means square-rigged boats are very much dependent on the direction of the wind. Their speed, too, is limited entirely by the strength of the wind.

This is why the invention of the fore-and-aft sail in the Middle East around 2,000 years ago was such a huge technological breakthrough. Unlike the simple square rig, which stretches across the boat at right angles, the fore-and-aft sail is set up in line with the boat. Although fore-and-aft sails can be square, the earliest were all triangular 'lateen' sails,[31] still seen today in Arab dhows. The top side of the triangle was hung from a yard mounted on the mast and slanting down at an angle from the aft of the boat. The bottom aft corner was left free and secured by ropes.

Sails like these work in an entirely different way to square sails. With lateens, the sail acts like an aerofoil. When the sail is at a right angle to the wind, the sail bows out. As the air rushes over it, it creates pressure differences either side. Just as these provide lift with an aerofoil (see page 31), so they draw the sailing boat on. The pressure on the sail tends to tip the boat over sideways, so a keel on the bottom of the boat is essential to reduce the chances of the boat capsizing. But with a lateen sail, a boat can 'beat' much closer to the wind – that is, it can sail almost into the wind. Early lateen boats could sail just 40° from the wind direction; some modern yachts can sail less than 20°.

Lateens were much more manoeuvrable than square rigs, and were not so dependent on wind direction. The way the

---

[31] They were called lateen because they were identified with the Mediterranean and the Latin world.

sails worked also meant that in the hands of a skilled sailor they could actually move faster than the wind. They were not as safe, though, and bigger boats would require a larger, more highly trained crew. So merchant boats often persisted with square rigs for reliability and economy.

By 1200, many ships had two masts, one with a lateen sail and one with a square sail, which gave them the best of both worlds. On the whole, though, merchants still preferred the square-rig because a big square rig sail could drive a ship with a heavier cargo. Lateens were preferred for small fishing boats, because of their versatility. Then in the fifteenth century, the Portuguese developed a little three-masted lateen-rigged ship called a caravel. The caravel was the fastest, most manoeuvrable ship of the age, and perfect for exploring unknown seas such as the coast of Africa, where sailors would encounter variable winds, strong currents and unknown shoals. All the great Portuguese explorers including Bartolome Diaz and Vasco da Gama used caravels for their voyages of discovery.

Interestingly, though, when Columbus made his historic voyage across the Atlantic in 1492, he chose to put square sails on the foremast and mainmast of his trio of caravels, and had a lateen only on the mizzenmast (the mast behind the mainmast). He was clearly confident that he was going to find following winds. As it turned out, he was right. He was able to take advantage of the easterly trade winds in the subtropics for the outward journey, then sail back further north driven by the westerly winds. This became the standard route for sailing boats on the transatlantic journey. But how did he know? Was he just lucky?

With new routes and new worlds discovered, the merchants followed to open up trade in anything from spices and silks from Southern Asia to tobacco from the Americas. The voyages were long, so merchants wanted big ships to make the journey worthwhile. But to drive big ships, you needed a large area of sail, and it was a much harder task to make lateen sail ships big. Moreover, lateen ships needed a large crew. In the sixteenth century, Venetian maritime statutes required lateen-sailed 'busses' of 240 tons to have a crew of 50; a square-sailed 'cog' of the same size was allowed a crew of just 20. So, of course, square sails and cheap crews won out over lateens.

Soon, masts were growing taller, and each carried not just one sail but two, three, four or even five. They had small triangular sails aft and to the fore, but they were essentially square-riggers. The classic was the East Indiaman, which plied the routes between India and Europe between the seventeenth and the nineteenth centuries. The culmination of these square riggers were the glorious 'clippers' of the nineteenth century.

Designed to bring back tea and other low-volume, high-value goods from China to Britain with the utmost possible speed, the clippers were narrow, very streamlined boats with a huge sail area, and only a fairly small cargo space. The American clippers were astonishingly fast for such big ships. They could frequently reach speeds of nearly 20 knots, and sail 400 nautical miles in a day. The record of 465 miles (861 km) in a single day was held by the clipper *Champion of the Seas*, which achieved this remarkable feat on its maiden voyage in 1854 – a record only finally beaten 130 years later in 1984 by a specialist racing yacht. While Columbus took

66 days to return across the Atlantic, clippers were expected to do it just fourteen days.

Yet just as clippers gave sail its finest hour, so the writing was on the wall. Steamships were already beginning to compete because, although slower, they were less dependent on the vagaries of the wind, and needed fewer crew. The death knell was the opening of the Suez Canal, which cut a huge distance off the voyage from Asia to the west, but couldn't be used by sailing boats. As steam boats got faster, and needed ever fewer crew, the sailing ships disappeared. Nowadays, of course, sail is essentially for recreation or sport, but for those sailors the magic is as alive as ever it was in Coleridge's day:

The fair breeze blew, the white foam flew,
The furrow followed free.

#39 Copper and Iron

If there is anything that clearly marks the end of prehistory and the beginning of history, it is the discovery of metals. The millions of years of prehistory, when humans relied on painstakingly sharpened stones and bones for tools, are aptly known as the Stone Age. The first transition into the historical era is tellingly the Bronze Age. The second is the Iron Age. And the modern age could well be called the Metallic Age.

Without metals, our cities would fall apart, since the nails and screws that hold things together are metal and the beams that strengthen buildings and bridges are metal. So are the trains, and cars and planes and ships that carry us and all the goods we need for living. So are the tools and machines we need to fabricate it all. And so are many humbler objects from saucepans and washing machines to knives and door handles. A world without metals might be appealingly rustic but would be primitive indeed.

The idea of metals and metal production is so much a part of our world that it's easy to take for granted. Yet the idea that metals could be obtained from the ground and fashioned into objects was astonishingly clever. Even today, knowing what metals are and where they come from, it is very hard for any-one but a highly trained mineralogist to even identify a rock that might yield metal. Just think what a discovery it would be if you didn't even know that ordinary-looking rocks actually contained metal.

Gold is one of the few metals that occur naturally in a pure state. It is also very distinctive and shiny. So it is not surprising that gold was among the first metals to be used. Yet it was too rare, and too soft, to be used as anything but ornament. The same must have seemed true initially of copper. Pure copper is, if anything, harder to find in the ground, because oxidation covers it in the sheen of dull green known as verdigris. And it is almost as soft as gold. So the earliest copper artefacts are mostly ceremonial or decorative, such as the small copper plates found at Çatal Höyük in Anatolia dating from around 8,500 years ago. The only tools were simple copper hooks and awls, like those from Çayönü Tepesi in eastern Turkey from 9,000 years ago.

The great breakthrough was the discovery that certain rocks, now known as ores, contained substantial quantities of copper that could be 'smelted' out by heating. It may have been an observant potter who noticed what happened when he fired the brightly coloured minerals green malachite and turquoise azurite in his kiln. If the kiln was hot enough, little drops of copper would have melted out of the stones. Once ores and smelting were discovered – maybe about 6,500–7,000 years ago in Anatolia and about 5,000 years ago in China – a copper industry began to develop, and copper tools began to gradually be used more and more in place of stone tools in what is called the Chalcolithic era.

The copper made in these smelters was very rarely pure, and often contained impurities such as arsenic, tin, zinc and antimony. Around 5,000 years ago in Western Asia, some smiths must have begun to realise that copper with the right quantity of arsenic or tin[32] in it made a metal that while not necessarily as pretty as pure copper, was both very hard and easy to cast into particular shapes by melting and cooling.[33] These impure arsenic or tin coppers, or alloys, are, of course, bronze.

It's hard to overestimate just what a technological breakthrough the discovery of bronze was. Making bronze was

---

[32] It was probably some time before smiths became aware of the dangers of arsenic and switched to tin bronze. Prolonged exposure to arsenic fumes damaged nerves to limbs and may have given rise to the later image of the maimed smith, such as the Greek god Hephaestus and the Roman Vulcan.

[33] The first bronze items such as axe heads were probably made in a single mould hollowed out in stone. But by the middle Bronze Age, smiths were making more complex items such as daggers by pouring the molten metal through a small gap into two hollowed-out stones put together and then pulled apart when the metal had cooled and solidified. By the end of the Bronze Age, smiths were making wax or fat models then putting clay round them and heating the clay to melt the wax. They then poured in the molten metal, waited for it to cool and solidify, and chipped away the clay.

the world's first major industry. Bronze axes, spearheads and daggers were so vastly superior to their stone equivalents that everyone wanted them. And bronze allowed for the creation of the first swords and suits of armour. The bronze industry spread quickly west across Europe from Asia and east into India, making fortunes for those with the skill to fashion bronze and creating the first large-scale, organised trade in minerals and the first major mines, as people dug for the valuable ores in places from Timna in Sinai to Mount Gabriel in County Cork.

Bronze gave humans an ability to shape the world, raise the standard of living and bring the fruits of civilisation in a way that stone never could. But it also brought many of the problems that we associate with the rise of civilisations. Its huge value, and the fact that some places had the resources and technology and others didn't, created enormous differences in power and wealth for the first time, and with those differences, inevitably, came war. The real motive behind the Ancient Greek attack on Troy, so memorably described in Homer's epic *Iliad*, may well have been the lure not of Helen's matchless beauty but control of the city's famous bronze trade.

The rise of the bronze industry, too, may have provoked the first real ecological crisis, as vast areas of forest were cleared, not just to make way for farms but to provide wood to fuel the voracious demands of the smelters. Plato lamented, for instance, how vast swathes of the countryside round Athens were ravaged by deforestation. Cyprus, the island that gave copper its name, was completely stripped of its ancient cedar forests.

As smiths' skill and ability to handle bronze improved, and they learned to exploit the subtly different mixtures of ores and alloys, they must have tried out other ores too. Eventually, about 4,500 years ago, Hittite smiths in Anatolia discovered that at very high temperatures, they could smelt certain ores to produce iron.[34] Iron was tougher than bronze and could make even better blades – and, crucially, iron ores were much more widely available than copper and tin. With carbon from the charcoal included in the iron, it made steel, which remains the best tool- and blade-making metal of all.

The technology of iron-making was much, much harder to master than bronze-making, though, and the first iron suffered from being too weak or too brittle. So for 1,000 years or more, bronze was still preferred to iron and steel. The first breakthrough, dating from about 1100 BC, was 'quenching', which means plunging the newly forged blade into cold water while still hot. The second was tempering, which means gently reheating the blade after quenching. Quenched and tempered steel gave a combination of hardness, strength and flexibility that proved far superior to bronze, and the Iron Age began.

Poets like Homer lamented the shift from the gold beauty of bronze to crude grey iron and steel, but it changed the balance of power. Bronze had been too expensive for all but elite soldiers to use. With iron, vast armies of foot soldiers could be equipped with swords, spears and armour. Moreover, iron was so cheap it could be used for more prosaic, peaceful purposes from cooking pots and spoons to drills and nails. Iron opened

---

[34] Iron was known well before this, but only from rare meteorite iron. This kind of iron was so precious that in Tutankhamun's tomb, a single iron dagger held pride of place amid the tonnes of fabulous gold objects.

up a huge range of everyday technology from the mundane, such as locks and keys, to machines held together by iron nails and braces. When the Romans abandoned the fort of Inchtuthil in central Scotland, they buried 750,000 nails to prevent them falling into the hands of the Picts.

Further key breakthroughs in iron- and steel-making technology in the eighteenth century quite literally underpinned the Industrial Revolution, and in some ways the Industrial Revolution is as much an Iron Age as the prehistoric era. Making cast iron using coke in blast furnaces enabled iron to be made on an industrial scale, so that iron became a major structural material. The famous Iron Bridge in Shropshire, built in 1778, was just the first of many fantastic iron structures from the Forth Rail Bridge to the Eiffel Tower, not to mention the hundreds of thousands of miles of rails that drove the industrial and urban explosion of the nineteenth century and beyond.

Anyone who feels that industrialisation is at the roots of all that is wrong with the modern world will feel that the discovery of metals was a disaster for humanity. With bronze and iron came swords and shields, soldiers and large-scale warfare. In the Bronze and Iron Ages came the beginnings of large-scale trade, mines where people slaved in dark and danger, industrial spoil, pollution from smelters and deforestation. In the age of the Industrial Revolution and on, blast furnaces added Blake's nightmare vision of dark Satanic mills, mines dug deeper and darker to supply coke, the landscape was scarred by railways, and iron was used to create the battleships and tanks for the world wars.

And yet all these things cannot necessarily be laid at the door of the metals themselves. Metals are fantastic discoveries, enabling us to make all kinds of wonderful things, from aeroplanes and spacecraft to robots and computer circuits. It is hard to conceive of any of the technology we so rely on today without metals and in particular copper and iron. Metals have given humankind the ability to shape and rebuild the world in a way that would be unimaginable with stone and clay and wood. Like any powerful idea, however, they can be misused, and it has been our choice that metals have been used to damage the world, and to damage ourselves, as well as improve it.

#38 Banking

There are few ideas in this book that have come in for so much stick over so long as banking. In the past few years, in particular, the banking crisis has aroused so much fury against the banks that it seems they are being attacked for the first time. Yet the attacks go back to antiquity.

The trade of the petty usurer is hated with most reason: it makes a profit from currency itself, instead of making it from the process which currency was meant to serve. Their common characteristic is obviously their sordid avarice.
– Aristotle

And Jesus went into the temple of God, and cast out all them that sold and bought in the temple, and overthrew the tables of the money changers ... and said unto them, 'It is written,

My house shall be called the house of prayer; but ye have made it a den of thieves.' – The Bible

When a government is dependent upon bankers for money, they and not the leaders of the government control the situation, since the hand that gives is above the hand that takes. Money has no motherland; financiers are without patriotism and without decency; their sole object is gain. – Napoleon Bonaparte

Banks have done more injury to the religion, morality, tranquility, prosperity, and even wealth of the nation than they can have done or ever will do good. – John Adams

I sincerely believe that banking institutions are more dangerous than standing armies; and that the principle of spending money to be paid by posterity ... is but swindling futurity on a large scale. – Thomas Jefferson

It is well enough that people of the nation do not understand our banking and monetary system, for if they did, I believe there would be a revolution before tomorrow morning. – Henry Ford

By comparison, Mark Twain's pungent assertion that 'A banker is a fellow who lends you his umbrella when the sun is shining and wants it back the minute it begins to rain', seems positively friendly.

So how have banks survived so long? What is it that makes them so apparently necessary?

From the customer's point of view, they have three main uses. The first is to facilitate money transfer – making it simpler for people to pay you and for you to pay others for goods and services, and to give you access to money when and where you need it. The second is to look after your money until you need it. The third is to extend credit to you or your business so that you have the money you need when you need it. In the developed world, it is still possible to function without a bank account, and many people do, but life without a bank account is much more of a struggle (not that life with one is exactly easy sometimes).

On the larger level, banks are deemed pretty much essential for the capitalist system to work. A few very rich people have the capital to start a business without bank funds. But otherwise entrepreneurs need starting capital, and capital to tide them over until cashflow builds up. In theory, banks gather together money from savers and other depositors and funnel it towards those who need it to run businesses.

This freeing up of money that would otherwise sit doing nothing is essential for economic growth, it is argued. Without this flow of money, economies would stagnate. With it, businesses have the money to start producing goods. They pay wages and salaries that people use to buy things, and the goods that they make can be sold, increasing the flow of money. Hence the recent worry over the way in which banks, in the wake of the banking crisis, have begun to restrict loans in order to build up their reserves. If this restriction goes too far, economic growth could be really damaged – and ironically the money available for building up bank reserves will also be curtailed.

The origins of banking lie in the ancient world, when people began to put their corn and other goods, and later their gold and silver, in temples and similar places for safe-keeping. Using their store of goods and gold, temple priests in eighteenth-century BC Babylon would make loans to merchants. By the time of Ancient Greece, temples and other private institutions were performing a full range of banking services – loans, deposits, money changing and transfers. The island of Delos became a banking centre. In return for deposits, many banking institutions started to give people receipts or credit notes. In the third-century Persian empire of the Sassanids, for instance, traders were using credit notes called Ṣakks. In effect, all the elements of modern banking were in place thousands of years ago.

It was in the Crusades, though, that modern banking began to emerge in Europe. Rather than risk carrying large sums of money on the long journey to the Crusades, wealthy soldiers and pilgrims would deposit their money with organisations such as the Knights Templar at the start of their journey, then use a demand note to pay for things at any of the Templar castles and holdings across Europe. The Templars made a great deal of money out of this, and became the first multi-national banking organisation, and it may have been their financial clout that eventually provoked the French king to dissolve them in 1307.

By that time, though, the first of the great Italian banks were beginning to appear – run by families such as the Medici, Bardi and Peruzzi. They avoided the Christian sin of 'usury' (charging interest on loans) by creative accounting.[35] Interest was presented in accounts as a voluntary gift or a reward for risks taken. These banks began increasingly to be not just places for keeping money or making transfers, but the major sources of finance in the world. Even kings and queens went to the banks to raise money for wars or building palaces. And because of the high rates of interest charged on finance – 12–45 per cent – the banks became increasingly rich and powerful. With the rise of trade in north-west Europe from the late 1500s on, banking became absolutely central to national economies as merchants borrowed money to buy goods and then paid it back, with interest, when the goods were sold.

In simple terms, the banks worked liked this. People deposited their gold or other valuables in the bank for safekeeping. In return the bank gave them a 'promise to pay' note should they ever want to retrieve their gold. Soon people began to buy things with these banknotes, rather than paying directly in gold. Even today, of course, banknotes are worthless bits of paper, just a 'promise to pay.'[36]

---

[35] A key innovation at this time was the 'double-entry book-keeping' system of accounting that allowed banks to keep a constant track of money coming in and going out – the cashflow – at the same time as giving a constant update of the assets, and the money available. Some experts regard this innovation alone as being the great idea that made capitalism possible – because, for the first time, it showed that there was such a thing as capital, which was defined as the wealth entered in accounts that was available for profit-making business.

[36] Originally, banks issued their own notes and in each country there was a kaleidoscope of sizes and designs. Eventually, governments began to standardise currency. In the USA, a single national currency was introduced in 1863. In the UK, the currency was standardised piecemeal throughout the

At first, since banknotes are just receipts, the value of notes in circulation matched the value of gold held in the bank. But for economies to grow, the amount of money in circulation needs to grow – and banks can make this happen directly simply by printing more banknotes, or by making loans and investments. They need to hold only a small amount of gold for emergencies. This is called 'fractional reserve banking' because the gold reserve is a fraction of the value of notes they print, or the loans and investments. Typically, a modern bank will hold on to only 10 per cent of every deposit and use the other 90 to generate more money.

Fractional reserve banking works fine as long as savers don't all ask for their deposits back at the same time. In troubled times, of course, or if people hear nasty rumours about the state of a bank's finances, there may be a 'run' on the bank as people rush to withdraw their savings. The bank's small reserve will be quickly lost and the bank could go bust, leaving nine out of ten of its savers high and dry.

No one wants to risk losing their money like this, yet if people don't put their money in banks, the banks will have no money to invest or lend, and the economy, most theorists believe, will seize up. So in most countries, the banking system is supported by central banks that act as guarantors to prevent people losing out if banks collapse. This way people can, in theory, feel safe depositing their money with a bank, though the recent banking crisis has revealed that even this

---

nineteenth century, and it wasn't until 1921 that the last private issue of banknotes ceased.

isn't enough when the imbalance between a bank's assets and its exposure (its loans and investments) gets too great.

As governments' response to the banking crisis revealed, banks are considered just too vital to the economies of developed countries to be allowed to fail. Governments stepped in because the ramifications of a bank collapse spread far and wide. Fractional reserves mean banks are so interdependent, with interlinked loans and investment – extended from quite small reserves – that a collapse in one place can bring others down like a house of cards, just as a public run on a bank would.[37]

It seems a dangerous system, and in some ways it is. It means most of the world's economies are built on expectation rather than present reality. Banks lend money that they haven't yet got to finance the continued growth of the economy. Yet the extraordinary thing is that it has worked for centuries. Without this system, Western economies would probably never have delivered the prosperity they have. There are inevitably massive hiccoughs every now and then, which bring recessions or worse. But for those who continue to prosper, the price is worth it. Maybe those who lose their homes and their jobs would not agree.

---

[37] It's interesting, given the fact that everyone in the banking industry knows this, that the failure of American subprime mortgages that triggered the crisis was allowed to happen. It doesn't, at first sight, make sense. But during the US government Financial Crisis Inquiry Commission's examination of the role of investment bankers Goldman Sachs in the events, Goldman Sachs made it clear that they had not hidden from clients the risk that securities based on the subprime mortgages could fail. Instead they were 'hedged', so that if they did fail, the clients would actually benefit.

#37 The Steam Engine

Right from the start, steam engines have attracted a quite unique mixture of affection and awe. Their continual bursts of steam make them seem like living, breathing animals, panting faster and faster as they work harder. With just fleeting out-bursts of snorting unpredictability, these proud, wild beasts have willingly submitted their strength to our bidding, and we feel grateful that they have.

In August 1830, the young actress Fanny Kemble,[38] fresh from her triumph as Juliet in *Romeo and Juliet* at Covent Garden, travelled on a trial run of the world's first steam pas-senger railway, the Liverpool and Manchester Railway. Much to her delight, she rode on the footplate of the locomotive with the line's creator, the engineer George Stephenson. Fanny found it all tremendously exciting. 'A common sheet of paper is enough for love,' she wrote in a long, enthusiastic letter to a friend, 'but a foolscap extra can alone contain a railroad and my ecstasies.' She goes on to describe the locomotive as a 'fire-horse' and 'this snorting little animal, which I felt rather inclined to pat':

---

[38] Four years later, Fanny Kemble married American Pierce Butler, heir to a fortune based on tobacco, cotton and rice grown by slave labour. When Butler inherited, Fanny saw to her horror the reality of slavery for the first time. When Butler refused to do anything about the slaves, she left him. Some years later she published her account of the plantations, one of the best eyewitness views of the reality of slavery in the Deep South, and became an outspoken critic of slavery, writing: 'I have sometimes been haunted with the idea that it was an imperative duty. Knowing what I know, and having seen what I have seen, to do all that lies in my power to show the dangers and the evils of this frightful institution.'

She goes upon two wheels, which are her feet, and are moved by bright steel legs called pistons; these are propelled by steam, and in proportion as more steam is applied to the upper extremities (the hip-joints, I suppose) of these pistons, the faster they move the wheels; and when it is desirable to diminish the speed, the steam, which unless suffered to escape would burst the boiler, evaporates through a safety-valve into the air …

What's so striking in Fanny's description is not just the animal qualities she bestows upon the locomotive, but her wonderful explanation of how it works. Fanny was a bright girl and she had George Stephenson to instruct her, but it is clear she understood it all well. It's this visibility of the steam engine's workings that seems to inspire that sense of both familiarity and awe that people feel for few, if any other, machines.

The idea of steam power is surprisingly old. Indeed, it dates back well over 2,000 years. As long ago as the third century BC, a Greek inventor in Alexandria called Ctesibius realised that steam jets from the spout of a kettle quite powerfully. He began to play with the idea of an aeolipile or wind ball, a round kettle on a pivot that could be set spinning by jets of steam gushing from nozzles either side. About 350 years later, another Alexandrian, named Hero, created a working design for an aeolipile, which a recent reconstruction shows works perfectly.

Hero's device, though, was simply a plaything, and although various inventors experimented with steam, it was another 1,600 years before the first practical steam engine was built. The breakthrough was the discovery of the vacuum and the power of air pressure in the mid-seventeenth century. In a famous demonstration in 1663, Otto von Guericke showed that atmospheric pressure was powerful enough to hold the two halves of a sphere drained of air against the pulling power of eight strong horses. This discovery opened up a completely different way of using steam to Hero's jets. Instead of using steam's expansive power, it could use the massive contraction when it cools and condenses. French inventor Denis Papin realised in the 1670s that if steam is trapped in cylinder, it will shrink dramatically to create a powerful vacuum as it condenses.

In 1698, English inventor Thomas Savery built the first full-scale steam engine using this principle. He created a pump by blowing steam into the pump's pipe, then cooling it to make it condense and shrink and so draw water up the pipe. Savery's engine was used in a number of the new deep coal mines of the time where flooding was a problem, but the high pressure in the system led to an explosion that eventually put an end to his invention.

When Devon ironmonger Thomas Newcomen built his new engine in 1712, he avoided this danger by boiling the water separately and sending the steam at low pressure into a cylinder with a piston. Steam was let into the cylinder to push the piston up, then a valve closed, cold water was sprayed in and the steam condensed, creating a vacuum that pulled the piston down. The piston was attached to a pivoted beam, and as the piston pulled down, it pulled the other end of the beam up, drawing water from up to 45 metres down in the mines where the engine was installed.

Newcomen's engine was so successful that soon thousands of them were installed in mines across Britain and Europe. The steam engine had arrived. But the key technological breakthroughs had not yet come, and the man who made them was Scottish inventor James Watt. Watt's first innovation was to add a separate condenser to condense the steam outside the cylinder and save chilling it down continually and wasting a lot of heat. His second innovation was to introduce steam from both sides of the piston, so that it could condense and contract from either side alternately. With Boulton & Watt's[39] double-action steam engine, the Age of Steam began.

It's hard to overstate the impact that the steam engine had. Steam gave people a previously unimaginable source of power. Linked to the new machines of the age, it enabled a few men to produce in a few hours what might have taken an army a month to produce. Indeed, it created a new breed of man: the industrial magnate. When Samuel Johnson's amanuensis Boswell visited the Soho, Birmingham mill of Matthew Boulton in 1776, he wrote: 'I wish Johnson had been with us … The vastness and the contrivance of some of the machinery would have "matched his mighty mind". I shall never forget Mr Bolton's expression to me: "I sell here, Sir, what all the world desires to have – POWER."'

The factory age had already begun with water wheels driving the belts that ran the weaving and spinning machines in northern textile towns in Britain. But the steam engine took the factory revolution to a whole new level. Water wheels

---

[39] Boulton & Watt was the partnership established in 1775 by James Watt and his English business partner, Matthew Boulton, to manufacture Watt's revolutionary engine design.

could be installed in only a very few places where the river was wide and deep enough, and they were highly dependent on the flow. Steam engines provided much more power, reliably and consistently, and could be installed pretty much anywhere they were needed. Soon they were being put into factories and workshops, mines and mills, pumping water, running machines, lifting weights. Chimneys venting the fumes from the engines filled the skies with smoke as factories marched across the landscape, and new towns mushroomed around them. For the first time in the history of the world, powered by steam, industry was becoming the driving force of society.

At the start of this Industrial Revolution, horse carts and waterways were quite enough to carry raw materials to the mills, and finished products away. But soon the mill owners began to look for a way to move things faster, farther and in larger quantities – both to cope with rising demand and to beat the competition. And that's where a new kind of steam engine came in.

This first generation of engines was all static – too big and heavy to ever be used for transport. But then in 1799, Cornishman Richard Trevithick created an incredibly compact, powerful little engine by using high-pressure steam to force the piston down rather than the vacuum of condensing steam to pull it. In 1804, Trevithick mounted his engine on a carriage and set it on a rail track to create the first steam locomotive. It was George Stephenson and his son Robert, though, who initiated the railway age with the Stockton and

Darlington Railway, which opened in 1825, and the Liverpool and Manchester Railway five years later.[40]

For a century, the steam engine was the driving force behind the most dramatic transformation of the human world in history.[41] Static steam engines powered the vast factories that churned out everything from girders to cotton trousers in mountainous quantities. Steam trains carried raw materials and finished goods to and from the factories, as well as a rising tide of passengers, able to travel considerable distances to work every day for the first time in history.

Starting in Britain, nation after nation saw an astonishing growth in wealth creation, industrial might and, especially, cities. In the USA, for instance, the urban population, which totalled just 7 per cent of all Americans in 1820, rose to over 51 per cent by 1920, during which time New York grew from just 124,000 people to almost 8 million, while Philadelphia grew from 64,000 to 2.4 million. And in the barely inhabited

---

[40] Investors were by no means convinced of the future of steam locomotives at first, and loco engineers had to prove their machine's worth in a series of public show trials. In America in 1830, Peter Cooper had to run his locomotive Tom Thumb against a horse-drawn train. The horse won, but Cooper did just enough to keep investors on board. In Britain, before the world's first passenger railroad opened between Liverpool and Manchester in 1830, company directors were not convinced that stationary engines hauling trains with cables might not be better than locomotives. So on 6 October 1829, they held a celebrated trial at Rainhill, in which five locomotives competed before a crowd of over 10,000. The trials were won by Robert Stephenson's *Rocket*, which covered 35 miles in 3 hours 12 minutes. Hauling 13 tons of loaded wagons, the *Rocket* averaged over 12 mph and at one point reached 25 mph.

[41] Not every scholar agrees that steam was the key factor in urbanisation. Washington academic Sukkoo Kim argues that it was the factory process, not steam, that was key.

West, hundreds of new cities sprang up as the new railroads marched across the landscape. Railroad pioneer Charles Francis Adams commented enthusiastically: '[T]he young city of the West has instinctively … flung herself, heart, soul, and body, into the movement of her time. She has realized the great fact that steam has revolutionized the world, and she has bound her whole existence up in the great power of modern times.'

Then, in the early twentieth century, steam suddenly seemed to go into decline, superseded, it seemed, by electricity and the internal combustion engine. Railways appeared to be fighting a losing battle against the rising tide of traffic on the roads, and even on railways steam locomotives gave way increasingly to diesel and electric. In Britain, the birthplace of steam railways, the last steam train ran in 1968. In the USA it ran in 1962 and in China in 2005. Meanwhile, factories switched even more rapidly to electricity to power their machines. The cloud-filled Victorian landscapes of chimneys and smokestacks are now a distant memory.

Yet steam power has not vanished at all; it has simply slipped behind the scenes. All but a tiny proportion of the world's electricity is generated by steam. Some power stations burn coal, others oil or gas, or consume nuclear fuel, but they all use the heat to create steam to drive the generator turbines.[42] So when you switch on your computer, the chances are you are using steam power. When you put your laundry in the washing machine, you are using steam power. When you

---

[42] Many power companies, such as Con Edison in Manhattan, even pump the steam from generators into houses around the power station for heating.

travel in the electric metro, it's really steam-powered. So are the city lights, the electronic displays at the airport, and every other aspect of the modern world that relies on electricity. Steam may now be invisible where you are, but its power is everywhere.

What's more, the steam engine has far from disappeared. Cracks are beginning to widen in the image of the internal combustion engine, with its raging thirst for oil, and the huge wodge of carbon and other pollutants it belches into the atmosphere. Many engineers are arguing that twenty-first-century steam technology, known as Advanced Steam, could offer something much better. Steam engines are not restricted to burning high-grade oil like petrol and diesel engines; they can be made to run on virtually anything that burns. Moreover, they produce maximum turning force from the word go, so they don't need clutch and gears, which sap efficiency. And they can run on much less fuel than petrol and diesel engines, so could be cheaper to run and much less polluting. In Switzerland and Austria, steam trains have recently been reintroduced with some success.

Back in 1781, soon after James Watt created his first steam engine, Erasmus Darwin (the evolutionist's grandfather) wrote this startling evocation of the future of steam:

Soon shall thy arm, UNCONQUER'D STEAM! afar
Drag the slow barge, or drive the rapid car;
Or on wide-waving wings expanded bear
The flying-chariot through the fields of air.

None of these predictions quite came true, though people did experiment with steam cars and steam-powered planes, but steam is indeed unconquered as the source of power that drives our modern world.

#36 Pottery

Pottery is ever our companion when we eat and drink. Pottery cups and mugs hold tea and coffee in a way that is secure and warm. Pottery plates and dishes provide a smooth, hygienic and non-tasting container or support for our food. Other interlopers have come and gone – glass, metals, wood, plastic, paper and even bread[43] – but now it seems we have settled on pottery for most of our dining needs. It's simple, cheap, long-lasting and even in its plainest form, attractive.

Pottery has been around such a long time that archaeologists have often used it as a way to identify different prehistoric cultures. A late Neolithic people who lived in north and west Europe some 3,800–4,400 years ago are now known as the Beaker people, for instance, because of the distinctive bell-shaped pottery beakers they made – mostly for drinking beer but also for storing food and even smelting copper ores.

---

[43] In medieval times, people in wealthy houses used to eat from squares of hard, stale four-day-old bread known as trenchers. At the end of the meal, the trencher could be eaten with sauce or perhaps collected by the almoner to give to the poor people who waited outside the door for scraps and leftovers. It was certainly cheaper than a dishwasher. By the end of the fifteenth century, however, particularly in northern Europe, trenchers were more typically wood or pewter, and wooden trenchers were in use into the nineteenth century alongside pottery plates.

Another group, which lived in northern Europe 4,450–4,900 years ago, is known as the Corded Ware culture because of the rope patterns on their pottery. It's not necessarily that pottery was absolutely central to these cultures; it is simply that distinctive fragments of their pottery have survived when most other traces have long vanished.

It used to be thought that pottery was invented only once people had begun to settle down on farms. Archaeological discoveries in the Middle East seemed to confirm that, with no evidence of pottery until about 8,000 years ago, some time after the first farms and cities appeared in this part of the world. In the Zagros Mountains in modern-day Iraq, for instance, people did not start to make pottery until 6300 BC, some 2,000 years after beginning to cultivate wheat and barley, keep cows and sheep and live in villages. But then pottery was found at Odai Yamamoto in Japan that dates back 12,500 years, long before the coming of farming. The hunting and gathering people who created this pottery,[44] which is surprisingly delicate and well-made, are known as the Jomon culture because of the distinctive cord marks or 'jomon' on their pots. In 1998, improved dating techniques put the date for some shards of Jomon pottery back a further 4,000 years, making them 16,500 years old. Clearly, having pots and an unsettled lifestyle were not incompatible.

---

[44] Excavations have uncovered evidence that the Jomon people ate smoked fish and drank wine made from elderberry, wild grape and strawberry. So, maybe far from leading a primitive subsistence life as archaeologists have often supposed, some hunter-gatherers were prehistoric connoisseurs, living the good life with no ties and few chores.

Until recently, the Jomon pots were thought to be the world's oldest pots, which surprised experts as much as the association with hunting and gathering, since they believed that pottery originated in mainland Asia. Then in 2009, fragments of charred pottery were found in Yuchanyan cave in China's Hunan province. By carbon dating fragments of bone and charcoal found close by, experts have dated this pottery to between 17,500 and 18,300 years old. If they are right (though the disturbed nature of cave floors means they cannot be sure[45]) then this is now the world's oldest pottery.

That doesn't mean it's the first ceramic. People were moulding clay into figurines long before. The oldest are the 'Venus figurines', little statuettes of naked women, found in northern and eastern Europe. The Venus figurine found at Dolní Věstonice in the Czech Republic dates back 27,000 years. The first pots came some time later.

Surprisingly few of the earliest pots show much sign of the soot that would suggest that they had been used for cooking. Nor are they the large pots that would later be used for storing food long-term. It seems the first pottery was actually crockery – bowls for serving food, or perhaps deeper dishes for heating shellfish with a hot stone. It may be that the early pots just weren't up to much more. In time, however, bigger,

---

[45] In a BBC news report, one of the researchers at Yuchanyan, David Cohen, admitted there are often problems dating cave floor artefacts. 'The way people move around and mess up caves is very difficult to see archaeologically … Imagine you have a fire and then people come in again have another fire and another, so you have the ashes of all these fires building up but at the same time people are digging and clearing, pushing things to the side; this messes things up.' But he believed they had taken care to make sure the dated fragments and the pottery matched.

tougher pots were made that could be used for cooking, for containing liquids and for storing food properly. These had a profound effect on our relationship with food.

Meat could be baked or roasted on hot stones or on a spit, but pots dramatically increased the range of foods that could be cooked by boiling them in water. Many otherwise inedible plants could be cooked this way. Pulses, cereals and root vegetables quickly became staple foods.

Pottery also, for the first time, provided good containers for liquids. It can't have been long after the creation of the first storage jars that people noticed what happens when fruits and other plant material are stored in moist conditions. Whenever they contain sugars, they start to ferment, and as they ferment the sugars are converted to alcohol. Perhaps it was an accident at first, but people soon began to show a remarkable knack for creating alcohol from just about anything – honey, grapes and other fruits, cereals and so on. It's probably fair to say that without pottery, there'd be no beer or wine.

The first pots were probably simple pinch-pots, made by pinching damp clay out between fingers and thumbs into the required shape.[46] Once shaped, the pot was simply left in the sun to dry and harden. Sun-dried pots will eventually collapse if filled with water, as the clay absorbs the water and softens. Before long, though, potters were making larger, deeper pots by rolling the clay into a long sausage shape and coiling it

---

[46] This technique is still used in the highly prized Japanese Raku ware, traditionally used in the Japanese tea ceremony. Raku pots are hand-moulded, then fired at low temperatures for a short period before being withdrawn while still glowing hot to be plunged into cold water or left to cool in the air.

around to make a pot. These coiled pots were often fired, simply by putting them in an open campfire.

No one knows quite when the potter's wheel first came into use, or where. Estimates of dates vary wildly, from 10,000 years ago to just 3,400 years ago, and varying experts say that it first appeared in Europe or China or Mesopotamia. The strongest early archaeological evidence – a stone potter's wheel and fragments of wheel-turned pots – comes from Mesopotamia. These early wheels were what are called slow wheels. These are simply little round platforms for the clay that you can turn by hand to save yourself having to move as you shape the pot, and that help keep the pot always at the same distance from you. They dramatically increase the speed and accuracy with which a potter can make batches of very similar, and much larger, pots.

It was the appearance of the fast wheel about 2,700 years ago, though, that was the great technological breakthrough. This is the wheel, essentially, that most craft potters use today. With the fast wheel, the platform is raised on an axle so that the potter can work standing. Wrapped around the axle is a heavy stone wheel which can be set spinning with a push or kick. As the stone's momentum keeps it spinning, the potter can run his hands over the clay to keep shaping it as it turns. To shape easily, the potter needs a softer, finer clay than with a slow hand wheel, so the pot needs to be fired in a kiln at a higher temperature to make it hard.

Using a fast wheel, a good potter can make a simple pot every minute or so, each pretty much identical. With the advent of the fast wheel, pot-making became an industry, and the volume of pots churned out in Greek and Roman times is astonishing. The Greeks in particular turned pottery-making into high art, with their decorations in black and then red.

For everyday crockery, though, pottery seemed rather cheap and crude compared with glass and metals, and for a long while pottery fell out of use at the table. Then in the ninth century, a new and beautiful kind of pottery arrived in the Islamic world from China, now known as porcelain. Porcelain had been made in China for some time but was just reaching perfection under the Sui and T'ang dynasties (581–907 AD). Instead of being coarse-grained, thick, dull and opaque, this Chinese pottery or porcelain was white, smooth and so delicately thin and translucent you could see the shadow of your drink inside it. It also rang beautifully when you tapped it.

Chinese porcelain reached a degree of exquisite perfection in the Ming dynasty (1368–1644), when the distinctive blue and white decoration so associated with Chinese porcelain was developed. It was in the sixteenth century, during the Ming, that Europeans began to see china, as it became known in England, for the first time. They were so captivated by its beauty that they immediately set about trying to imitate it. The Chinese secret, though, proved hard to crack.

Because of its translucence, European potters thought they could match it by mixing powdered glass in with the clay. This looked quite similar but was softer and thicker, so inevitably it looked cruder. English potters added powdered bone to toughen it up, and created bone-china, which while attractive couldn't match the delicacy and beauty of porcelain from China. It wasn't until the 1760s that French and English potters discovered what made Chinese porcelain special.[47] It contains two substances known from their Chinese names as *kaolin* (a very fine white clay) and *petuntse* (a rock that fuses at a high temperature to form natural glass). Once they discovered the ingredients, they at first imported them from China and then realised that local china clay and china stone would work almost as well.

Since then, the production of pottery has changed dramatically. Very little is now made on potters' wheels. Instead, it is made on a vast industrial scale by various automatic processes such as granulate moulding, which means pressing the clay into moulds while semi-hard and granulated. Most mass-produced plates are made like this. Though there is little art or skill involved in the production of the vast bulk of pottery sold in the shops, the pottery emerging from factories is attractive and does its job supremely well, and exquisite hand-made pottery can still be bought at a premium.

Meanwhile, ceramics may prove to be the wonder material of the century. For most people, ceramics, when they aren't expensive works of art, are materials for the bathroom and kitchen. But ceramics technology is being developed

---

[47] The secret of china was actually discovered in Meissen half a century earlier by the young genius Johann Friedrich Böttger, but only through the extraordinary cruelty of Augustus the Strong, the elector of Saxony. Hearing of the teenage Johann's alchemical skills, Augustus had him locked up until he found how to transmute base metal into gold. Taking pity, Dresden scientist Ehrenfried Walther von Tschirnhaus persuaded Augustus to allow the boy to stay with him and work on the secret of china instead. Still under guard, Johann solved the problem in a year in 1708, and Meissen porcelain went into production in 1709. All the same, Augustus released Johann only in 1714. By that time, he was very ill from the effects of working in his laboratory, and in just five years he was dead.

for everything from bomb-proof shields for aircraft to high-efficiency engines for cars. Special ceramics are even being developed to work as replacement body parts. Maybe the phrase 'feet of clay' could one day be literally true.

#35 Coffee and Tea

Can you imagine going through a week or even a month, let alone a lifetime, without the steaming charms of coffee and tea? Rudyard Kipling couldn't, writing of tea:

> We had a kettle; we let it leak:
> Our not repairing made it worse.
> We haven't had any tea for a week …
> The bottom is out of the Universe.

Tea and coffee are such a part of the fabric of everyday life that it is easy to forget what amazing drinks they are. If they were in a fantasy novel, they'd seem almost like magic potions – richly tasting, delicious, warm drinks that instantly make you more alert and ready for life.

It's no wonder, then, that legends have grown up about just who had the idea for each. It's fairly certain that tea originated in China. There are historical records of tea farms dating back at least 3,000 years. There is genetic evidence, too, that all the modern varieties of tea plant are hybrids of the evergreen *Camellia sinensis*, which can be traced back to the mountains of northern Burma and the western Chinese provinces of Yunnan and Sichuan. Indeed, it seems likely that tea originated in Yunnan, where wild tea trees thousands of years old can be found in the rainforests high in the mountains. It was in the west of China where 2,500 years ago the great Chinese philosopher Laozi met a customs official who encouraged him to write down his thoughts in the *Tao Te Ching* over his first cup of tea, a drink he later described as 'the froth of the liquid jade'. And it may be here in the west of China that the Chinese legend of tea's origin is set.

According to the legend, the Emperor Shen Nong was famous for his interest in herbal medicine. In 2737 BC, so one story goes, Shen Nong, out in the west with his army, was sipping a bowl of boiled water, when a few leaves of nearby tea fluttered into it. As the water turned brown and the emperor sipped on, he was pleasantly surprised by the flavour and the restorative qualities of the strange brew. Apparently, Shen Nong also discovered that tea was an antidote to various poisonous herbs. Whatever the truth, it seems likely that tea-drinking was widespread in China by 2,500 years ago, both for medicinal reasons and simple pleasure among ordinary people, as well as a status symbol at the Emperor's court.

Coffee is much more recent in origin. The first historic records come from the Sufi monks who grew coffee in their gardens in Yemen in the fifteenth century. But the two main coffee plants, *Coffea arabica* and *Coffea caneophora* (which gives the 'robusta' beans), are natives of Ethiopia and sub-Saharan Africa respectively. And it is in Ethiopia, one legend has it, that coffee was discovered.

The coffee legend, perhaps tellingly, comes from the opposite end of the social scale. While it was the Emperor of China who is credited with tea, we owe coffee, apparently, to a poor goatherd named Kaldi, who lived in Ethiopia about 1,200 years ago. Apparently, Kaldi noticed his goats getting rather frisky after eating the red berries of a certain bush and decided to try them himself. Excited by the effects, Kaldi went to a holy man, who disapprovingly tossed them on the fire. Kaldi rescued the beans, by now roasted, ground them to a powder and added water to make the first cup of coffee.

Interestingly, despite their very different origins, coffee and tea both arrived in Europe within a decade or so, in the mid-seventeenth century. The first European coffee house opened in Italy in 1645, and England's first, the still-running Queen's Lane Coffee House in Oxford, just nine years later. Tea arrived in Europe around the same time, and came to England in the 1660s with King Charles II's wife Catherine of Braganza, who picked it up as the new fad in her native Portugal.

Right from the start in Europe, it's clear there was something of a divide between tea and coffee despite the coincidence of their arrival and their similarity as hot, pleasantly bitter, aromatic drinks full of stimulating caffeine. Tea was brought to England by the royals and was always very respectable, as befits its imperial Chinese origins. Coffee was first drunk by Oxford students and its image has always fallen on the louche side, a natural follow-on to its beginnings with an upstart goatherd.

Even before it came to Europe, tea was often the drink of the refined, sipped in reverence in Japanese and Chinese tea ceremonies. And few people doubted it was good for you on every level. For Buddhists, it had even spiritual value, while the first Japanese tea manual, dating from the thirteenth century and entitled *How to Stay Healthy by Drinking Tea*, asserted boldly that: 'Tea is the ultimate mental and medical remedy and has the ability to make one's life more full and complete'; while a Japanese proverb says: 'If man has no tea in him, he is incapable of understanding truth and beauty.'

Coffee, on the other hand, always walked on the wild side. Like tea, coffee was drunk religiously, not for Zen-like Buddhist calm but to stimulate the spiritual excitement of the Sufis. It's perhaps not surprising then that non-Sufi Muslims began to regard it as rather dubious or even *haraam* (forbidden), no doubt horrified at the sight of all those frenzied Sufi monks high on coffee. Indeed, unimaginable as Turkey without it would be today, coffee was actually banned there in the early seventeenth century. And ironically it was banned in its place of origin, Ethiopia, by Orthodox Christians until 1889.

In Europe and North America, while ladies took tea in their stately homes, students and intellectuals gathered in disreputable coffee houses to discuss revolutionary ideas or simply poke fun at the tea-drinking classes. In France, Voltaire, Rousseau and Diderot quaffed coffee to the Enlightenment and washed in the dreams of the French Revolution in Paris's Café Procope. In America, countless cups of coffee in Boston's Green Dragon coffee house fuelled the American rebellion as John Adams, James Otis and Paul Revere planned their campaign. And after the rebellion came around, and Americans dumped tea in Boston harbour in defiance against British taxes in the infamous Tea Party, many Americans refused to drink tea as a protest. Tea was tainted as a drink in the USA until quite recently when many Americans began to dip into high-end teas as a mark of refinement. The end of the revolution?

Tea was tainted in another way too, besides its association with British tea taxes. Just as the English poor adopted tea with affection to make it the national drink, and a 'nice cuppa' became the epitome of homely, unpretentious working-class life, so the tea trade was the crux of Victorian colonialism. In the early 1800s, the British were growing opium in India, then illegally importing it to China to get the Chinese hooked and willing to part with their tea at rock-bottom prices. Eventually, the British smuggled some tea plants out of China and planted tea all over India to earn Indians the money to buy British manufactured goods. Countless Indians lost their traditional farming way of life to become wage slaves.

While the real consequences of growing and producing tea had a profoundly negative effect on millions of people under the British Empire, at home it became associated with the most cherished and gentle sides of British culture – from tea on the lawn in an English summer to a mug of warm comfort in the Blitz. For the British, tea has always been the great remedy in a crisis. If you've had a nasty shock, a good cup of tea is the answer. If your boyfriend has just left you, it's time to put the kettle on. Not everyone in England succumbed to tea's spell, though. J.B. Priestley muttered cantankerously: 'Our trouble is that we drink too much tea. I see in this the slow revenge of the Orient, which has diverted the Yellow River down our throats.'

Coffee, meanwhile, remarkably managed to maintain its reputation as the devil's drink, as America's Beat Generation and those first recalcitrant Teenagers of the 1950s hung out in espresso bars and defied their elders to the hiss of the Gaggia and the thump and wail of the jukebox.

Now the issues are slightly different. Coffee has lost any left-field association, as waves of low-level American colonialism sweep the world under the Starbucks logo, along with espressos and cappuccinos, not to mention lattes, mochas, and all kinds of other elaborate variations to pander to the discerning consumer. If anything, tea, drunk more by liberals and campaigners against poverty in reaction to the global culture of coffee, has become the protest option.

There are two things that seem to matter now in relation to tea and coffee. The first is the part they play in the global economy. The second is health issues. Are tea and coffee bad or good for your personal well-being?

Coffee and tea are now huge industries worth hundreds of billions of pounds. Around the world, there are some 25 million farmers involved in growing coffee alone, and countless more depend upon it for their livelihood. Indeed, it's hard to overestimate the importance of tea and coffee in the economic fortunes of many Third World countries. But there's a problem. Despite the massive demand for coffee in the West, the world grows too much of it. In the early years of this century, there was a glut of coffee on the world market that led to a dramatic slump in price. Prices have slightly recovered in recent years, but coffee-growers still find it hard to get a decent price for their coffee.

As you sip your cappuccino, you might think coffee seems too expensive, not too cheap. The problem is 'added value'. Foodsellers can make only so much profit on raw, unprocessed food. But processing food adds value and opens the way to big profits. When it comes to added value, instant coffee is a real winner, but so too are cappuccinos and espressos and lattes. Moreover, much of the global coffee industry is concentrated in a few giant corporate hands. Nestlé and Altria, along with Sara Lee and Procter & Gamble, buy almost half the world's coffee. Such concentrated buying power, such a glut of coffee, and such massive potential added value shifted the money made from coffee dramatically away from the growers to the big multinationals. Back in 2002, in a report aptly entitled 'Mugged', Oxfam traced the prices paid for a kilo of coffee grown in Uganda, and showed that the price in UK shops was 700 times what the farmer got. The rise of the Fair Trade coffee movement has done quite a bit to highlight and remedy the problem, but it remains essentially there. The picture for tea is not so different.

When it comes to health, the issues are more complex than you might imagine. Chemically, both tea and coffee work primarily because they contain caffeine, a psychoactive drug that in small quantities can lift your mood and make you mentally more alert. In bigger quantities, however, caffeine can trigger anxiety, panic and insomnia. It can also cause headaches and raise blood pressure and cholesterol levels. Until recently, experts recommended that the ideal dose for raising mental alertness was one or two strong cups of coffee a day (100–200 mg), and people were frightened into switching to decaf because of the supposed increased risk of heart disease from all this stimulation. However, recent research has shown that more may not do as much harm after all, and may actually do you good. Indeed, there may have been something of the hoary caution about too much stimulation being Bad For You.

Nonetheless, tolerance to caffeine quickly builds up. Studies show that if you drink 400 mg (4–5 cups) of coffee a day for just a week, caffeine no longer keeps you awake. Meanwhile, stopping your caffeine intake suddenly can cause withdrawal symptoms including headaches, irritability and tiredness lasting from one to five days, and typically peaking after 48 hours. Interestingly, caffeine increases the effectiveness of pain relievers in dealing with headaches by up to 40 per cent, which is why many over-the-counter pain relievers include caffeine.

The caffeine content of coffee varies considerably. Typically, though, a single cup of instant coffee contains 65–100 mg of caffeine, while an espresso shot contains 100 mg and a cup of strong drip coffee contains 115–175 mg. Decaf, by comparison, contains only about 3 mg. Tea contains about half as much caffeine as coffee (30–60 mg). But none of these figures is definitive. There's a huge variability in the caffeine content of a cup of tea or coffee prepared by the same person using the same ingredients and equipment day after day.

Besides caffeine, coffee and tea also contain another chemical – theophylline – which in drug form is good for asthma in relaxing bronchial muscles. Tea also contains another stimulant, theobromine. Theobromine's effect is milder but more lasting than caffeine's, and is the mood-enhancing chemical found in chocolate. So when someone says, 'There's nothing like a good cup of tea for cheering you up', the effect is real, not imaginary.

But perhaps it is good to conclude with the paean of Jerome K. Jerome in *Three Men in a Boat*:

After eggs and bacon [our stomach] says, 'Work!' After beefsteak and porter, it says, 'Sleep!' After a cup of tea (two spoonfuls for each cup, and don't let it stand for more than three minutes), it says to the brain, 'Now rise, and show your strength. Be eloquent, and deep, and tender; see, with a clear eye, into Nature, and into life: spread your white wings of quivering thought, and soar, a god-like spirit, over the whirling world beneath you, up through long lanes of flaming stars to the gates of eternity!'

Time to put the kettle on.

#34 Wine

What a sad place the world would be without wine. As Victor Hugo so memorably put it: 'God made only water, but man made wine.' We can certainly manage without it. It's completely unnecessary. It has no nutritional value. Even the cheapest bottle costs a fair amount and the most expensive costs a fortune. And drunk in any more than moderate amounts it causes people to misbehave at the time and suffer pain and remorse later.

Worse still, wine in any quantity can cause accidents when people drive after drinking, and can lead to violence as people who've drunk too much become belligerent. And continued heavy wine-drinking over long periods can create alcoholic dependency and all its associated ills from social problems to liver damage.

Wine is, in fact, one of the most useless inventions ever, and it seems likely that it is to blame for more days off work than even the common cold. But of course all this is to miss the point. Saying that wine is useless is like saying pleasure has no use. True, maybe, but who'd want to forgo it altogether?

And, of course, it isn't all about pleasure. TV comedians Mitchell and Webb have a wonderful sketch in which they liken drinking a little wine to a Masonic rite. Their big secret is that drinking just under two glasses of wine solves all problems and gives you the confidence to do anything. The punchline of the sketch is that the hero, having come to rule the world in a spirit of wonderful bonhomie, feels so on top of it all that he finishes his second glass. Of course, he's drunk just too much and the world descends into chaos.

This is the point about wine. In the right quantities, it is a balm that smoothes away anxiety. It takes away the sense of unease we have in so many social encounters. And it turns a simple meal into an occasion. There is probably a psycho-chemical reason for this. Scientists believe that alcohol works through affecting neurotransmitters such as serotonin and GABA – by its disinhibitory effect – but there is certainly more to it than this. Wine, of course, is not just alcohol but when at its best a richly flavoured, deliciously aromatic, vividly coloured creation – the end result of a long labour and maybe years' preparation to bring the drinker maximum pleasure.

Wine inspires the kind of interest that no other drink does. Many vintners devote their lives to growing and creating the best possible vintages. Just as many drinkers are equally dedicated connoisseurs, relishing every nuance of taste and history. Many more simply enjoy knowing a little and tasting a lot. 'Wine is one of the most civilized things in the world and one of the most natural things in the world that has been brought to the greatest perfection,' wrote Ernest Hemingway in *Death in the Afternoon*, 'and it offers a greater range of enjoyment and appreciation than, possibly, any other purely sensory things.'

Wine has been drunk (and probably people have been too) for over 8,000 years. Indeed, people started drinking wine not long after the invention of the pots that would have been needed to hold it. The oldest signs of wine-drinking have been found at Shulaveri in the Caucasus Mountains in Georgia, where infrared spectroscopy has been used to identify wine residue in the form of tartaric acid on jars dating back to 6000 BC. Wine jars almost as old have been found at Hajji Firuz in the Zagros Mountains in Iran.

There's no way of telling what fruit this early wine was made from. Wine can, of course, be made from just about anything that is rich enough in sugar to ferment. Wild grapes (*Vitis vinifera* subsp. *silvestris*) certainly grow in the area but they seem too small and bitter to be used for wine. It's not clear when grapes were domesticated – the earliest seeds found date from about 3000 BC – but they have two huge advantages over wild grapes. First, the fruits are much bigger and sweeter. Second, the vines are self-pollinating. The Chinese started with a slightly different wild grape, the mountain grape (*Vitis thunbergii*), until they too imported the domesticated grape, which has gradually been carried around the world and is now, of course, grown wherever the climate is suitable, including Australia, New Zealand, Chile, South Africa and California, far from its native home in the Caucasus.

In the Ancient World, the great masters of wine-making were the Greeks, and the *amphorae* (jars) that contained Greek wine have been found all over the Mediterranean and beyond. The seventh-century Greek poet Alkman sang the praise of Denthis wine from the slopes of Mount Taygetus with its flowery aroma, while Aristotle talks of Lemnian wine, from Lemnos, which is still produced today. Yet the Greek wine industry declined with its civilisation, and the realm of the master vintners shifted west to Italy, Spain and in particular France, where the chateau system reached a Golden Age in the mid-nineteenth century when Bordeaux wine achieved a pinnacle of taste. The last 50 years, of course, have seen the emergence of New World wines, with Australian and Chilean wines sometimes taking the connoisseurs' crown away from the traditional French vintages.

The French remain great drinkers of wine. It is often claimed that in spite of their very fatty diets, French people suffer less from heart disease because they down a lot of red wine in particular. What they neglect to point out is that other countries where they drink a lot of red wine, such as Bulgaria and Hungary, have quite high rates of heart disease.

Nevertheless, in recent years, some neuroscientists have been singing the praises of red wine, or rather a key ingredient of red wine called resveratrol. Italian scientist Alessandro Cellini found that fish given high doses of resveratrol lived 60 per cent longer, and when other fish died of old age at twelve weeks, these Methuselah fish still had the mental agility of young fish. Resveratrol seemed to protect the fish's brain cells against age-related decline. Similar studies show that resveratrol is an antioxidant, protecting cells by mopping up free radicals, while others show that it actually encourages nerve cells to re-grow. One group of researchers even suggested that a glass or two of wine a day can increase neural connections sevenfold. It may even protect against Alzheimer's.

However, before you hit the bottle, it's worth remembering that alcohol is a major brain toxin. Even quite small amounts of alcohol can slow your thinking, ruin your sense of balance, wreck your judgement and completely obliterate your short-term memory. Long-term heavy drinking shrinks the brain and leads to memory loss and mental disorders. And the fish that benefitted from those high doses of resveratrol were on the equivalent of 72 bottles of wine day! A glass of red wine a day for women and two for men won't do any harm, but it's far from proven that it really will do you good.

Of course, some people have always attacked wine for the moral damage it does, not the physical. Some Muslims are firmly against drinking any kind of alcohol, and through the ages many Christians have preached abstinence. On the other hand, there are those like Cardinal Richelieu who retorted: 'If God forbade drinking, would He have made wine so good?' But perhaps we should all heed this warning from the Roman playwright and clown Plautus: 'The great evil of wine is that it first seizes the feet; it is a crafty wrestler.'

#33 Romance

Softly, he touched her on the arm and pointed to the little wooden boat that fluttered gold on the water in the sun's last rays. As she turned, she saw it was filled with red roses, her favourite flowers, and written clumsily on the side was her name in silver letters. 'It's yours,' he said, as her eyes brimmed with tears. 'That's so romantic,' she whispered. And it was.

Romance has become such a cliché, yet it is a cliché that seems to seduce us all – not just the millions of (mostly) women who read romantic novels (a market worth $1.37 billion a year in the USA alone), but everyone who longs for that climactic moment of love, that perfect fantasy moment when time stands still and your head spins with the magic of it all. It's estimated, though who knows how, that a billion cards are sent every year on Valentine's Day, which has now become one of the most widely celebrated of all festivals around the world. And yet there are many people, perfectly loving, to whom the whole idea of romance is baffling.

Over the last few decades, scientists have devoted countless hours of research to finding just what love is, but it remains elusive. Some scientists have wired up lovers to see what romance does to the brain. Their findings suggest that it all happens in three stages. First of all, there's 'lust', which makes you go looking, boosting your sex hormones: testosterone for men and oestrogen for women. That's apparently quite short-lived.

Then there's 'attraction'. When two people fall in love, chemical nerve transmitters go haywire in their brains. MRI scans show that floods of dopamine light up the pleasure centres in their brains, rather like cocaine does. A surge in norepinephrine sets their hearts aflutter and makes their cheeks flush and their mouths go dry. It can also make them restless and unable to eat or sleep. And a slump in serotonin makes them fixated – people suffering obsessive compulsive disorder apparently have the same serotonin slump. This, they say, lasts much longer, up to eighteen months.[48]

Finally, if all goes well, it settles down into 'attachment'. The pleasure chemicals no longer kick in, but instead as the lovers bond they get a mutual rise in oxytocin, the so-called cuddle hormone, which is released after sex and also helps cement the bond between mothers and babies. They also get a boost in vasopressins. Experiments showed that if pairs of prairie voles, which normally bond for life, were given a drug to suppress vasopressin, they quickly lost interest in each other.

Other scientists have tried taking a psychological tack on romance. Some talk about romance being a 'commitment device' that has evolved to keep parents together for long enough to raise their children. Some psychologists insist that you get a year of 'romantic' love followed by years of 'companionate' love; others have found that 'romantic' love can last a lifetime. And the newspapers are full of research results that seem to show exactly what makes people attracted – and that all seem to prove nonsense when put to the test.

So science has a long way to go before it quite manages to take the magic out of romance entirely.

Of course, the sex drive is a primal instinct as powerful as the need for food. Love, too, is natural bond as old as humanity. But romance is something different and rather special. It adds something exciting and wonderful to the attraction

---

[48] Of course, you can get similar chemical changes by eating a sticky bun, going for a run, lying in the sun, having a nap, and having a drink. So if that's all it is, love isn't that special.

between two people that is nothing to do with natural drives.[49] For the people who experience it, it opens the most extraordinary and beautiful time of their lives – a time when life has a meaning and one meaning only, a time when all the worries of life slip away, a time of unimaginable bliss, a time when time stands still ...

It seems so transcendent, and runs so deep, that it seems as if people must always have felt this way. Yet the chances are

---

[49] Philosophers and poets have been talking about it for thousands of years, of course. In Plato's *Symposium* on love, in which Plato asks characters to say what love is, the comic playwright Aristophanes tells a story to make fun of those who say they only feel 'whole' when they're in love: In the beginning, there were three kinds of human, one male, one female and one half man and half woman, but they each had four limbs and two faces. They might have been strange, but these jolly creatures were brave and strong and even challenged the Gods. Zeus, of course, got cross, and decided to split them all in half to diminish their strength. And of course, he created us, lonely creatures forever searching for out other halves. It was probably meant as a joke, yet this image of love as finding your other half still has touching echoes today.

Another contributor to the *Symposium*, Socrates, also thought that love fills a human lack, but for him the lack was the beautiful and good. Love is the desire to possess the beautiful and good for ever – and is, then, a desire for immortality. We can achieve this through creation, inspired by a beautiful beloved, in three ways, each better than the next – having children, performing heroic deeds and winning lasting fame, and finally, and best of all, by creating works of science, education, law and art. For him, human love was simply a necessary step on the way to higher things.

The prophetess Diotima argued that the beautiful love inspires the mind and soul to focus on higher things, in particular Divinity, which is the source of Beauty. This kind of love came to be called Platonic love (after Plato) and merged into the courtly tradition of love, which was also in many ways Platonic, and which became immensely popular in the seventeenth and eighteenth centuries. Now it can often be used as a euphemism for unrequited love, or a kind of pretend love.

that the idea of romance is quite new. People fell in love, of course, and passionately at that, but they never aspired to this idyllic state called romance. The very name gives a clue to romance's relative youth. Romance only really began to bloom after the fall of Rome. The word comes from the Old French *romanz* or *roman*, which originally just meant 'slangy', and in turn came from what Romans called the colloquial version of Latin, *Romanice*.[50]

Some time around the twelfth century, writers scribbling away in the French cathedral schools, who were of course well versed in Latin, decided to tell their own, popular versions in French of old Latin and Greek tales of love and adventure. Some were simply adaptations of the Greek versions of thrillers; others were cut-down versions of the great epics such as Virgil's *Aeneid* and Homer's *Odyssey*. They worked so well that soon the French scribes were telling new stories, based on knights and fairies, dragons and lost love. One of the most famous is Chrétien de Troyes' *Roman de la Rose*.

There was a very special quality to the love in these stories, however, which was entirely new and may well come from the songs of unrequited love and inspirational stories of knightly honour that were emerging from the Islamic world through Spain.[51] Love is never easy in the romances. Lovers are parted, they suffer, they go through enormous difficulties, but their

---

[50] It's quite strange to think that when we long for a bit of romance, to an Ancient Roman, that would be like saying you long for a bit of Cockney.

[51] Shakespeare's *Romeo and Juliet* is said by some, with little actual proof, to have been inspired by the tragic Arabic love story from the seventh century of *Layla and Majnun*, also the subject of guitarist Eric Clapton's most famous track.

love sustains them through all their trials – until finally they are reunited, even if it is only through suicide or death through grief on finding their beloved dead. The epitome of these is the beautiful and tragic story of Tristan and Isolde, which was retold many times. The love they share has a very special quality. It is idyllic, high-flown, ecstatic, passionate yet at same time remarkably pure.

The nature of love in the romances is partly inspired by 'courtly love', a love modelled on the feudal relationship between a knight and his liege lord. The knight serves his lady with the same deference and loyalty that he would his lord. She controls the relationship, but he is ennobled by his submission, since he is inspired by her to do great deeds to be worthy of her love.

From these medieval stories emerged the wonderful literature of romance in Western Europe, which both shaped and reflected our changing experience and expectations in love. The bar was set high by Shakespeare with his remarkable sonnets and plays, especially *Romeo and Juliet*. Love in Shakespeare is idealised, a miraculous emotion that endures all. 'Love is … an ever-fix'd mark,' Shakespeare writes, 'That looks on tempests and is never shaken.' So too is a lover. 'Shall I compare thee to a summer's day?/Thou art more lovely and more temperate.'

It is this idealisation that marks out romance as something different from ordinary love. It is never common. It is rare and transcendent. One's beloved has to be so unique, so special that all else in the world melts away. If it seems like adoration, not simply love, then that's probably because it is. The star of romance rose in the West as religious faith was at first beset by doubt, then began to wane.

It rose, too, as the blossoming of the self and individualism in the Enlightenment and beyond told us that each of us is, in some way, special, but then left us feeling alone and very small. Romance provided both freedom and self-realisation. Romance, sociologist Anthony Giddens argues, gives us our own story in life.

And of course, while we are waiting for our own love story to begin, we can fill our heads with the romances of others. It is surely no coincidence that the idea of romance has flowered along with a wealth of romantic writing.

Poets often made romance transcendent and noble and even tragic in the courtly tradition. The man suffered and the woman looked down from her pedestal. Love is frequently unrequited. Novelists such as Jane Austen ingeniously turned it around to the woman's point of view, and showed that the woman suffered or was foolish in love, and so created a much more intimate, much more tender kind of romance. And invariably a happy ending: 'Reader, I married him,' sighs Charlotte Brontë's Jane Eyre finally.

Romance is cherished because it is perhaps the best and most exalted experience we can ever have. We do not always love well. We do not always pin our love on the right person. We may get jealous or foolish or angry or sentimental or smothering or obsessive. But when we do love well, when we do indeed find the person of our dreams, even if that dream is just a little more grounded in reality than in the stories, then it reminds us, maybe briefly, maybe lastingly, that the world is

a wonderful place. It's a precious gift that needs and deserves
a lifetime of care.

> See! the mountains kiss high heaven,
> And the waves clasp one another;
> No sister flower would be forgiven
> If it disdained its brother;
> And the sunlight clasps the earth,
> And the moonbeams kiss the sea: -
> What are all these kissings worth,
> If thou kiss not me?
>
> — Percy Bysshe Shelley, 'Love's Philosophy'

As Oscar Wilde said, who, being loved, is poor?

#32 Mass-production

'Time loves to be wasted', said Henry Ford epigrammatically.
'From that waste there can be no salvage. It is the hardest
waste of all to correct because it does not litter the floor.'

No wonder, then, he was so ecstatic about the innovation
introduced in 1913 at Ford's Highland Park car factory in
Detroit by one of Ford's managers, Charles Sorensen. Indeed,
he was so ecstatic that he later claimed the idea was his own.
What Sorensen had done was to introduce an assembly line
to build the Model T Ford. The effect was so startling that
it inspired what some people called the second industrial
revolution.

Mass-production had been around for some time before the Ford experiment. It meant breaking the production process into standardised components. Instead of making a finished item, each factory hand added just a single component or performed a certain routine task, again and again, passing it on each time to the next hand. That way, the item was built up bit by bit. The specialisation and repetition speeded up the industrial process dramatically.

Back in the sixteenth century, the vast Venice arsenal had managed to build a complete ship each day using this kind of system, and in the American Civil War, the Springfield Armory churned out different guns at an unprecedented rate to keep the army supplied by using interchangeable parts and breaking the assembly process into stages.

In the 1860s, the extraordinarily innovative meat processor Gustavus Swift had made sure his Chicago abattoir lived up to his name. Inside the plant, an overhead trolley whisked each carcass to various process stations where workers would lop off a particular part and deal with it appropriately as it passed by. This is, Ford later said, what gave him the idea, and perhaps there is something rather disturbing in thinking that the process behind our modern consumer lifestyle was inspired by mass slaughter.

So mass-production and assembly lines were not new when Ford introduced them. What was new, and revolutionary, was that no one had attempted it on such a large and complex item as a car, which had always previously been coach-built by hand. Nor had anyone tried it on such a massive scale or with such a high degree of organisation. At first, Sorensen experimented just with a conveyor belt that carried radiators around to be assembled in one place, then soldered in another. But before long the entire assembly of the Model T was organised like this, with each car being whisked past overhead, briefly pausing as workers added their particular component or completed their task until finally the finished car rolled off the assembly line. The factory was a vision of non-stop motion.

It all focused, Ford said, 'upon a manufacturing process of the principles of power, accuracy, economy, system, continuity, speed and repetition'. The result was astonishingly effective. In August 1913, it took an average of twelve and a half man hours to assemble a Model T; a year later, after Sorensen had introduced the assembly lines, it took just one and a half hours.

The impact of this was genuinely revolutionary. It meant that Ford could sell the T at such low prices that it opened up motoring, previously the preserve of the rich, to the ordinary American. 'Every time I reduce the charge for our car by one dollar,' Ford declared excitedly, 'I get a thousand new buyers.' And the speed of the production line meant that Ford could keep up with demand. In 1908 Ford had just 10 per cent of the American car market. By 1914 it had pretty much half and was rolling out more than a quarter of a million cars every year.

The first and most obvious impact of Ford's innovation was on the car industry. Without mass-production, the motor car would have remained a specialist item for the rich, no more affordable than a luxury yacht. Mass-production meant that cars could be made cheap enough and in sufficient numbers for them to become a standard purchase for people even on relatively modest incomes.[52]

The figures are staggering. Today, there are some three-quarters of a billion cars on the world's roads and the car industry worldwide makes a million new ones every year. The mass ownership of cars has transformed cities and people's ways of life. Many cities in the USA are built entirely around the car, with such vast distances between residential and shopping, leisure and business areas that the only way of travelling between them is by road.

But it is not just the car. Countless items in our homes and offices are affordable and abundant because of mass-production. Very few items have escaped the relentless pull of the assembly line. Computers and TVs, washing machines

---

[52] Such was the charismatic personality of Henry Ford, and the huge impact of the mass-production, mass-consumption approach that a range of social theories known as Fordism sprang up. The key idea was that not only should goods be produced cheaply in massive quantities using standardisation and assembly lines, but that factory workers should also be paid well so that they provide a mass market for the products they make.

The Ford approach became such an extraordinary phenomenon in the 1930s that Hitler had a picture of Henry Ford on his desk and Stalin took Ford's ideas as a role model for Soviet industry in the Five Year plans. 'American efficiency is that indomitable force,' historian Thomas Hughes quotes Stalin as saying, 'which neither knows nor recognises obstacles; which continues on a task once started until it is finished, even if it is a minor task; and without which serious constructive work is impossible ... The combination of the Russian revolutionary sweep with American efficiency is the essence of Leninism.'

For Aldous Huxley, this mass-production, mass-consumption world was such a profound and dispiriting change that in *Brave New World* he sets up the coming of Ford as the dawn of a new age like the dawn of the Christian era. Dates in his new world are given AF (After Ford) and people praise Our Ford.

and microwaves, and numerous other quite complex items are built at prices ordinary people can afford. Even items such as food are packaged using the same principles. So many of the things we take for granted would be restricted to the homes of the super-rich if it were not for mass-production.

Of course, there is a downside to all this. First of all, mass-produced items are often less well-made than hand-crafted items – though there are some items that cannot be hand-made at all. They are also dully identical and have none of the interesting individuality of hand-made items. Secondly, they have taken away much of the job satisfaction of factory workers, and in many cases taken away their job altogether. Instead of the contentment of completing a job, factory workers have simply to add their part, routinely and repetitively without often ever getting to see the product finished. And of course many factory jobs have been lost to automation and robotic assembly systems.

There is a sense that mass-production has helped us both become voracious consumers and fill our lives with the soullessness of gently buzzing factories. There is something quite wasteful about a system that seems to generate masses of products that we don't necessarily need in order to fuel economic growth.

And yet it's easy to sit in one's ivory tower and get rueful over the passing of craft items and skilled labour. But in the pre-mass-production era, life for most people was grim. Poverty was widespread, and life expectancy was shockingly low. The houses of the working class were empty of all but the most basic items, since those beautiful hand-made items were unaffordable even to those who made them. And jobs were often dangerous and demanding.

The coming of the mass-production, mass-consumption approach transformed the lives of millions of working-class people in the Western world. The consumer goods factories gave them, for the first time, reasonably well paid and secure jobs and a lifestyle that their grandparents could barely imagine. And though the work may have been dull, at least it was pretty likely you would get through the day without being maimed and not so exhausted that you couldn't enjoy some of the new pleasures on offer.[53]

#31 Laws of Motion

'Truth is ever to be found in simplicity,' Newton is said to have written in *Rules for Methodizing the Apocalypse*, 'and not in the multiplicity and confusion of things.' And with his three fundamental Laws of Motion, along with his law of gravity, he

---

[53] One of the inherent qualities of mass-production, though, is the division of tasks and labour, and this has proved a problem for many more developed countries. Over recent decades, more and more production tasks and finally entire manufacturing processes have been transferred to factories in places like India and China. The low cost of wages in these countries means that goods can be made for the developed world cheaper than ever before, but of course jobs in manufacturing in developed countries have been lost, while the factory workers in places like China and India are often paid too little for them to become large markets for the goods they are turning out themselves. The complete split between producers and consumers is contrary to the basic thrust behind Ford's ideas, and although there is always something worrying about the ideas of a man who says 'History is bunk', it does seem as if this is an ultimately unsustainable situation.

reduced the entire history, present and future of the universe to a few simple premises and a couple of simple mathematical equations.

Although a few minor adjustments are needed at the very extremes of the scale – for Einstein's relativity on a gigantic scale and for quantum theory on the subatomic – Newton's 'System of the World' provides a simple and powerful tool for studying and predicting every motion in the universe. Using Newton's laws, scientists can work out anything from the way a motorbike will corner to the trajectory of a space probe around Jupiter, from the force on a butterfly's wings to the tidal motion of the oceans. It is a quite astonishing idea, and has underpinned many of science and technology's greatest achievements in the last three centuries.

To see how elegant and far-reaching Newton's laws are and what a crucial part they continue to play at the cutting edge of science, you only have to look at two key recent discoveries in astronomy: dark matter and extra-solar planets.

The universe is a wonderful clockwork of circling objects, with moons orbiting planets orbiting stars, stars orbiting galaxies, and galaxies circling each other. Newton's laws of gravity and motion demonstrate quite simply that the further out an object is circling, the slower it needs to travel to give it the momentum to keep a steady course. So astronomers were very surprised to discover in the 1970s that stars at the edges of a galaxy are orbiting just as fast as stars near the centre. The only good explanation was that the stars are not at the edge of the galaxy as they appear.

They are actually held within a much larger disc of matter that we simply cannot see. Astronomers now call this invisible matter dark matter. Using only Newton's laws, astronomers have been able to calculate that all the stars in each galaxy are embedded in huge haloes of dark matter stretching way beyond the visible disc of the galaxy in all directions. In fact, the disc of stars is like a scattering of pepper in between the halves of a gigantic invisible bun of dark matter. We cannot see this bun at all; we just know it is there because of the huge effects of its gravity.[54]

Similarly, in 1995, astronomers confirmed that they had detected for the first time a new planet far beyond the solar system, orbiting a distant sun-like star, 51 Pegasi. Since then many more of these extra-solar planets have been discovered orbiting distant stars, and the total as of July 2010 was 466. These planets are so distant and so dark compared to their parent star that it is almost impossible to see them directly, even with the most powerful telescopes in space. Indeed, only ten have actually been imaged directly. Nearly all these amazingly distant planets are being discovered using Newton's laws. Astronomers look for the slight wobble in the parent star's motion caused by the planet's gravity – and Newton's laws allow them to calculate the size of the planet and its distance from the star. There is no greater testament to the power of the laws than this, applied to some of the furthest extremes of space we know of.

---

[54] No one knows quite what dark matter is, but it's not just invisible; it hasn't even enough substance to cluster into stars. It's a bit like an incredibly thin gas that we can walk through without noticing. The sun and stars are probably racing through a mist of dark matter all the time. Indeed, dark matter particles may be so tiny that a billion particles may be slipping straight through you right now.

Newton claimed during a lunch with William Stukeley in 1726 that the inspiration for the idea of gravity came to him one late summer day 60 years earlier as he sat thinking in the garden at Woolsthorpe, and saw an apple drop from a tree.

It is not entirely clear what the falling apple made him think, but Newton's real insight was to understand just why it fell. In the previous half century, Kepler had shown that planets have elliptical (oval) orbits, and Galileo had shown that things accelerate at an even pace as they fall towards the ground. Yet no one had thought of connecting these two events, let alone showing they have the same universal cause.

Newton realised that the apple was not just falling but being pulled by an invisible force – and later wondered if this same force might be holding the planets in orbit. Just as gravity pulls the apple to Earth, so gravity keeps the Moon in its orbit round the Earth, and the planets round the Sun, and stops them flying off into space. From this simple but brilliant idea, Newton developed his theory of gravity, the universal force that tries to pull all matter together. With his extraordinary mathematical proofs, he showed that this force must be the same everywhere, and that the pull between two things depends on their mass (the amount of matter in them) and the square of the distance between them.

Over the next twenty years, Newton refined his idea of gravitation into a comprehensive system including the three great Laws of Motion. The first law was the idea of inertia or momentum. It basically means that things stay still or keep moving at the same speed in a straight line unless something pushes or pulls on them, that is, a force. He applied this to the Moon – showing that the Moon tries to carry on in a straight line, but gravity pulls it into an orbit. The second is the idea that the rate and direction of any change – an object's acceleration – depends entirely on the strength of the force, and how heavy the affected object is. If the Moon were closer to the Earth, the pull of gravity between them would be so strong that the Moon would be dragged down to crash into the Earth. If it were further away, gravity would be so weak that the Moon would fly off into space. The third law showed that every action and reaction is equal and opposite – so when two things crash together they bounce off with equal force.

The key, perhaps, to Newton's success was that he did not attempt to explain gravity; he simply presented a mathematical description, writing: 'I have not been able to discover the cause of those properties of gravity from phenomena, and I frame no hypotheses … it is enough that gravity does really exist, and act according to the laws which we have explained, and abundantly serves to account for all the motions of the celestial bodies, and of our sea.' He was criticised for this lack of explanation at the time, but it was gradually realised that this was actually his greatest insight – to simply describe with mathematical precision rather than attempt to lift the veil and, as he put it, try to read God's mind.[55]

---

[55] This mathematical view of the universe seemed to some so cold and abstract and clockwork that a century later many Romantics turned against it. At a famous literary dinner on 28 December 1817, which included the poets Wordsworth and Keats, the artist Benjamin Haydon reported that Charles Lamb, 'in a strain of humour beyond description, abused me for putting Newton's head into my [Haydon's] picture; "a fellow," said he, "who believed nothing unless it was as clear as the three sides of a triangle." And then he and Keats agreed that Newton had destroyed all the poetry of the rainbow by reducing it to the prismatic colours. It was impossible to resist

We take Newton's view of the ways things move so much for granted nowadays, that it is hard to imagine just what an extraordinary breakthrough it was. Before Newton, there had been no notion that the movement of the fish in the sea or papers disturbed by a breeze had anything in common whatsoever with the movement of the heavens, let alone that they were predictable in any way. They were at best seen to be controlled by unique, local factors; at worst by the whim of the gods. The universe was, essentially, a mysterious, capricious place.

With his law of gravity and his three Laws of Motion, Newton showed that every movement, large or small, on the ground or in the furthest reaches of space, behaved according to the same simple, universal laws. In his book *Philosophiæ naturalis principia mathematica* (*The Mathematical Principles of Natural Philosophy*), or simply *Principia*, probably the greatest science book ever written, he suddenly blew away the universe's chaotic mystery and showed that everything, everywhere behaved in an orderly, entirely understandable way. It was as if the whole universe had been revealed at last as some great, incredibly complex clockwork machine, and Newton's laws were the key to its working. Incredibly, it showed that the laws we work out with experiments here in labs on the ground can be applied right across the universe.

Even more significantly, it showed how every single movement in the universe can be analysed mathematically, and Newton provided the mathematical tools to do it, with the two

him, and we all drank "Newton's health and confusion to mathematics".'
Two years later, Keats was to memorably describe the process in his poem
'Lamia' as 'unweaving the rainbow'.

entirely new branches of mathematics that he created – differential and integral calculus. Armed with Newton's laws and Newton's maths, it became possible, in theory, to predict the movement of everything in the universe from the greatest star to the tiniest molecule, for ever into the future.

No wonder then that as Newton's ideas began to sink in, he came to be regarded with awe in the eighteenth century. His revelation that the universe behaves according to predictable, universal laws ushered in a whole new, optimistic age, the age of Enlightenment, in which people believed we humans can, by our efforts alone, learn to understand and improve the world. As the poet Alexander Pope said, in his famous satirical verse, 'Nature and nature's laws lay hid in night;/God said, "Let Newton be!" and all was light.'

If this optimism seems clouded today, it is only by the doubts that we will do the right thing – not that things are ultimately beyond our understanding in the way Newton initiated. And if Einstein's insights have shown a subtler, deeper conception of how universal laws work at extremes, Newton's laws underpin our basic understanding of how everything works on a day-to-day scale.

#30 Universities

The word university comes from the Latin *universitas magistrorum et scholarium*, which means, essentially, a community of teachers and scholars. It is a wonderfully simple and apt description, which sums up the spirit of universities right from the earliest days. They are not schools where pupils simply go to take instruction. They are communities, where learning is exchanged. Teachers impart their knowledge not only to students, but also to each other, and there is the sense that they are places where ideas are shared and cherished.

Of course, universities don't always live up to this ideal, and as universities have multiplied in number in recent years across the world, standards and approaches have inevitably varied, with some quite clearly being education factories, or worse, while others foster an outdated elitism. Nonetheless, the word university has a powerful aura that still inspires both administrators and students to regard them with just a little more reverence, just a little more sense of something rather special, than they would a college.

The first three universities, Bologna, Paris and Oxford, all date back to the eleventh century when the monastic tradition in Europe was at its height, and you can see the monastic links in the cloisters of many of the older universities. It's partly this that gives them their special quality. But the aura runs deeper than that. Universities had an urgent mission of learning. They were set up by the Church, the medieval historian Sir Richard Southern asserted, to save humanity with their learning. The perfect knowledge of the world that might have been mankind's was lost by the Fall. It was the scholars' task to recover some of what was lost and bring redemption to mankind before the imminent end of the world. So it was not surprising that these early universities had a deep commitment to learning, and if the original purpose has been lost, some of the passion for knowledge lingers on in universities today.

Although they were endowed by the Church, the learning the medieval universities undertook was essentially secular.

The tone was set by the influential and scholarly canon of the Abbey of St Victor in Paris in the early twelfth century, Hugh of Saint Victor. Although firmly in the monastic tradition, Hugh argued that secular learning and study of the natural world were a necessary foundation for proper religious contemplation. In other words, you needed to know about God's world before you contemplated the heavens. 'Learn everything,' Hugh insisted, 'later you will see that nothing is superfluous.'

Students at the medieval universities did not study theological matters as in the monasteries, but the liberal arts[56] – that is, the general knowledge meant to train a student's capacity for rational thought, rather than professional or vocational training. The idea of liberal arts dates back to Roman times, when it was the education right for a free man, hence 'liberal' arts. In the medieval arts, there were seven liberal arts to be studied, divided into the *trivium* (grammar, rhetoric and dialectic) and the *quadrivium* (arithmetic, music, geometry and astronomy). According to Hugh, learning these would help 'to restore God's image in us'. It was this higher purpose that inspired

---

[56] This is why universities such as Cambridge still award all their graduates the title Bachelor of *Arts*, no matter what subject they studied. The term bachelor, incidentally, comes from the Latin *baccalaureus*, which of course is also the origin of the French *baccalauréat*. It was the Latin name for a knight's squire, and there was a sense that university students were being apprenticed to do battle with the world of learning, just as the squire was being prepared for warfare. A degree was called a degree, because it was meant to be just a step, or degree, on the path to becoming a fully qualified master. The term graduate comes from the Latin *gradus*, which means 'step'.

university scholars to write *Summae,* which were intended as encyclopaedias of the whole of reality.

The medieval universities taught entirely in Latin, and students were expected to chat in Latin even outside classes, on pain of a fine. This served to emphasise the town/gown divide, and students attending university were often given phrase books to help them converse with the locals. But it made the universities entirely international. It was easy for an English student to go to Bologna or a German student to go to Salamanca in Spain and know they would have no language problems. So students did indeed study right across Europe. Europe was united intellectually as never since, yet while it helped the exchange of learning, it created a sense of elevation and remoteness from the ordinary people that has clung on to the universities ever since in the image of 'ivory towers'[57] of learning.

There is another fascinating strand to the origins of universities that is often forgotten. Visitors from the Middle East cannot fail to be struck by the similarity between the quadrangles of the old European universities and the ancient Islamic schools set up in places like Baghdad, Cairo and Fez in Morocco in the ninth and tenth centuries. The Islamic school of Qayrawan (al Karaouine) in Fez, established in 859 AD, might, indeed, be called the world's first university.

It seems likely that, before the divisive wars of the Crusades, the cultural interchange between Islam and the West was significant. Certainly, Arab learning translated into

---

[57] The phrase apparently comes from the Biblical 'Song of Solomon', where it is used to describe a woman's neck and suggest an aloof nobility.

Latin, with the authors given Latin names such as Avicenna, Geber, Averroes and Alhazen, played a key role in the early universities – along with the classical texts reintroduced to the West from Islam. Moreover, the whole teaching set-up of the early European universities seems to owe a lot to the early Muslim schools with their study groups or *halaqas*, their special master/student relationships and so on. Even today, university professors occupy academic 'chairs' – a 1,000-year hangover from the Muslim schools where only the professor sat on a chair or *kursi*, and all his students squatted around him on the floor.

As the divide between East and West deepened, these connections were forgotten; and in time, too, the Christian religious overtones faded and universities became entirely secular institutions. Many traditions lingered on, though, and so too did the heightened sense of purpose. And maybe also the idea that students leave home and throw their lives entirely into being at university owes a great deal to the monastic retreat to focus on higher things. Although religion is taught now only on specialist minority courses, and the teaching is rational, not revelatory, it's this quality of retreat that makes universities special. They are otherworldly, and meant to be – indeed need to be, to free teachers and students from everyday distractions to learn about life and the world in a very different way, which could be anything from long drunken nights chatting about the meaning of life to solitary hours poring over dense books in the university library.

The contribution of universities to our intellectual and cultural life over the centuries has been immense. Nearly all the greatest minds in science and philosophy, for instance, found their first inspiration and made their first bold explorations in their field at university.[58] Scientists like Newton, Darwin, Maxwell and Dirac, philosophers such as Erasmus and Wittgenstein, and poets such as Wordsworth and Coleridge all began their careers at Cambridge University, for instance.

The universities continue to play a pivotal role in our society. For all the vacuous discussions and social flutter, many of them are major hubs of research and academic advancement. They may not always provide the hands-on, practical work that specialist research institutes give, but they provide the new ideas and the theoretical underpinnings without which the specialist institutes could never start. While much of the research on genetics, for instance, is in the labs of biotech companies and government research establishments, the breakthrough discovery of the structure of DNA by Watson and Crick in 1953 that made it all possible took place at universities in Cambridge and London.

For the students who study at them, the best of universities provide a unique chance for learning, not just about the details of their subjects, but how to think for themselves. They are oases, too, where students can explore their ideas, investigate their hopes and dreams and learn about themselves in a way that they can at no other kind of educational establishment. They meet intelligent people and can exchange ideas both

---

[58] Often, the brightest, most original minds didn't learn directly from the tutors, but sought things out for themselves. While at Cambridge, the young Isaac Newton was so concerned to follow up his own research that he barely bothered with the coursework and was almost failed. Unknown to his tutors, though, he was already going far beyond them, developing the latest revolutionary mathematical and scientific ideas of the French genius René Descartes, which were only just beginning to filter into England.

profound and trivial, share pivotal moments in their lives and pointless drunken nights, and make friends and love. Most, though by no means all, people who have been to university agree that it was a defining moment in their lives.

#29 Simplified Chinese

Writing is one of the hottest and most politically charged debates in China. The People's Republic is backing a much simplified version of Chinese writing; Taiwan is currently seeking World Heritage status for Traditional Chinese writing to stop it being eradicated. Of course, it's not just a battle about letters, but over the very future of China and its culture.

Over 90 per cent of Chinese people speak Chinese, the language of the Han people (the dominant ethnic group in China), which makes it the most widely spoken language on Earth (845 million native speakers, compared with 329 million Spanish and 328 million English). But Han comes in various dialects, and those dialects are so different that in the past, people speaking the Beijing dialect would find it as hard to understand someone from Guangzhou as a Portuguese would find it to understand someone from Romania.[59] The words are often the same in the various Chinese dialects but the tone with which they are spoken, and the word order, can be so different that they are mutually unintelligible. In the northern Chinese dialect (Mandarin), for instance, there

---

[59] The reason for this particular comparison is that both Portuguese and Romanian are 'romance' languages with an underlying connection because they are both derived from Latin.

are four different tones or pitches that distinguish words that would otherwise sound the same. Southern Chinese has nine of these tones.

There are seven major dialects of Han Chinese. Six of them are spoken by less than 20 per cent of people in China, including the Wu dialect of Shanghai (about 8 per cent), the Kejia or Hakka Fujianese dialect of Fujian (4 per cent), and the Yue (Cantonese) dialect of Hong Kong and Guangzhou (5 per cent). Many of the vast diaspora of Chinese people around the world, especially in South-east Asia, also speak Cantonese or Fujianese. However, by far the most widely spoken dialect in mainland China now is Mandarin, spoken by some 70 per cent of Chinese people.

In the past, Mandarin was the language of officialdom and got its name from the Portuguese, who used the word to describe the dialect of the 'mandarins' (governors) of Beijing. Its use spread as government officials moved around the country and it paid people wherever they went to learn Mandarin to get on. In the 1950s, the government decided to promote its use as a common, national language and called it *Putonghua* (which means 'common speech'), rather than the foreign name Mandarin. *Putonghua* is the form of Chinese taught to foreigners and is the language Chinese children are taught in at school, the language of government and the language of the media. In the major cities, almost every young person can read *Putonghua* because they learned it at school. Not everyone who reads it, though, can necessarily speak it, and in rural areas knowledge of *Putonghua* is much patchier.

Interestingly, many of the vast differences between the various Chinese dialects vanish when they are written down.

The dialects may sound very, very different, but the words are written down with many of the same Chinese characters, so the sentence will mean the same whether the reader is from Beijing or Shenzhen. Because of the way Chinese characters work, they mean the same regardless of the way they are sounded – just as the written figure 4 means exactly the same whether you are French or German. All the same, most written Chinese is in the form of *Putonghua* anyway. It is very rare to try to write any of the dialects down, except for Cantonese.

Traditional Chinese is the world's most complex written language. Whereas in most Western alphabets there are fewer than 33 letters to cope with, plus a few accent marks, Chinese has 50,000 or so characters. Highly educated Chinese people will probably be familiar with 10,000 of these, and anyone who is literate will know at least 2,500, which is what you need to know to read a newspaper.

The reason why Traditional Chinese has so many characters is that it doesn't really work phonetically, so words cannot be built up from single sounds. Instead, there is a separate character for each word or syllable. Originally, written Chinese was based on simple graphic pictures (pictographs) of natural objects. There are pictographs like this dating back to the eleventh century BC. Many written languages started like this and moved towards a phonetic alphabet, but Chinese characters only have a hint at pronunciation. Instead, as it developed, Chinese combined pictures to create new abstract meanings or ideographs. Thus a combination of the pictures for sun and moon meant 'bright' while a combination of the pictures for woman and child meant 'happiness'. Tellingly, three pictures of women together mean 'treachery'. Chinese characters also developed as pictures came to be used for words that sounded the same when spoken. So the picture character for an ear of corn developed into the character for the verb 'to come' because these words sound similar when spoken.

Several different writing styles developed as China split into different kingdoms between the seventh and third centuries BC, but when the country was unified under the Qins in 221 BC, the Qin style was imposed everywhere. The Qin style was substantially modified under the Han (206 BC–220 AD), but modern 'Traditional' Chinese characters are essentially no more than a development of the ancient Han characters.

Chinese characters look impossibly complex at first, but they are always made up from a particular number of strokes of the pen in a particular order. So the character for 'mouth', which is basically a square, is written with three strokes: first the left side, then the top and right together in a single stroke, and lastly the base. Typically, too, the character has two parts, with the right-hand side signifying the meaning in some way and the left, called the radical, signifying the sound. In the most common system, there are about 214 of these radicals, which are the closest thing Chinese has to Western letters.

Written Traditional Chinese is hard even for Chinese children to learn, and in the 1950s, it was felt that this was holding back any improvements in literacy. So the government introduced two controversial measures. The first was to simplify the most commonly used few thousand characters, making them easier to learn and quicker to write.[60] It also used just

---

[60] The second, even more drastic, measure was to try to dispense with Chinese characters altogether and write Chinese instead in the Roman alphabet. This Romanised Chinese was called pinyin and essentially

one simple character in place of several elaborate traditional characters. This is a dramatic reduction of course, and while making Chinese hugely easier to write, it loses some of the richness and complexity of the language.

But Simplified Chinese wasn't just about literacy. This was Mao's China, and it was all part of the attack on China's bourgeois intellectuals that reached a head in the Cultural Revolution between 1966 and Mao's death in 1976. The complexity of Traditional Chinese was so tied up with the intellectual elite that teachers of it were persecuted and even murdered. Taiwan came to regard the imposition of Simplified Chinese as a communist plot and banned it until 2003. Even on the mainland, many did and still do regard it as a terrible betrayal of Chinese heritage.

The enforced introduction of Simplified Chinese, however, was highly effective. Literacy rates did soar, although this was maybe more because of the wider spread of education than the writing system. Indeed, China has some of the highest literacy rates in the world – an astonishing achievement for a country where the vast majority of people were barely educated peasants little more than half a century ago.

----

involved using 25 letters of the Western alphabet (excluding the letter 'v') to create the sounds of Mandarin Chinese, along with accents above each syllable to create the four different tones. Pinyin never caught on in China, and the idea was quickly dropped, but pinyin is very useful for foreigners since it allows any Westerner, after a little basic instruction, to read and pronounce Chinese words without knowing any Chinese characters. It was the widespread adoption of pinyin that led to the change of Peking to Beijing and Mao Tse-tung to Mao Zedong. The pinyin version is much closer to the way Chinese people would say these words, and street signs in China are often written in pinyin as well as in characters.

Simplified Chinese is now the dominant form of writing in mainland China. Indeed, less than 5 per cent of Chinese people on the mainland write in Traditional Chinese – although in places like Taiwan and Hong Kong the Traditional characters are still used, and they are making something of a comeback among intellectuals on the mainland where they are seen as more sophisticated. Officially, the law on the mainland sanctions the use of Traditional writing only for ceremonial purposes and for historical literature, but shops and businesses often use it for displays and logos, even though it is not strictly legal.

The debate over the relative merits of Simplified Chinese and Traditional Chinese is detailed and intense. Some argue that Traditional Chinese is just unsuited to the modern world, with the character for 'electricity' symbolising rain to link it with lightning, whereas now, of course, electricity comes from a wide range of sources. Others say that Simplified Chinese loses much of the richness of Traditional Chinese, with the Simplified Chinese character for 'love' losing the heart that made the Traditional character so evocative. This is a perfect symbol, say critics, for the limitations of Simplified Chinese – it is a writing system without a heart.

Simplified Chinese is now massively dominant but there is still considerable energy behind Traditional Chinese, especially coming from Hong Kong and Taiwan. Whichever wins out ultimately, if either does, it is more likely to be because of its political backing than its genuine merits. A traditional Chinese proverb says: 'Listen to both sides and be enlightened; listen to one side and be left in the dark.' At the moment there is slightly more darkness than light.

#28 Refrigeration

Imagine a world with no cold beer. No ice cream. No butter or milk. Fresh fruit and vegetables for only a few months a year – and even then outrageously expensive. No fresh fish, and definitely no sushi. Meat a costly luxury. No cut flowers for that romantic date …

All of these things we could well manage without, but what a loss to our modern lifestyle! Refrigeration has transformed the way people in cities eat and drink. Foods that you might once have been able to get only if you lived on a farm – and even then only at certain times of year – you can get night and day simply by opening the freezer. Exotic foods that come from the other side of the world, such as bananas or tropical prawns, are there in your local supermarket all year round, kept fresh as the day they were harvested by refrigeration. This variety of fresh food not only brings us immense pleasure but also provides us with a diet that is much healthier than we'd otherwise have.

Chilling preserves food by reducing the growth of microorganisms such as bacteria and mould that make food go off and be rendered potentially poisonous.[61] It also restricts and slows the activity of chemical enzymes and other chemical activity that spoil food, making fruit, for instance, go soft and mushy and brown, and butter go rancid. Complete freezing can preserve some foods[62] even longer because the freezing of water in

---

[61] Milk turns sour, for instance, because bacteria in the milk ferment the lactose (milk sugar) into lactic acid.

[62] Salad vegetables and soft fruits don't freeze well because the formation of ice crystals breaks down the cell membranes, turning the food soft and mushy.

the food into ice makes it unavailable to the microorganisms that need it for growth. It may also preserve the food's nutrient content.[63]

It's been discovered how all this works only recently, but people noticed how cold and ice could keep things fresh for longer thousands of years ago. At least 3,000 years ago, the Chinese were harvesting ice in winter and storing it in caves to preserve food, while the Romans collected snow from the high mountains and kept it in straw-covered pits to cool water and wine, and for cold summer baths known as *frigidaria*. For centuries, people preserved food by keeping it in cooler cellars and larders. Sometimes, the wealthy had ice brought down from the mountains to store in thickly built ice houses, ready to add to cool drinks or make ice cream.

In the nineteenth century, demand for fresh food soared even while the growth of cities was increasing the distance between farmers and consumers, and food merchants began to experiment with ways of keeping food fresh in transit to the customer. Specially insulated trucks with ice bunkers at either end or on top kept fish and dairy products fresh on their journey, while insulated food stores were set up in cities and kept cool with ice shipped in from considerable distances. Norway became a major supplier of natural ice to Western Europe.

---

[63] Just how well, varies from food to food. Before some fruits and vegetables are frozen commercially they are blanched by brief immersion in boiling water to deactivate enzymes and yeasts that would otherwise continue the spoiling process, even in the freezer. The blanching reduces the vitamin C content by as much as 20 per cent. Freezing has almost no effect on the nutrient content of meat and fish, though water-soluble vitamins and minerals are sometimes lost from fish during defrosting.

New Englander Frederick Tudor became known as the Ice King, shipping North American ice all around the world.

In the USA in the late nineteenth century, millions of ordinary households acquired 'iceboxes' – insulated metal boxes with ice compartments that could be used for keeping meat, fish and dairy products fresh, and for cooling beer. Ice carts became a familiar sight in many neighbourhoods. Whenever the ice melted, people would put out a note for the iceman saying 'Ice today, please' and he would drop off a big block of it. Such was the demand for ice that every river, lake and pond was raided in winter, including Walden Pond in Concord, Massachusetts, made famous by the writer Henry Thoreau. Unfortunately, many of the sources of ice were polluted by sewage and industrial waste, and soon natural ice began to be seen as a health hazard.

The idea of artificial cooling dates back thousands of years. The Ancient Egyptians, for instance, would put boiling water in pots on the roof at night, so that it might cool as it evaporated. The Persian polymath Ibn Sina (Avicenna) created a coil in which aromatic vapours evaporated and cooled the coil. In sixteenth-century Italy, people often cooled wine by smearing the bottle neck with saltpetre (sodium nitrate) and rotating it in water, a process described in 1550 by Blasius Villafranca, a Spanish physician living in Rome, in a book entitled *Methodus Refrigerandi ex vocato Salenitro Vinum Aquanque ac Potus quodvis aliud Genus*. As saltpetre dissolves, it takes the heat out of water and makes it cooler. English natural philosopher Francis Bacon (1561–1626) heard about this technique and began to apply it to other food. He caught pneumonia in 1626 while testing the effect of freezing on meat preservation by going out in a blizzard and stuffing a chicken with snow. Bacon had his chips a month later but the chicken was preserved. It was the great Irish chemist Robert Boyle who began to work out some of the science behind it all, and wrote an important treatise called *An Experimental History of Cold* (1665).

We now know that artificial cooling can work in two main ways. Chemical cooling (as with saltpetre) works because of the heat taken out of the water as the salt dissolves. Mechanical cooling can be either evaporative or vapour-compression. Evaporative cooling occurs because liquids take heat energy from their surroundings in order to evaporate, which is why sweat keeps us cool as it evaporates from our skin.[64] Evaporative cooling is especially effective with volatile liquids such as alcohol and ether.[65] Vapour-compression cooling, discovered by John Dalton (1766–1844), works by compressing a gas or vapour then letting it expand. As it expands, it draws heat from its surroundings.

Most modern refrigerators use a combination of the two. First the vapour is compressed (usually with a piston), before being passed through a cooling coil where it is cooled and condensed into a liquid by contact with water or air. When

---

[64] Self-cooling drink cans work by evaporative cooling. As you open the can, a desiccant inside a special compartment within the can spills into the liquid. As it does, it evaporates, cooling the liquid sharply.

[65] American scientist and statesman Benjamin Franklin and British professor John Hadley used bellows to evaporate alcohol quickly from the bulb of a thermometer and discovered that they could bring the temperature down dramatically, well below freezing point. 'From this experiment,' Franklin wrote wryly, 'one may see the possibility of freezing a man to death on a warm summer's day.'

it emerges from the coil, the vapour expands suddenly and partially evaporates, drawing in heat from its surroundings. Finally, it goes to an evaporator unit where it evaporates completely, causing further cooling, and returns to the compressor to begin the cycle again.[66]

In the nineteenth century, inventors experimented with various techniques to create a mechanical refrigerator. The first successes were with vapour-compression. American inventor Oliver Evans designed but never built a vapour-compression refrigerator in 1805. An American living in Britain, Jacob Perkins, made the first artificial refrigerator in 1834, also using vapour-compression. And in 1842, American physician John Gorrie created the first ice-making machine. Doctor Gorrie also had the idea of using refrigeration to cool the air and help his malaria patients recover, but this pioneering air conditioning was never built.

The commercial breakthrough for refrigeration came in the 1850s, with machines such as those devised by Alexander Twinning in the USA and James Harrison in Geelong, Australia. By the 1860s, a dozen meat-packing houses across Australia were using Harrison's refrigeration system. Within twenty years, refrigerator ships such as New Zealand's *Dunedin* and the English SS *Selembria* were plying the oceans, carrying

---

[66] Recently, inventors have been experimenting with different systems such as sonic and magnetic refrigeration. Sonic refrigeration, developed in the Sounds Cool refrigerator, uses high-pressure sound waves to compress (and expand) helium gas and create a cooling effect. Magnetic refrigeration relies on the discovery that an alloy of gadolinium, germanium and silicon gets cool when exposed to a magnetic field. When a wheel made of this powdered alloy is spun next to a magnet, it creates a simple, cheap refrigeration unit.

frozen meat and dairy products right around the world from New Zealand and Australia and South America. Livestock farming began to boom on a massive scale in Australasia and South America, and Europeans started to enjoy the pleasures of plentiful and cheap meat and dairy products – even though they originated on the other side of the world.

The impact on farming was dramatic, since particular areas or countries could now specialise in products they were especially suited to, no matter how far their markets. And countries no longer had to feed themselves, but could rely instead on the abundance of particular foods in other countries far away, allowing an upsurge in industrialisation and development right across the globe. The brewing industry, too, was installing its own refrigeration units, and ice cool German lagers began to spread across the world.

For a while, refrigeration remained largely in commercial and industrial units, because the ammonia used as a refrigerant was far too toxic for homes, which continued to rely on natural iceboxes. But in the 1920s, the Frigidaire company created CFCs (chlorofluorocarbons) that went under the trade name Freon. Of course, now we know that CFCs, while harmless to humans, damage the world's protective layer of ozone in the atmosphere, without which we'd be exposed to harmful UV rays from the sun.[67] But back in the 1920s, CFCs seemed like a miracle – cheap and harmless and perfect as refrigerants because they evaporate at low temperatures. Domestic refrigerators became a reality, and by the Second

----

[67] CFCs have now been replaced by refrigerants such as R134a, R-407C ('Suva') and R410a ('Puron').

World War, millions of homes across Europe and North America had their own personal refrigerators, allowing people to keep food fresh as never before. It was like having a farm full of fresh food in your kitchen, as well as ice cool drinks even on the hottest day of the year.

Now, neither our lifestyle nor the global food industry could function at all without refrigeration, and refrigeration has found numerous other uses, too. The oil business uses it to help refine oil. The metal industry uses it to temper and improve steel.[68] The pharmaceuticals industry uses it to make drugs such as blood-pressure-lowering statins. Hospitals use it for everything from safely storing live vaccines and blood samples, to keeping donor organs in good condition long enough to reach transplant patients. Morgues use it to preserve cadavers in good condition for the funeral or for a police investigation. The woollen business uses refrigeration to reduce moth attacks. Munitions factories keep explosives cool. Some people even believe they might preserve their bodies by freezing for a future time of immortality. A chilling thought.

#27 Marxism

The impact of Karl Marx's ideas on the twentieth century is incalculable. A century after his death more than half the world's population lived under governments that claimed to draw their inspiration from Marxism, and both monstrous

---

[68] In the late 1990s, cryogenic (below −150°C) tempering of metals was developed to make better baseball bats, golf clubs, amplifiers and much more.

tyrants such as Stalin and Mao and professed freedom fighters like Che Guevara saw themselves as his followers. Millions of people of myriad political intents and persuasions once called themselves Marxists. And if the high-water mark of his influence seems to have passed with the collapse of Soviet communism, it does not diminish the extraordinary power of Marx's ideas.

For a century, Marx divided opinion to such an extent that people went to war, killed and betrayed to bring what they believed were his ideas to life, while others, equally determined, went to war, murdered and plotted to prevent what they saw as Marxism ever happening. To his supporters, he invited the devotion of a Mohammed or Jesus Christ, a leader who would deliver them from the evils of oppression. To his opponents, he was the devil incarnate, to be blamed for everything from the collapse of house prices to the atrocities of the gulags. All this may well have surprised Marx himself who, on hearing a new French party declare itself to be Marxist, commented that 'I, at least, am not a Marxist'.

Marxism was the creation of two men, Karl Marx and Friedrich Engels, but as Engels himself generously acknowledged after Marx's death in 1883: 'Marx was a genius; we others were at best talented. Without him the theory would not be by far what it is today. It therefore rightly bears his name.'

Although both men were deeply aware of the political consequences of their ideas, they believed that what they created was a startling new scientific theory – a new way of looking at the world based on evidence. It was this new theory that would give revolutionaries the tools for creating a new world.

That was why, even though the main thrust of their ideas was summarised briefly in the famous *Manifesto of the Communist Party* of 1848, Marx laboured in the British Library for decades producing his great work *Das Kapital*, in which he examined the evidence in detail and propounded his theory. The changes that would come were nothing to do with morals and ideals, which are as changeable as fashion, Marx argued, but the inevitable outcome of natural processes.

Marx was a materialist – that is, he argued that the mind doesn't exist independently of matter, and that the material world, the world of matter, shapes human thought. For Marx, there is no such thing as an ideal above and beyond the material world. Thus human nature, ideals and beliefs are always shaped by the circumstances in which they are formed.

The impetus for Marx's writing came from the very visible suffering of the working class in England and elsewhere. When he arrived in England from Germany, Marx picked up on what Eric Hobsbawm describes as 'the universal discontent of men who felt themselves hungry in a society reeking with wealth, enslaved in a country which prided itself on its freedom, seeking bread and hope and receiving in return stones and despair'. He was deeply moved by Engels' vivid portrait of the suffering of labourers in Manchester in his 1845 book *The Condition of the Working Class in England*. It became their joint mission to explain how this situation had arisen and how it might be changed.

The central thesis of Marx's ideas was that lives and social relationships are driven not by ideals or beliefs or individual ideas but by economics. Indeed, he argued that ideals and beliefs are entirely shaped by economics. Studying history revealed it as a constant struggle between classes of people with conflicting economic interests, a theory Marx called 'historical materialism'. In the feudal era, for instance, the barons wanted to get the most out of the serfs in terms of labour, and the serfs wanted to get the most out of the barons. So conflict was inevitable, sometimes personal, sometimes class-driven as with the Peasants' Revolt of 1381. As feudalism gave way to capitalism, so the focus of the conflict shifted to the industrial capitalist class and the industrial working class, or rather the bourgeoisie and the proletariat.

Marx argued that most ideas are class ideas, and in particular the ideas of the dominant class at each moment in history. It was, for instance, the rise of the merchant middle class that led to the challenging of feudal restrictions on freedom of trade and a demand for freedom of action. In Marx's own time, it was the ideas of the industrial capitalist class that were in the ascendant. In the *Communist Manifesto*, he and Engels asserted that the state under capitalism is 'a committee for managing the common affairs of the whole bourgeoisie'. You could look at everything in terms of 'production', they asserted, and ideas are simply 'mental production'. 'The class which has the means of material production at its disposal,' they wrote, 'has control at the same time over the means of mental production.'

Marx shifted Rousseau's famous assertion that 'man is born free yet everywhere is in chains' by talking of alienation. People, he argued, may appear to be free in their work, but in reality are chained, because they are alienated from themselves. With no control over what they do, they become automatons, unable to fulfil their human potential. Workers are often unaware that they are alienated because of the prevailing beliefs in society – beliefs, for instance, about human nature, which, of course, serve the interests of the dominant class. Organised religion is a perfect example. 'Religion,' Marx famously stated, 'is the opiate of the people.' Nowadays, a prevailing belief might be that we are all ultimately selfish, which keeps us forever striving to better our material circumstances, making us both eager labourers and insatiable consumers.

Perhaps the crucial part of Marx's theory, though, was the idea that changing economic relationships drive revolutions at certain points in history that completely alter the power balance between the classes. Just as the origins of the modern world lay in the revolutionary shift from feudalism to capitalism, so the economic instability and class conflict inherent in the modern capitalist world would inevitably result in revolution and a final shift to communism, in which private property would vanish and everything would be held in common. In this future state, people would no longer be alienated from themselves and would at last be able to fulfil their human potential.

Although Marx regarded the downfall of capitalism and its replacement with communism as something that must happen, his purpose was not simply to describe the historical process. He believed that once people understood how history works, they could begin to take hold of it and direct it in a way that was good for all.

Marx's ideas caught the mood of the times, and revolutionaries and working-class movements across Europe took them up with a passion. What had seemed just personal or local grievances suddenly had a universal explanation. It was a wonderful and exciting revelation. At last people felt that they understood what was going on, and what's more they knew what they had to do to change it. In 1864, activists from all over Europe met with a common purpose at the Working Men's International Association, later called the First International, and the term Marxism was used for the first time.

Interestingly, though, the places where Marx's ideas were ultimately taken up with the most enthusiasm were Russia and China, neither of which fitted his picture of the industrial society on the brink of collapse. Both were still dominated by their rural peasantry, who were enslaved in a far more tangible way than the wage slaves in the factories. So first Lenin and then Mao 'adapted' Marxism to their own circumstances. Lenin, for instance, argued that the proletariat can be led to the right frame of mind for change – revolutionary consciousness – by a vanguard of professional revolutionaries. If these professionals overthrow the government and establish a dictatorship of the proletariat, they can educate the masses and leapfrog Marx's stages to bring on the bright communist future.

Of course, the disastrous cost of these kinds of argument is written in the blood of millions across the twentieth century. The purges of Stalin and the atrocities of Maoism, followed by the collapse of the Soviet Union and the gradual economic opening of China, seemed the ultimate proof of Marxism's failure. Marx's critics gleefully announced the demise of the most tragically wrong idea in human history. Yet this could be a mistake.

Although Marxism is now a platform for political action for only a tiny minority of people in the West, Marx's analysis of history has not necessarily been disproved. Marx might argue that neither China nor Russia, nor for that matter Cuba, fitted his picture of the industrial proletariat ready for change. All were still stuck in what could be described as a feudal state when their communist revolutions took place, so the revolution was directed against feudalism, and so maybe their current capitalist (or pseudo-capitalist) phase is inevitable. Even now, China's population is predominantly rural.

So, Marx might argue, the conditions for the lasting communist revolution around the world have simply not yet been reached. Certainly a world in which a fifth of the population are living in what the World Bank calls 'extreme poverty' and a further quarter are living in what is euphemistically called 'moderate poverty' is far from a glowing endorsement of the triumph of capitalism. The recent banking crisis and all-too-obvious flaws in the world financial system call capitalism even more into question.

Whatever the political future of Marx's ideas, they have seeped permanently into our consciousness. We take it as a given that our ideas and culture are shaped by the times. Although the Marxist academic with his dismissal of the notion of individual creativity and emphasis on scientific analysis of the arts and media has been caricatured and ridiculed, the essence of Marx's arguments shapes academic thinking now more than ever. Philosophers of science like Karl Popper, for instance, argue that science theories are essentially reflections of their socio-historical context, while historians are careful to avoid 'Whig' history – history written from a contemporary point of view that implies a continuous progress to the present.

Interestingly, even right-wing thinkers have been embracing Marx in recent years, now that the spectre of communism has vanished, claiming that he is really a capitalist. In his biography of Marx, Francis Wheen quotes an issue of the *New Yorker* magazine from 1997 in which Marx is hailed as 'the next big thinker' and the man to tell us about the nature of political corruption, inequality, global markets and much more. 'The longer I spend on Wall Street, the more convinced I am that Marx was right,' a wealthy investment banker is quoted as saying. 'I am absolutely convinced that Marx's approach is the best way to look at capitalism.' Of course, when someone so clearly in the rich camp endorses Marx, one is instantly suspicious. But maybe he is right, and maybe Marx's best time is yet to come.

#26 Government

In 1791, the great libertarian campaigner Thomas Paine wrote in *The Rights of Man* that 'society is a blessing, but government is evil'. In his typically robust fashion, Paine argued that governments bring nothing but harm. Ordinary men can live quite happily together without government, he felt. Governments were essentially criminal. 'If we would delineate human nature with a baseness of heart, and hypocrisy of countenance, that reflection would shudder at and humanity disown,' Paine fulminated. 'It is kings, courts, and cabinets that must sit for the portrait.'

Paine was writing at the time of the American and French Revolutions, and he argued that America had managed to live for two years without any form of government at all, without society collapsing into chaos. Take away government and people's natural adaptability comes to the fore and they organise things quite well for themselves.

The founders of the American constitution did not agree with Paine, however much they admired him. They felt that government was necessary. James Madison, often called the Father of the US Constitution, later replied to Paine's assertion in this vein: 'It has been said that all Government is an evil. It would be more proper to say that the necessity of any Government is a misfortune. This necessity however exists; and the problem to be solved is, not what form of Government is perfect, but which of the forms is least imperfect.'

Anarchists, however, have continued to argue that people would live much better without government. It would not, they argue, descend into what is colloquially called anarchy because people's self-interest, even if not their communal spirit, would soon mean that mutual support networks would be set up. Unfortunately, it is almost impossible to imagine their ideas ever being really tried out.

Nowhere in the world do people live without government, and every time governments have collapsed, such as after the French, Russian and Chinese revolutions, the chaos has been so frightening that many people almost welcomed the brutal regimes that stepped in to take charge. More recently, the financial disarray that followed the fall of the Soviet Union meant that most Russians sighed with relief when Vladimir Putin asserted control. Similarly, the continuing turmoil in Iraq has made some Iraqis look back almost nostalgically on the time of Saddam Hussein, when, at least, the lights worked and the streets were safe. For most people, even bad government is better than no government at all because it provides the basic necessities of life.

It is sometimes said that government is a necessary evil because people are essentially selfish and so, without government, would descend into the terrible dog-eat-dog world described by seventeenth-century philosopher Thomas Hobbes as the 'war of all against all'. Anarchists would rightly challenge this argument. First of all, there can be no such thing as a 'necessary evil'. If it is evil, it is unnecessary; and if it is necessary, it cannot be evil. Secondly, there is no convincing evidence to show that people are so madly out of control that without government to rein them in, they would be at each others' throats. It is not government at all that allows 50,000 people to stand at a parade without everyone fighting for the one best place at the front. It is not government that makes people look after the sick or donate to charity. It is not government that forces millions of people in cities to interact daily and continually without strife for all but a fraction of the time.

So why is government necessary, or even desirable, then? The prevailing opinion for the last few centuries has been the idea of the social contract,[69] first fully articulated by

---

[69] Perhaps one of the first of all established governments was that of King Hor-Aha ('Fighting Hawk') set up on the banks of the Nile about 3100 BC. What makes it interesting is how clearly it showed elements of the social contract, in which an educated elite are allowed to rule, in theory, for the benefit of all. At the heart of Hor-Aha's royal control lay an unwritten bargain between the king and his people. In exchange for control over their loyalties and labours, the king offered security. This was much more than just physical safety; it was *maat* – a term used to describe the Egyptians' entire sense of order and well-being. Without *maat*, the world would descend into

philosophers such as Thomas Hobbes, John Locke and Jean-Jacques Rousseau.[70] Hobbes argued that in a 'state of nature' people act so selfishly and aggressively that life is 'solitary, poor, nasty, brutish and short', and so people mutually agree to be governed to bring some order to life. This is little more than the less-than-convincing 'necessary evil' argument. Locke took a different stance, arguing that in the state of nature there is a natural order but people are still fearful of each other and so agree to be governed for mutual protection.

Rousseau had yet another take, arguing that we each could willingly put aside our egoism in order to shape society for the best through the general will: 'Each of us puts his person and all his power in common under the supreme direction of the general will; and in a body we receive each member as an indivisible part of the whole.' In this way, popular government, Rousseau argued, is a civilising force, helping to mould people's characters; we have to give up some of our natural independence, but in return we get real freedom.

---

isfet, or chaos. The smiting of enemies and wild beasts to keep chaos at bay was a crucial symbol of the king's role. The king was the living Horus, *maat* personified, opposed by Seth, the god of chaos. It was this sense that the entire state of the world depended on the king that helped the pharaohs maintain control for over 3,000 years. Without the king, Egypt would become an unthinkable, *maat*-less nightmare.

[70] The origins of the idea are much older, though. In *Crito*, Socrates argued powerfully that he must stay in prison and accept the death penalty. The Laws of Athens, he says, are what made his entire way of life possible, from the marriage of his parents to his education and upbringing. So he is obliged to live, and die, by the laws he has benefited from. Plato argued that people want government to ensure justice and avoid being treated unjustly by others.

The social contract theory has been enormously influential,[71] and many governments use this kind of idea as their mandate for government whether truthfully or deceptively. It doesn't necessarily imply that the type of government should be democratic in form. People could mutually consent to be governed by a tyrant. However, as soon as tyrants behave tyrannically, they lose consent. So the only form of government that can really work with the social contract is one that renews consent continually – that is, a democratic government.

This is the theory. The practice is, of course, often very different, firstly because very few governments, if any, are genuinely democratic; and secondly because there are other forces in play such as the power of money and global corporations. And of course, for people to give their consent genuinely, they must know what they are consenting to. In reality, they rarely do. That was the philosopher David Hume's objection to the social contract theory back in the eighteenth century – not that the idea of consent was wrong, but just that in practice it didn't really happen. This is a fair and important criticism and one that needs to be addressed all around the world.

In fact, it is the central problem with government. Libertarians argue that because of the problems of government, government should be scaled back. The 'smaller' government is, and the fewer restrictions we have on our life,

---

[71] Forty years ago, American philosopher John Rawls proposed a variation of the social contract in line with game theory, in which rational, entirely self-serving people in an 'original position' (which was his take on the state of nature) agreed on government in their own best interests. Irish philosopher Philip Pettit argues that because consent can always be 'manufactured' by governments, agreement to the contract should be signified instead by lack of rebellion against it.

the freer we are. But often what they are really arguing for is freedom to pursue their own agenda, regardless of the cost to some sections of society. Their argument, in fact, comes surprisingly close to that of the anarchists, even though they are, on the surface, from opposite ends of the political spectrum.

Government is needed to deliver justice for all, to ensure that the world is fair, both in the sense of even-handedness and attractiveness. Most people can manage well and happily together, without any government or laws. But we need a government to ensure that the weak and vulnerable are properly looked after and that everyone is fairly treated. We need laws to protect us from disruptive minorities such as criminals and profiteers. We need a framework of order that gives us the confidence to do anything from buy a house or a car to negotiate a business deal. And we need society to be ordered so that each of us has the best possible opportunity to live safe, comfortable and fulfilled lives. In other words, we need society to be well governed.

#25 Calculus

In his book *Taming the Infinite*, Professor Ian Stewart declares that calculus was 'the most significant advance in the history of mathematics'. It is a bold claim, but there is a strong case to be made in its favour. Calculus was the mathematics that drove the scientific revolution which began in the seventeenth century and continues to this day. It turned out to be the mathematics of the natural world, and allowed everything from the trajectory of planets to the growth of ant populations to be analysed mathematically.

Previously, mathematics had only been really good at coping with things that don't move, or that stay moving at exactly the same rate, which is why, before calculus, mathematics had pretty much only been used for abstract logic, financial and architectural calculations and basic mechanical calculations. Calculus opened the way for maths to explore things that are changing and moving at a varying pace. Since that applies to just about everything in nature, this change was profound and far-reaching. It gave scientists a uniquely powerful tool for exploring and explaining the natural world.

The door to calculus was pushed open in the early seventeenth century when Fermat and Descartes realised that algebra and geometry could be tied together simply by using co-ordinates – two or more numbers that pinpoint a location in relation to reference lines, such as the axes on a graph. Using co-ordinates, all geometry can be summed up in algebraic equations and, in theory, every equation can be conveyed geometrically as curves and lines on a graph.

Bringing algebra and geometry together in an entirely new kind of mathematics called analytic geometry allowed, for the first time, mathematics to be used to analyse how things move and change. But there were two fundamental missing elements. Analytic geometry could not study the rate at which things were changing nor analyse the amount of change that happened. It could show, for instance, how far an object travels in a particular time, but not its velocity and acceleration at a particular point. That's like studying a bird's flight by observing only where it takes off and lands. That's where calculus comes in. It allows you to analyse what's going on in between.

Imagine knocking a flowerpot from your windowsill. Newton's law of gravity tells you that it accelerates earthwards before smashing on the pavement below with some force. But how fast will the pot be travelling after falling for a second? You can work out its average speed by measuring how far it travels in a second. But that doesn't tell you how fast it is going – the pot's instantaneous speed. Calculus provides the answer by using limits. If you measure the average speed between two limits – or points either side of the point it reaches after a second – you get very close to the instantaneous speed. The closer your limits are, the closer you get to the instantaneous speed.

You might think that if you were to reduce the limits to nothing you would then get the instantaneous speed exactly. But if the limits were nothing, then the pot wouldn't have moved at all in between them. It would have moved no distance and taken no time to do it. That would give you a speed of zero.[72] Irish philosopher Bishop Berkeley famously criticised calculus because of this problem, describing it as 'the ghosts of departed quantities'. Solving the conundrum took mathematicians two centuries, but by then calculus had more than proved its worth.

---

[72] The problem was initially overcome using 'infinitesimals' – numbers smaller than any given number, yet not zero. If an infinitesimal is added to itself, no matter how many times, it always remains less than a given number. This system made the calculations possible, but was vague and imprecise, which is why most calculus since the nineteenth century has used limits instead. For some mathematical operations, though, infinitesimals have been proven to work better.

The credit for the invention of calculus was fiercely debated almost immediately. Was it the German polymath and mathematical genius Gottfried Wilhelm Leibniz?[73] Or was it the towering figure of English science, the creator of the laws of motion and the theory of gravity, Sir Isaac Newton? Probably in terms of sheer chronological priority, the winner was Leibniz. It was Leibniz, too, who gave calculus the notation it uses today, such as the terms 'delta' x and 'delta' y. But his writings were so fragmented and obscure that even one of his supporters, the Italian Bernoulli brothers Jacob and Johann, wrote of his first description of calculus that it was 'an enigma rather than an explanation'.

Newton created a much clearer and fuller description. His ideas were first summarised in 1671 in a book entitled *Method of Fluxions and Infinite Series*. He called calculus 'fluxions' because the idea of the limits was of a quantity 'flowing' towards zero, the instantaneous point, but not actually getting there. Newton was notoriously cautious and cagey, so used only simple maths in his great *Principia* outlining the laws of motion and gravity, but there is every chance that he created calculus in order to develop these great theories – since mathematically they need calculus in order to be fully expressed.

---

[73] Leibniz was one of the great figures of German science and philosophy, and his interests were wide-ranging. Besides creating calculus, he devised the binary number system and made significant contributions to everything from geology to the study of logic. But his reputation suffered a terrible blow when he was satirised by Voltaire in *Candide* as the absurdly optimistic Dr Pangloss, who even in the face of catastrophic miseries and suffering insists that 'all is for the best'. Only in recent years has his brilliance been fully recognised again.

Calculus, as developed by Leibniz and Newton, involves two principal operations: differentiation and integration. Differentiation comes from the idea of taking apart and integration of bringing together. They are opposite sides of the same coin, even though each has led to its own branch of calculus: differential calculus and integral calculus. Differentiation is about calculating rates of change, just as in the case of our precipitous flowerpot. In terms of the geometry of graphs, it's also a way of finding tangents to curves. Integration is about the opposite; finding the quantity of something, if you know only its rate of change. In terms of the geometry of graphs, it's about finding the area under the curve between two points.[74]

The fight over who first thought of calculus, Leibniz or Newton, created an intellectual rivalry between Britain and Europe that was great for British empirical philosophy but something of a disaster for British mathematics. Although Newton's system of calculus was much more coherent and fully developed than Leibniz's, its focus on geometry proved, ironically, to be a handicap. In the meantime, continental mathematicians made more rapid progress with Leibniz's more algebraic calculus. It was only once the differences were resolved, though, and the problem of Berkeley's ghostly zero was solved by the development of analysis in the early 1800s,

---

[74] If you find this hard to follow, it's not surprising. When the great mathematician Johann Bernoulli was trying to get his head around Leibniz's ideas, he wrote: 'But just as much as it is easy to find the differential [derivative] of a given quantity, so it is difficult to find the integral of a given differential. Moreover, sometimes we cannot say with certainty whether the integral of a given quantity can be found or not.'

that the full power of calculus was finally unleashed. From then on, calculus was at the forefront of science.

The roll call of scientific breakthroughs made possible by calculus is extraordinary. Without it, there would probably have been no Laws of Motion and no law of gravity. There would have been no theory of electromagnetism, relativity or quantum physics. No Big Bang theory or knowledge of black holes. All of these and many more key scientific theories depend on analysing rates of change.

Calculus is equally important in technology, too. The process of calculating the trajectory of space probes depends on it. So does calculating how an aircraft will fly. Or how a bomb will explode. Even our understanding of how animal populations change, or how financial instruments will fare, can be explored using calculus. In medicine, calculus is used to plan the most effective way to intervene and stop epidemics spreading, or to calculate the timing and dosage of drugs, or the angle to insert an artificial blood vessel to ensure the best flow.

Of course, calculus is a great idea not just because of the sheer range of uses it has, especially in science, or even the key role it played in bringing the key scientific theories of the last two centuries to fruition – even though this is quite astounding. What makes it so great is the beauty of such an ingenious, brilliant mathematical tool that can explain to us the laws of nature – and reveal patterns we just never knew were there. Newton and Leibniz are rightly considered geniuses for their creation of calculus – and although maybe someone else would have thought of it if they hadn't, it was they who had the insight to work out how to analyse something as fundamental, yet as hard to pin down, as how things change. It turned our view of the natural and physical world from one that was essentially static to one that was dynamic. By the late nineteenth century, Gilbert and Sullivan's Modern Major General could proudly boast in *The Pirates of Penzance* about the heights of his achievement:

> With many cheerful facts about the square of the hypotenuse.
> I'm very good at integral and differential calculus.

Thank goodness someone is.

#24 Arable Farming

In 2008, amid talk of a world food crisis, with global shortages of basic foods and rising prices, the UN met in Rome to work out how to feed the world. The participants agreed that it was wholly unacceptable that 862 million people worldwide were malnourished, given the resources available. They also resolved that global food production must be doubled by 2030.

There are two points here that are especially remarkable. The first is that there is enough food to feed the world's entire population well right now – if only it were more equally distributed. The second is that experts consider it entirely realistic to talk of doubling world food production over the next two decades.

This is an incredible testament to farming. Farmers are already producing enough to feed more than 6 billion people, not to mention a vast quantity of livestock (70 per cent of the world's maize crop is fed to animals). By 2030, if the UN's goals are actually achieved, they will be producing enough to feed 8.5 billion.

There is no other way besides farming that even a tiny fraction of the food needed to feed so many could ever be found. Arable farming is a simple but brilliant idea. Where hunter-gatherers must be constantly on the move in search of elusive sources of wild food, arable farming provides food on tap simply by the farmer collecting the seeds or tubers of particular wild food plants such as grasses, then planting them together near at hand, so enough grow where one has easy access to them. The variety of foods may be restricted, but the supply is reassuringly predictable.

Over history, by planting selected seeds and improving techniques, farmers have boosted crop plants' ability to yield food far above that of their wild counterparts. The result is that farmers can now typically grow 120 bushels of wheat on a single acre – which is enough to keep 120 people in bread throughout the year (a bushel of wheat gives flour for about 100 loaves). Some farmers get well over 400 bushels.

Other methods of getting food can't come even remotely near this. The few remaining hunter-gatherer tribes around the world, such as the Yora and Awa Guaja of the Amazon, need vast areas to find food even for a small tribal group. And of course, there is now very little wild food left. So now farming is literally a matter of life and death. If farms stopped producing food, most of us would be dead within a very short time.

Of course, part of the reason there are so many people in the world today is because farming has made more food available. The beginning of arable farming 10,000 or so years ago triggered the world's first population boom.

A second boom – the massive urbanisation of the Industrial Revolution – is linked to the eighteenth-century revolution that replaced ancient subsistence farming with commercial farms, using new techniques to produce food to sell to city folk at a profit.

A third boom, that has seen the global population double since the 1960s, has been enabled by a massive increase in global food production through new intensive farming techniques involving specialised crop strains, fertilisers and pesticides, including the so-called Green Revolution.[75]

---

[75] The Green Revolution began with Norman Borlaug's experiments with wheat in the mountains of central Mexico in the 1940s. Borlaug's great idea was 'hybrid' wheat with short stems, created by adding pollen from one crop strain to the seeds of another. Boosted with additional fertilisers, pesticides and water, these dwarf hybrids grow quickly and produce a huge grain yield since less of the plant's energy goes into the stem. When Borlaug introduced his idea to India in 1968, the effect was little short of miraculous. Up until that time, India had been notorious for its dreadful famines. But with the hybrid grains, annual wheat production soared almost overnight from 10 million to 17 million tonnes – and went on rising. By 2006 India's fields were yielding a staggering 73 million tonnes of wheat every year, and far from being riven by famine, the country was actually a wheat exporter. Elsewhere in southern Asia, hybrid grains were introduced with similarly impressive results, not just with wheat but also new hybrids of rice, corn, sorghum and other staple crops. It now seems as if the rise in production may finally be running out of steam, however, because of the massive drain

The traditional view was that farming began in response to a shortage of food for foraging and hunting in the dry conditions after the Ice Age about 10–8,000 years ago. But most experts now agree that this doesn't account for the variations in the times when farming first appeared around the world – 11,000 years ago in the Middle East, 8,000 years ago in China and 10,000 years ago in South America. If anything, crop farming may have developed in times of plenty.

What's more, recent findings have pushed the first crops well back before the end of the Ice Age. Previously, the oldest known arable farms were in the Middle East, where people were growing things such as emmer and einkorn wheat (the forerunners of modern wheat strains), barley, rye, vetch and lentils up to 11,500 years ago. Then in 2005, researchers working near the Sea of Galilee in Israel discovered a site labelled Ohalo II. Here, at least 23,000 years ago, people were collecting seeds of wild grasses such as emmer wheat and barley, and grinding them into flour to make bread.

In fact, it seems that the origins of farming are very much older than once thought and emerged gradually rather than all together. People domesticated dogs as hunting companions and may have tended herds of sheep and goat tens of thousands of years ago. They may also have nurtured wild fruit and nut trees. The idea of planting selected seeds of wild plants such as grasses in order to grow crops probably developed from practices like this separately around the world.

---

on India's scarce water resources, and because of the cumulative effect of build-up of pesticides and fertilisers in the soil.

When arable farming did begin, the effect on the human way of life was dramatic. No longer would people move around hunting and foraging. To plant, tend and harvest their crops, people had to settle permanently in one place and build stable houses and villages. The need to organise labour, planting, harvesting and storage, and the availability of surpluses for trading, soon led to the development of the first towns, the first governments, building, writing and everything we associate with the development of civilisation.

Interestingly, though, not everyone agrees that this makes farming a great idea. Recently, Cambridge academic Jay Stock described the invention of arable farming as 'the worst mistake in human history'. The idea that primitive man was superior is an old thread, typified by Rousseau's picture of the 'noble savage' uncorrupted by the complexities of the civilised world, and sprouting up in 1960s hippy anthropology. But the idea that farming in particular was a retrograde step was put forward by Jared Diamond in his 1997 book *Guns, Germs and Steel*. We may think that farming has brought us health, wealth and long life, Diamond contended, but it has in fact brought us misery. Farming not only replaced a very varied and healthy diet of wild food with a poor diet of a few staples; it also led to the development of soldiers, warfare, class divisions and all the bad aspects of civilisation, because of the way it allowed the food to be stockpiled, and freed some, but not others, from the necessity of looking for it.

Moreover, a sedentary lifestyle and the proximity of animals and shared water resources led to the spread of infectious diseases. Jay Stock made his damning comment after he studied the bones of hunter-gatherers living in Egypt just before farming developed and found that these people were significantly taller and healthier than the first farmers were. Yet there is plenty to suggest that a hunter-gatherer lifestyle, too, was far from idyllic. And, although the first farmers were unhealthy and stunted, things have improved. A huge number of people today are taller and live much longer, healthier lives than their hunter-gatherer ancestors.

And, of course, it is not simply about health. The food surpluses and division of wealth may indeed have brought us warfare, taxes, robbery, murder and a whole host of other problems. But they have also brought us wonderful civilisations, beautiful buildings, ingenious craftsmanship, amazing technology and pretty much every significant scientific and artistic achievement of humanity. In fact, it has, you could say, delivered us the whole of human history, since history only began once farming allowed people to settle long enough in one place to record it. Of course, there is indescribably bad in human history along with the incontestably glorious, but one cannot wish it away. It is in the way we live and practise farming rather than in the idea of farming itself that any faults lie.

Farming continues to give us the indispensable gift of food. Thanks to the efforts of farmers, 5 billion people are able to eat well every day. Those who lack food lack it because they are unable to farm or gain access to the fruits of farming.

Yet delivering all this food is taking an enormous toll on the environment. Over more than one third of the world's land surface, the natural ecosystem has been replaced by the artificial landscape of farms, with their meadows and enclosures, their ploughed lands and crops. And farming acreage is still growing. Every year an area of the Amazon rainforest the size of Scotland is chopped or burned down to create new farmland. Modern intensive farming can damage the natural environment in other ways too, from poisoning the land and the oceans with pesticides and fertilisers to adding carbon to the atmosphere with energy intensive practices.

Farming is a hugely important idea, vital to the world as we know it. The old hymns which praised and gave thanks for the miracle of the harvest each year were right to acknowledge its wondrous power to sustain our most basic need. And the farmer, specifically the idea of the farmer labouring through the year to bring food from the land, is rightly an elemental, mythic image, at the heart of our relationship with the world for more than 10,000 years. But it is an idea that still needs to be treated with care and reverence if it is to bring us the maximum good.

#23 The Self

As the inscription to his great 1855 poetry book *Leaves of Grass* the American poet Walt Whitman wrote a short poem, which opens with the line: 'One's-self I sing, a simple separate person.'[76] It was a conceit. Whitman did not really regard the

---

76   One's-self I sing, a simple separate person,
        Yet utter the word Democratic, the word En-Masse.

        Of physiology from top to toe I sing,
        Not physiognomy alone nor brain alone is worthy for the Muse, I say
        The Form complete is worthier far,
        The Female equally with the Male I sing.

        Of Life immense in passion, pulse, and power,

self as either simple or entirely separate, yet it was in keeping with the beginning of an age, our age, in which people claim individuality as a right.

Our modern world revolves around the idea of self and individualism. We don't simply accept our individuality; we are thoroughly committed to it. We expect our individual rights to be respected – our right to vote, our right to equality, our rights as consumers, our right to express our opinions, to make a choice, to follow our own careers, to freedom, to peace, to a decent retirement and much more. Psychiatrists treat us as individuals with our own problems. Economists regard us as self-interested consumers. Game theorists work out strategies on the assumption that we are entirely separate entities working only for ourselves. Governments and businesses set incentive targets in the belief that individuals need them to perform well. Advertisers tailor their commercials to appeal to that sense of self, because you're worth it. It's an age when even our genes are selfish and clamouring to join the Me generation.

There's a political dimension to this, of course. Capitalism needs us to have a strong sense of individuality. It needs us to heed Margaret Thatcher's infamous remark: 'There's no such thing as society.' There is an argument that we have been encouraged to believe in our selfhood by commercial (and political) interests who take the maxim 'divide and rule' to its logical extreme by dividing us right down to the level of our singularity. Divide and sell might be more accurate.

Cheerful, for freest action form'd under the laws divine,
The Modern Man I sing.

– Walt Whitman

This sense of self and individuality we have is so powerful, and so utterly convincing in its demands to be listened to and respected, that it's easy to take it for granted. Yet this outlook is actually quite new. It's not something that people in previous ages would necessarily recognise, let alone understand. It's a psychological concept, this view of the self, and is uniquely modern.

It seems likely that there was a time early in history when people had less sense of self than they do now, and that self-awareness, maybe even self-consciousness, only began to emerge once many people began to live close together in cities – and perhaps became more conscious of the need for personal space and a separate identity.

Maybe the emergence of monotheism, the replacement of many gods and spirits with one, played a part. It encouraged people to focus inwards rather than outwards – on abstract thoughts inside your head, thoughts separate from the outside world. Christianity and Islam both turned the moral responsibility of how to live and behave on to the individual, rather than the community or tribe. They asked you to make your own choice.

Maybe, though, these monotheistic religions themselves reflected a growing need for self-definition across the civilised world. Some of the most profound explorations of how to live life came from thinkers in cultures that were not in any way monotheistic – Laozi and Confucius in China, Prince Siddhartha in India, and the philosophers of Ancient Greece such as Aristotle, Plato, Socrates and Epicurus. Laozi, for instance, emphasised the importance of self-knowledge.

'Knowing others is wisdom,' wrote Laozi. 'Knowing the self is enlightenment.'

Meanwhile Plato, maybe an exact contemporary of Laozi, argued that the true self is the reason, or the intellect. The intellect is the soul, and is separate from the body. We might call it the mind. Aristotle, on the other hand, agreed that the soul is the essence of self but insisted that it cannot be separated from the body and is, instead, defined entirely by what it does. The debate over whether the mind or soul can exist separately from the body has been a constant strand in Western philosophy ever since. Roman philosophers became interested in the difference between the inner self and the self you present to the world – the *persona*, a term which originally described the character mask in Greek theatre.

The next great shift in the perception of self emerged from the bustling commerce and bruising politics of the cities of Renaissance Italy. Having a strong sense of self wasn't just an idea but became a practical necessity. In this turbulent world, people began to realise that you would sink or swim on the strengths of your own talents and choices in life. Humanist thinkers placed humanity, with all its extraordinary talents and limitations, its huge possibilities and many problems, at the centre of the picture. Meanwhile, on a practical level, merchants and politicians began to embrace a life of personal ambition.

Gradually, there began to develop a distinctive new Western personality. 'Marked by individualism, secularity, strength of will, multiplicity of interest and impulse, creative innovation, and a willingness to defy traditional limitations on human activity,' Richard Tarnas writes in *The Passion of the*

Western Mind, 'this spirit soon began to spread across Europe, providing the lineaments of the modern character.'

That new sense of individual potential, of freedom of choice, was, on the one hand, incredibly liberating. It drove a religious revolution as Protestants rejected the mediation of priests and the Catholic hierarchy to seek their own personal relationship with God. It triggered a scientific revolution as thinkers began to understand the importance of looking at the world for themselves. And it unleashed not only the individual pursuit of fame and fortune that unfolded into the capitalist version of society, but also the increasing expectation of control over one's own destiny which led to political revolution and demands for democratic and other human rights.

But just as it was liberating and motivating, this new sense of self was also unnerving. Suddenly, instead of just being part of a bigger community, or a child directed by God, you were on your own. What could you be certain of? Philosophers started to explore our place in the world urgently, just as natural philosophers were exploring the natural world.

In this world of doubt, René Descartes believed that the only thing you could be certain of was your own consciousness; everything else might be illusion. *Cogito ergo sum*, 'I think therefore I am', was the one irreducible fact of existence, Descartes argued, and so he separated the thoughts from the body. It is in one's thoughts that one's unique self resides and the body is like an avatar directed from within.[77] He believed in this way that he had, literally, saved our souls.

---

[77] Descartes has been criticised for the ultimate illogicality of his position, which leaves the mind in limbo, but the recent growth in the power of computers and the internet throws up the intriguing possibility, however remote,

Many philosophers rejected this mind-body dualism, as it came to be called. Yet the idea of self remained connected to thoughts. A tree maintains its identity as a tree, John Locke argued, even though new particles pass through it all the time, because it is always organised like a tree.[78] What is crucial is the continuity of organisation.

Thus our identity is the continuity of our thoughts, the assembly or experiences, beliefs and, above all, memories, not the material our bodies are made of. You are the person who remembers falling over in the street or that embarrassing occasion when you were caught singing out loud to your iPod in the middle of the otherwise silent library. But what if some trauma made you forget all your past life?[79] Would you still be the same person? Locke argued that you wouldn't.[80]

---

of being able to upload all our thoughts into cyberspace when we die. It doesn't necessarily matter whether or not this can be done – it probably can't – but the question is, are your uploaded thoughts you or not? If they are, then Descartes may have been right.

[78] A famous illustration of this principle is the ship of Theseus. During the course of his long voyage, Theseus replaces worn-out parts bit by bit until eventually the whole ship has been replaced. Is it still the same ship? Some would say so, but what if some salvage expert had gathered up the discarded parts and built another ship from them? Which then would be the real ship of Theseus?

[79] Scottish philosopher Thomas Reid objected to Locke with the famous illustration of the brave officer who remembered being flogged as a child. After he took the enemy standard he was promoted to general but forgot the childhood flogging. Surely, argued Reid, the general and the child are the same person, even though he has entirely forgotten the flogging?

[80] This is a philosophically defensible position, but it's much harder when it comes to criminal law. Could we really decide not to prosecute a criminal just because he had lost his memory of the crime and so was a different person then from now?

The Scottish philosopher David Hume took this argument even further, after noticing just how elusive the self is. Whenever you try to look inside at your own mind, he argued, it seems to slip away and all you get is a bundle of perceptions, experiences and memories. In other words, there is content but no container – just a bundle of thoughts.

This a bit like a wave without water, other philosophers objected. Ludwig Wittgenstein suggested that the mistake is to think of the self as something you can be aware of; we just assume it must be because we use the word 'I' to express experiences. In other words, it is all about words: 'In fact this seems to be the real ego, the one of which it was said, "*Cogito ergo sum*". Is there then no mind, but only a body? Answer: the word 'mind' has meaning, i.e. it has a use in our language; but saying this doesn't yet say what kind of use we make of it.' Daniel Dennett goes even further, suggesting that selves are a convenient fiction, a centre of gravity on which we can hang stories but nothing more.

This kind of logical conundrum, however, can often seem far removed from the messy business of living. In the nineteenth century, a different way at looking at the self emerged in the form of psychology. Scientists began to look at the human mind and human identity as not a philosophical problem but a scientific one which could be subject to research and theory. They adopted an Ancient Greek word for the soul, *psyche*, to sum up the way thought, behaviour and personality are shaped. The task of the psychoanalyst is to analyse how the individual psyche is shaped.

The psychoanalytic theories of Sigmund Freud were of course enormously influential, and although many of his ideas have been challenged, they have seeped into our collective consciousness. We accept, for instance, the existence of a part of our mind of which we are not conscious, but which influences our behaviour. We take for granted that our actions are directed subconsciously by childhood traumas. We believe too that we subtly betray our innermost desires in our actions.

Psychology has enhanced our sense of our own consciousness, and capitalism, democratic rights and liberal values have combined with the analyses of social science to give us an entirely modern sense of individuality, and entitlement to freedom of choice. It's been exciting and has brought us many benefits. Yet at the same time, our sense of self-determination, of being able to choose the course of our lives, has become less certain. We are racked by self-doubt in a way previous generations weren't. We worry that we are not in control of our personalities, but driven by subconscious fears and psychological defects.[81] More than one in every four Americans now suffers from what is called a personality disorder. Two-thirds

---

[81] In one of the most disturbing developments of the twentieth century, Freud's nephew, Edward Bernays, argued that society could be shaped and controlled – indeed should be shaped and controlled – by exploiting the subconscious triggers that his uncle had revealed. He became the PR guru of the USA, operating behind the scenes to shape American society by ingenious image-building and PR campaigns. He helped American tobacco tycoons to make it socially acceptable for women to smoke and gave other titans of industry the tools to persuade us to pave over our countryside or switch to beer as the 'beverage of moderation'. He also engineered the overthrow of Guatemala's government, leading to a dictatorship that was guilty of genocide, by sowing the image of dangerous communism in Americans' minds. By exploiting the very things at the heart of our individuality, he proved us to be sheep.

of young American women suffer from some kind of eating disorder.

Even our sense of self seems to be becoming ever more slippery. A powerful strand of 'postmodernist' thinking insists that our modern self cannot bear the stresses placed on it by fragmented modern life. It forces us to respond by developing multiple selves, becoming different people in different situations and media. None of these is necessarily truer or more real than any of the others; they are all part of a protean, shifting ensemble which some can keep under control better than others.

The crystallising idea of self seems to have given many of us a degree of self-determination, autonomy, freedom of choice and freedom from persecution that is unique in history. We talk of self-made men. Of people being self-reliant, self-assured, self-confident or self-possessed. Yet it has also made us doubt that we know what to do with this possession. Is the self good, or is it selfish? Why should helping others be described as being self-less? The ghost in the machine is still just as spooky as ever.

#22 Electricity Grids

Flip the switch on your lights and immediately they burst into brilliance. Turn on the electric kettle and at once a surge of electricity flows through the kettle's heating coils. Open the fridge, and out wafts cool air chilled by the continual buzz of current through the fridge's heat exchangers. All this electricity, available on demand to power the varied range of electrical appliances in the home and office, flows from a power station located perhaps the other side of the country virtually instantaneously when you switch on. The supply is now so routine that it's easy to forget just what an extraordinary thing it is. Indeed, most of us get quite upset if the power goes off for a few hours, let alone a day or more.

Yet it is an extraordinary thing. Little more than 100 years ago, energy had to be brought physically into the house. Coal for the fires, oil for the lamps and wood for the stoves had to be fetched and carried, often with considerable effort, then stored until needed. Many early Victorian houses have coal bunkers the size of a small room to store the fuel needed for maybe just a few of the winter months. Filling it up was a physical, dirty job for the coal merchant, and carrying the coal for just the day's fires in from the bunker was a real chore for the houseowner, or the scullery maid. Electricity grids supply energy effortlessly, invisibly and without any need for storage whatsoever.

Although the electricity supply now provides energy for a huge array of appliances, it was the demand for electric lighting that got the grid created in the first place. Sir Humphry Davy created the first electric light as early as 1802 by connecting the ends of platinum wire to the terminals of the pioneering battery, the Voltaic pile. The current made the wire glow brilliant white before burning out. Over the next 70 years, various inventors tried to create a light using platinum or carbon filaments, but despite the high melting points of these materials, they always burned out.

The breakthrough was William Crookes' creation of a really good vacuum inside a glass bulb in 1875. With all the oxygen taken out of the bulb, the filament would glow but would not burn out. British physicist Joseph Wilson Swan was the first to take advantage of the new vacuum, demonstrating a carbon rod bulb at a meeting in Newcastle in 1879. The following year, Swan installed 45 lamps in Sir William Armstrong's country house, Cragside in Rothbury. The next year an electricity supply station was set up in Godalming in Surrey to supply nearby houses with electricity for the new lamps, but the cost was far too high to be profitable and it soon closed down. In 1882, a more successful station was set up in Brighton, which can thus claim to have the longest continuous public electricity supply in the world.

Meanwhile, in the USA, Thomas Alva Edison was creating his own electric light bulb. In 1882, Edison set up the Edison Electric Light Company in London and immediately started legal proceedings against Swan for patent infringement. The lengthy court battle ended with Swan and Edison agreeing to join forces in 1883.

Power stations were set up in a few towns to supply nearby houses, but restrictive legislation and erratic supply meant most people who wanted electric light had to generate their own electricity. One of the problems with the small local power stations was that the extra demand at night was often just too much for them.

For some time in the late 1880s, electrical engineers disputed bitterly over how to supply electricity in what became known as the Battle of the Currents. On one side were the DC (direct current) crowd, including Edison, Lord Kelvin and others who favoured a DC supply because it was safe at the low voltages suitable for domestic use and could be stored in batteries. For them, the power drop-off that occurred at distance from the power station was a minor problem. On the other side were men such as George Westinghouse, Charles Parsons and Charles Metz who believed in AC (alternating current), which, with the aid of transformers, could be transmitted at high voltages over long distances without losing any power.

At the heart of the battle was the bitter personal rivalry between Edison and a one-time employee of his, the brilliant Serbian-born inventor Nikola Tesla. Highly practical and lacking the maths to appreciate Tesla's sophisticated work on AC, Edison got rid of Tesla without compensation, saying: '[Tesla's] ideas are splendid, but they are utterly impractical.' Edison launched an intensive publicity campaign against AC, including spreading misinformation about supposed dangers. In 1902, his film crew made a film showing the electrocution by AC of Topsy, a circus elephant which had killed three men. Even more gruesomely, Edison secretly funded the development of the first electric chair, used on 6 August 1890 to execute condemned murderer William Kemmler. The execution was so badly botched that Westinghouse, commented grimly: 'They would have done better using an axe.'

In the end, despite Edison's efforts, Westinghouse and Tesla, who became known as 'The Wizard of the West', had the last laugh. On 16 November 1896, electric power generated by hydropower at Niagara Falls was sent 30 miles to the city of Buffalo without any detectable power drop-off, using Tesla's innovative polyphase AC system. Suddenly, big power was available for industry. Moreover, it became possible to get massive economies of scale by generating power at a single big power station, then transmitting it over huge distances with no significant power loss, by changing the voltage with transformers – something that can't be done with DC.

A few small power stations continued to supply local domestic use with DC. But as ever more homes switched on to electric light, and industry began to exploit this wonderful new source of on-tap energy, the pattern of electricity supply became dominated by the big power stations and AC delivery.

By the 1920s, a good electricity supply across the nation, for both domestic and industrial use, was seen as a basic necessity. The fragmented and uncoordinated networks, though, were not well equipped to supply it. So in the late 1920s, the UK, for instance, embarked on an ambitious plan to create a nationwide electricity network which became known as the National Grid. Before the Grid was in place, in 1931, barely 30 per cent of UK houses had an electric supply. Just seventeen years later, 85 per cent did. Similar grid systems were set up in most industrialised nations.

But the coordination of electricity supplies hasn't stopped there. Now 'synchronous grids' have been set up to link supply networks across national borders. The largest in the world is the synchronous grid of Continental Europe, formerly known as the UCTE, which covers most of the European Union and supplies over 400 million homes.[82] There is even a proposal to set up a SuperSmart Grid covering all of Europe, northern Africa, Turkey and the Middle East. It's called a 'smart' grid, because it would use two-way digital technology

---

[82] In 2020, China will complete a grid that will cover the whole country and dwarf the European grid.

both to control appliances at people's homes and to adjust the flow of electricity in the supply system to make sure its efficiency is maximised. The point of linking the European and African networks is that most of Europe's huge energy demands could be met not from polluting, carbon-producing oil- and coal-fired power stations in Europe, but at much lower cost from Africa's vast, clean renewable hydroelectric resources. One day, switching on a light in Glasgow might draw instantly upon power generated on a dam on the Nile.

This is the great beauty of electricity grids. They not only ensure that every corner of the country has a good electricity supply but they are so interconnected that they can instantly spread and balance supply and demand throughout the network. When there is a blip in UK demand, for instance, a massive hydropower station under the North Wales mountains kicks in, or power is drawn across the channel from the Continental Grid. Moreover, when production in one power station drops, others far across the country can instantly take up the slack to ensure the supply stays astonishingly constant right across the grid.

The electricity supply is so silent, so invisible and so readily available that it is easy to forget just how amazing it is that it is there so reliably. Everything from high-tech gadgets to basic lighting depends on the constant supply of electricity delivered to every house night and day by the grid. The idea of every home in the developed world being supplied together and instantly is quite astonishing when you think about it. The everyday miracle involved only becomes apparent if you get to see one of the computerised maps of the grid at a National Grid centre, showing the state of the supply. The grid visibly

links every corner of the nation and supplies it with vital
energy, just as surely as the blood circulation delivers life-
giving oxygen to the body.

#21 Quantum Theory

'If anybody says he can think about quantum problems without getting giddy,' Danish physicist Niels Bohr said, 'that
only shows he has not understood the first thing about them.'
Niels Bohr was one of the chief architects of quantum theory,
and he was right; quantum theory is one of the most bizarre,
mind-blowing theories of science ever devised. A century after
its creation it still sounds so weird that it seems like science
fiction rather than the long-established branch of physics it is.
Indeed, it is so weird that it has prompted even philosophers
to question the whole nature of reality.

Quantum theory is based on the discovery that at the
very smallest scales, smaller than atoms, things behave very
differently. The classical rules of physics, the rules that govern everything from how an ant crawls to how the universe
expands, just don't work at the sub-atomic scale, it seems. In
classical physics, things behave according to a strict pattern
of cause and effect. Quantum theory shows that at the sub-
atomic level, we have to abandon this strict cause-and-effect
relationship.[83] Instead, it is all about probabilities. It means you
can never say where something is (and by something we mean,

_____

[83] Quantum theory doesn't mean that there is no such thing as cause
and effect; it simply works in a different way. The effect is probable, not
predetermined.

essentially, a sub-atomic particle); you can only say where it probably is. Its position is fixed only once you observe it.

This is far more unsettling than it sounds at first. Even though it was Einstein's insights into the interaction of light and atoms that sparked the creation of quantum theory, Einstein hated it. It was not just that the universe was suddenly governed by not one set of laws, but two – one for the sub-atomic world and one for all the rest. It was the whole chancy nature of quantum theory that disturbed him.

Einstein's theories of relativity might seem extraordinary, but they always assumed that the universe behaved with certainty. He just couldn't relate to a universe directed by probability. 'God doesn't play dice,' he famously said,[84] and devised a thought experiment to prove quantum theory wrong. This experiment, known as the Einstein-Podolsky-Rosen (EPR) experiment, envisaged a pair of particles emitted simultaneously from an atom. According to quantum theory, Einstein said, the 'spin'[85] of the two particles is not fixed until they are observed. Yet the instant one is observed, quantum theory would predict, the other's spin becomes fixed too – even if it is on the other side of the universe.

Einstein thought this patently absurd since information can, according to classical physics, travel no faster than the

---

[84] What he actually said was: 'It seems hard to sneak a look at God's cards. But that he plays dice and uses "telepathic" methods ... is something that I cannot believe for a single moment.'
[85] Spin is a special quantum quality of all sub-atomic particles, but it's a mathematical concept rather than a physical rotation.

speed of light.[86] So quantum theory must be wrong. Then in 1982, amazingly, French physicist Alain Aspect showed that the EPR demonstrates a real effect. The two particles are said to be 'entangled'. It's as if they are twins that can telepathically communicate across space.

Astounding though it sounds, entanglement has been demonstrated again and again over the last few decades and can be used to create that science fiction marvel, the teleport. If you attach another particle to one of an entangled pair, the attachment is instantly recreated, seemingly magically, by the other one of the pair, no matter how far apart. In 1997, photons were teleported across a laboratory in Rome like this, and since then molecules as big as bacteria have been teleported. Some scientists, of course, talk of teleporting entire objects across the world, but that's a long way off. Nevertheless, even though no one has even the vaguest idea how entanglement works, it's real and it does.[87]

Another astounding effect is 'quantum tunnelling'. Because the location of a quantum particle is only probable, sometimes the improbable can happen. The particle can sometimes appear on the far side of an impenetrable barrier, as if it has tunnelled through in an instant.

---

[86] English poet Arthur Buller gently mocked Einstein with this limerick:

> There was a young lady named Bright
> Whose speed was far faster than light;
> She set out one day
> In a relative way
> And returned on the previous night.

[87] Recently, scientists in Singapore and the USA suggested that DNA, the master molecule of genetic instructions inside every living cell, is held together by quantum entanglement.

Quantum tunnelling is involved in the latest hard-disc drives in computers. It's what allows you to clear data rapidly from flash drives. Mobile phones and computers may soon have touch-screens that are pressure-sensitive, thanks to quantum tunnelling. And the effects are observable in nature. It's how the sun gives out light. It's how enzymes often speed up organic processes. In fact, the more scientists delve, the more widespread its effects seem to be, 'explaining' phenomena that no one quite understood before. Yet no one knows how it works. Scientists working in the field of quantum mechanics have simply to accept that it's real and go on exploring its effects without any real notion of how it works on a 'common sense' level.

The origins of quantum theory lie back in the late 1800s, when scientists were trying to figure out how light is emitted from atoms. Most agreed that light travelled in waves and that each colour has a different wavelength. They knew that each kind of atom emitted a particular range of wavelengths – a particular spectrum of colours. And they knew that the energy in light increases from the red end of the spectrum to the violet. It was the hunt for an equation that summed up this increase that led to the idea of quanta. In 1900, German scientist Max Planck found that he could create an equation that worked only by treating the emitted light not as waves but bite-sized chunks of energy which he called 'quanta', from the Latin for 'how much'.

For Planck, this was simply a mathematical trick. But Einstein soon showed it was much more than that. In 1902, Hungarian physicist Philipp Lenard noticed something rather strange about the photoelectric effect – the way a little electricity is created when certain kinds of light hit metal atoms and knock electrons off. The energy of the electrons knocked off doesn't vary with the light's intensity at all, only its colour. This seemed weird; it was as if waves washed exactly the same amount of sand away on the beach no matter how big the wave.

Einstein, in the third of his great papers of 1905, showed what was going on. Even though at the time the consensus was that light is a wave, Einstein realised that Lenard's observation made complete sense if light consists of chunks of energy like Planck's quanta, and that quanta were not a mathematical trick but actual particles of light, later known as photons.

Eight years later, the young Niels Bohr was puzzling over the structure of the atom. Recent experiments by Ernest Rutherford had revealed that atoms are largely empty space, with tiny electrons orbiting a minute, dense nucleus. But why, Bohr mused, did each kind of atom seem to emit light only at certain wavelengths (known as spectral lines) and not others? And why didn't electrons just gradually spiral in towards the nucleus like a roulette ball?

Then it dawned on Bohr. It all made sense if you thought in terms of quanta. Electrons must only occupy certain orbits or 'energy levels' around the nucleus, as if each has a ticket to sit only in certain tiers in a stadium. When photons hit atoms, they bump electrons up a few tiers; light is emitted when electrons drop down an energy level or two. The colour emitted depends on the size of the drop. Each atom has a unique pattern of energy levels, and so emits its own unique range of colours.

This extraordinary insight rightly earned Bohr the 1922 Nobel Prize in physics and gave us the basis of the model of the atom we have today,[88] although it has been modified considerably since then. Yet it threw up as many problems as it solved. Now we had light, which everyone had thought of as a wave, behaving like a particle. And then, in the 1920s, French physics student Louis de Broglie showed that electrons, which everyone had thought of as a particle, could behave like a wave. What's more, light and matter seemed to switch between the two according to how you observed them. It all seemed horribly contradictory.

Gradually, physicists realised that the contradiction disappeared if you thought in terms of quanta and probabilities. An ingenious German physicist, Werner Heisenberg, realised a puzzling fact. You can measure, for instance, the momentum of a photon as it moves as a wave. Or you can measure its position as a particle. But you can never be sure of both at the same time because, as soon as you try to pin a photon down as a particle, it starts behaving like a wave, and vice versa.

This insight, called the Uncertainty Principle, is not just a problem with measuring. It is a basic property of all sub-atomic particles. It means that quantum scientists have to think in terms of probabilities, not certainties. This assumption became the heart of the new science of quantum

---

[88] Amazingly, many science text books still depict the atom with a ball-like nucleus orbited by electrons like planets around the sun. This image was created by Japanese physicist Hantaro Nagaoka in 1904, and was outdated a century ago. In fact, electrons are not like orbiting planets at all, but more like multiple whirring propeller blades spinning so fast they seem to be everywhere at once.

mechanics developed principally by Heisenberg and Bohr in Copenhagen in 1927.

Over 80 years on, quantum mechanics, the field of science founded on quantum theory, has now branched out into every field of science, affecting chemistry, biology, optics, electronics and much more. It's been observed to work again and again, and predictions made on the basis of quantum theory have proved to be amazingly accurate. So scientists have no doubt that the basic thinking behind it is right. Yet repeated attempts to join it with classical physics in Grand Unified Theories have so far failed, and ideas such as the many-worlds theory (which suggests that all the possibilities of the quanta are actually realised, but in different worlds) remain nothing more than ideas.

For the moment, scientists accept that it works and use its rich insights to push their exploration of the sub-atomic world further and develop some amazing new technology. But a real understanding of how it works is as yet beyond us.

Because it seems to upturn the traditional laws of physics and the clockwork, entirely deterministic universe that they depict, some people have found all kinds of extraordinary things in quantum theory. The deterministic nature of classical science laws, for instance, makes it very difficult to see how humans could have free will – since every action is entirely predetermined by those that go before. Quantum theory, with its infinite possibilities, seems, to some, to permit it.[89] Others see the operation of mystical forces, and use (and misuse)

---

[89] But quantum theory doesn't actually allow any more control than classical laws; it simply switches you from the straightjacket of a programme to being the victim of chance.

quantum theory to explain or justify all kinds of outlandish ideas, some of which may be valid, but most of which are fluff. Some even see quantum theory as a way to finally unite scientific and religious, mystical thought. That seems unlikely, but there's no doubt that our journey into the extraordinary quantum world has barely begun.

#20 Printing

Printing has changed the world as much as any idea in the last millennium. Its effects are subtle. It's not like technology such as the aeroplane which you can see and hear. It's not even like banks which have a tangible effect on our lives all the time. But the impact of printing has been nonetheless profound, because of the way it has shaped our entire way of thinking and communicating.

The introduction of printing bound the human world together in a way that was never possible before.[90] It allowed vast numbers of people to share ideas, to read the same stories, to read the same language, to exchange experiences, to follow the same beliefs. Tens of thousands of people, across

---

[90] Before printing, ideas travelled slowly, and often touched only a few people. Very few people in the ancient world, for instance, actually read the works of even antiquity's greatest thinker, Aristotle, or even, for that matter, the Bible. There were only a handful of manuscript copies of even the most famous literary works, most tucked away in private libraries. So most ideas spread by word of mouth and many had to be preserved by memory alone.

the nation, across continents, were literally reading from the same page for the first time.[91]

In talking about the impact of printing, we're talking about a very specific kind of printing, the movable type printing of books introduced to Europe by Gutenberg in the fifteenth century. The origins of printing are actually quite ancient. At least 1,800 years ago, the Chinese and Japanese were carving images on the end of wooden blocks and inking them with the soot from lamps dissolved in liquid, then stamping the images on paper, silk or walls. The images they carved were holy symbols or texts, which gained in magical power by repetition.[92]

By the ninth century, though, the Chinese were printing entire books, including the famous *Diamond Sutra* of 868, the oldest surviving printed book, which is actually a selection of Buddha's sermons printed on sheets pasted together into a manuscript roll over 5 metres long. The purpose of printing books in China, however, was not to spread knowledge but to produce definitive, authorised versions that no one could challenge. So there were rarely many copies printed. It's

---

[91] In some ways, it did just what the internet is doing today, and perhaps human communication could be said to have moved in three great waves – the development of writing, the introduction of printing and the coming of the internet – each arriving and spreading around the world faster.

[92] In what must have been the largest early print run by far, the eighth-century Japanese Buddhist Empress Koken ordered the printing of 1 million copies of a charm to set in miniature pagodas to guard against a repeat outbreak of a deadly plague of smallpox which had devastated the country in 735–737. The charm didn't work, though, for the Empress herself died of smallpox just as the vast printout was completed in 770.

interesting that one of the first uses of wood-block printing for multiple copies was to print paper money.[93]

At first, the early Chinese block-printed books were painstakingly produced, with the block for each page individually carved by hand. Then in the tenth century, some printers began to experiment with movable type. With movable type, every page of every book can be built up letter by letter from the same ready-made collection of letters or characters. In Europe, later, the letters would be cast metal; the Chinese ones were ceramic or wood.

The problem for the Chinese with movable type, though, was that Chinese had over 50,000 different characters, so it was something of nightmare finding the right character when you needed it. To try and make selection easier, Chinese printers made vast revolving tables for the characters, divided into sections for characters with different tones. Even so most printers found it easier to stick with block printing. Interestingly, in the fifteenth century, the Korean king Sejong the Great commissioned the creation of a simple alphabet of just 25 letters from which words could be built up, but Korean scholars refused to budge from their traditional Chinese characters, and movable type in Asia languished.

In the end, printing travelled across to Europe not as books and type but perhaps as something as trivial as playing cards.

---

[93] When Marco Polo visited Kublai Khan's China in the thirteenth century, he observed of the paper notes that: 'Of this money, the Khan has such a quantity made that with it he could buy all the treasure in the world. With this currency he orders all payments to be made throughout every province and kingdom and region of his empire. And no one dares refuse it on pain of losing his life.'

Printed playing cards arrived in Europe in the fourteenth century and quickly became hugely popular. Indeed, by 1404 playing cards were such an obsession that the Church authorities tried, in vain, to ban them, as they were distracting people from work and sermons. It may have been with playing cards that the first great European printer, Johannes Gutenberg, first tried his hand at printing, before moving on to higher things.

Born sometime in the 1390s in Mainz in Germany, Gutenberg was a perfectionist, and he laboured for decades to get his process right – all the time fighting to keep his ideas secret and fend off investors who were impatient for some return. It's impossible to tell whether Gutenberg learned of it from China, or if he came up with it independently, but his great innovation was movable type.

Movable type was so much more practical with the European alphabet of just 26 letters. A full-length book, though, would need tens of thousands of copies of each letter, and Gutenberg devised a way of reproducing them all quickly and accurately by casting them from a special lead alloy in tiny wooden boxes, with a reverse imprint of the letter at the end (the origin of the term 'typecasting'). Gutenberg also had to redesign the letters of script to make them fit on neatly together.

Even with all these beautifully made and even letters, getting each of the thousands of them on a page to print properly was quite a challenge. Chinese and European block printers had simply brushed the paper over the inked block. This wouldn't really work for movable type when different letters might sit just a fraction higher or lower. So Gutenberg adapted a screw press from book binders, who in turn probably adapted it from presses made for crushing olives and grapes. The screw press pushed the paper down firmly on to the inked typeset to ensure a clean and even print.

Eventually, Gutenberg perfected his process and in 1444, the first major printed European book was created,[94] the Bible now known as the Gutenberg Bible. This was still a big, high-end luxury item, selling only to those with a lot of cash to spare, and the scribes who wrote manuscript books were still in business. Gradually, though, printers began to make smaller and cheaper books.

One of the pioneers was Aldus Manutius, the Venetian scholar who set up the world's first great publishing house, the Aldine Press, in the 1490s. Aldus not only introduced the small, elegant, easy-to-read Italic (from Italy) typeface, but also the handy Octavo size book – the size of a typical modern hardback book. Books, instead of being literally chained up in a few inaccessible libraries to be read only by dedicated scholars, were suddenly inexpensively available everywhere. They could be carried around and read in the home, on journeys, in cafés.

---

[94] We take for granted the book with its pages, but even that was an idea that was a long time coming. The earliest books were in fact scrolls which could be dozens of metres long. They were written on papyrus, the tough paper-like material made from the Egyptian papyrus reed. Consulting such a book was a real chore, since you might have to scroll and unscroll for ages to find the right place. In the second century BC, a shortage of papyrus led to the development in Pergamon of an alternative, parchment, which was made from thin stretched sheep and goat skins, and vellum made from calf skin. Parchment was much tougher than papyrus, and you could write on both sides. So books didn't have to be on scrolls. Instead they could be on pages bound together with a cover, and known as a codex.

It's difficult to overstate just how dramatic a transformation in the spread of ideas this was. Before Gutenberg, when nearly all books were manuscripts, the total number of books in all Europe was a matter of thousands. Within half a century of the first printing of Gutenberg's Bible, there were 10 million books, and the Aldine Press was launching books with first print runs of 1,000 or more.

The impact was both public, as ideas were shared rapidly among a large readership, and private as people could travel, in their imagination, in the solitude of their own homes. Interestingly, many of the ideas that were shared through print at first were not new ideas but ancient ones. The Aldine Press, for instance, concentrated heavily on publishing the great classics of the ancient world, and so the arrival of print didn't necessarily help contemporary authors but instead brought about a revival of interest in Virgil and Homer, Galen and Aristotle.

Nonetheless, the public effect of print was to standardise and preserve knowledge, which had been fluid, changeable and often simply forgotten. For the first time, there was a growing body of ideas, an authoritative consensus which people could add to or challenge. Ever since, there has been a sense of our knowledge of the world gradually building up, brick by brick, rather than coming and going with occasional flashes of brilliance. Knowledge became more democratic, too, with more and more people able to access it through text-books and encyclopaedias.

At the same time, print encouraged the expression of individual thought. Before printing, a writer was actually a scribe, someone who just copied a book rather than created it.

Many manuscripts were the creation of numerous anonymous contributors. Monks working on a manuscript, for instance, might all have the same adopted name, so that it is impossible to untangle who actually wrote it in the first place. Printing promoted, for the first time, individual authorship, and the expression of personal ideas and experiences to be shared with other people. Printed books came with title pages promoting their content and announcing the name of the author. American historian Elizabeth Eisenstein argued that this shift was a key factor in the three great revolutions in European thought – the Protestant Reformation, the Renaissance and the Scientific Revolution.[95]

One of the more surprising effects of printing, though, was to stimulate the development of single national vernacular languages like English, French and German. In the Middle Ages, people in France, England and Germany spoke such a variety of local dialects that someone from Paris was virtually unintelligible to someone from Marseilles. William Caxton, the pioneer of printing in England, told a tale of a housewife in Kent who assumed that the word 'egg' must be French because she hadn't heard of it. In order to print books for a

---

[95] The Victorian thinker Thomas Carlyle spoke of: 'The three great elements of modern civilisation, Gun powder, Printing, and the Protestant religion.' This is an interesting choice, but he was echoing the pioneer of scientific thought Francis Bacon, who in 1620 wrote: 'Again, it is well to observe the force and virtue and consequence of discoveries, and these are to be seen nowhere more conspicuously than in those three which were unknown to the ancients ... namely printing, gunpowder and the magnet. For these three have changed the whole face and state of things throughout the world ... no empire, no sect, no star seems to have exerted greater power and influence in human affairs than these mechanical discoveries.'

mass market, printers had to decide on just one dialect, and the dialect selected by the printers rapidly became the national language, such as Parisian French in France and London English in England. At the same time, though, Latin, which had been the international language of scholars, gradually began to fall out of use for literature (though much more slowly for scholarship), and every nation began to develop its own national literature and culture in a way that would have been unimaginable before.

It would be wrong to assume that the impact of Gutenberg's movable type was immediate. The effect spread slowly over centuries, rippling out across the world, as more and more people got to experience the printed word. Indeed, it was only in the last century, when governments began to provide universal education and hundreds of millions of people began to learn to read, that the print revolution finally arrived.

Today, 45 trillion pages are printed every day, and billions of people read books, magazines and newspapers, read shopping labels and bills, check tickets and much more besides. They make possible basic communication and the sharing of experiences and ideas in our hugely populated world that would otherwise have been impossible. Print at least partly brings humanity together and allows us to think as one, but only partly.

#19 Feminism

Anyone who doubts that feminism is a live, important issue needed only to listen to the news from Iran in July 2010.

There a woman called Sakineh Mohammadi Ashtiani had been sentenced four years earlier to being stoned to death for adultery. It was only after a wave of international protest that the Iranian authorities announced the sentence would not actually be carried out. But the fact that it was even a possibility bears grim testament to the status of women in Iran.

It seems that Iranian women, though, are fighting back, and Iran has one of the most active feminist movements in the world. The movement has no leaders or central office, but exists stubbornly in every household where women refuse to accept their role not just as citizens but as human beings whose lives are, ultimately, considered to be worth less than men's.

The household nature of the Iranian women's movement is typical of both the strengths and weaknesses of feminism. Unlike slavery and the exploitation of workers, the oppression of women across many different societies in the past was often barely visible. It went on behind closed doors where countless men sometimes subtly, sometimes brutally, repressed the women of their household. Sometimes, the oppression was physical, with legal condoning of rape and beatings within marriage. More often, the problem was one of exclusion and the complete loss of control over one's life. This too the law condoned, with women often being legally their husband's property. Millions of women suffered alone, unable to even share their misery, let alone express it.

Maybe many women did resist, but their cries were never heard. The first audible protest was Mary Wollstonecraft's *A Vindication of the Rights of Woman* (1792), and there were many more, some celebrated, some vilified, some just quietly ignored before the lone voices began to join together into a clamour in the late nineteenth century. That was when the word 'feminism' came into use in English. It was borrowed from the French word *féministe* to stigmatise the strident and bold women who dared to demand better treatment, and dared, in particular, to demand the right to vote. Even the word 'suffragette' was originally meant to demean these little women's campaign to join the suffrage.

British women finally got the vote in 1918[96] and very soon most of the Western world followed suit. It's hard in retrospect to appreciate just how much of an achievement this was. Many men, and even some women, put up a very determined resistance that was only gradually broken down. Getting the vote was not just a matter of allowing women to vote in elections; it was a symbolic acknowledgement that women had an equal stake in society.

For almost half a century, getting the vote seemed such a triumph that women stopped asking for more. Then in the 1960s and 1970s a new kind of feminism arose – this time addressed to the specific problems women faced both in the home and in trying to make a career. Ironically, the term feminism was widely taken up again by the women's movement after the labels 'Women's Liberation' or 'Women's Lib' gained notoriety from strident public demonstrations and 'braburning', when some women argued that bras were a cage for women's breasts invented for men's titillation.

---

[96] Women got the vote in New Zealand as early as 1893 and in Australia in 1902, in Finland in 1906 and in Denmark, Norway and Iceland between 1913 and 1915.

Despite the ridicule, these campaigns, too, achieved at least some of their goals. Under pressure, the UK, for instance, introduced laws to ensure equal pay for women and to protect them against discrimination, while the US government amended the Constitution to give women the 'right to choose' over abortion. By the 1990s, women began to take it for granted that they could choose pretty much any career that they wanted, and expect to make progress – though some complained about the 'glass ceiling' of prejudice that prevented women rising above a certain place in the workplace hierarchy, while others protested about sexual harassment. 'Sexism' came to be widely regarded as unacceptable, and maternity leave became a legal right in many countries.

Just as with the suffrage movement (sometimes called the first wave of feminism), success took the energy out of this second wave of feminism – so dramatically that feminism as a political movement seemed to fade away in the 1990s. Indeed, it faded so much that an article in *Time* magazine in 1998 by journalist Ginia Bellafante was run with the cover line, 'Is feminism dead?' One of the chief murderers, Bellafante claimed, was Camille Paglia's 1990 book *Sexual Personae*, in which she argued that female sexuality was humanity's greatest force and that it was up to women to realise its power. Bellafante lamented that in the wake of Paglia's highly publicised proclamation of female sexuality, feminism was melting away in a welter of self-indulgent sexual and romantic confessions, in which a woman only had to proclaim that she enjoyed sex – or lament that her love-life was bad – to be lauded by other women for expressing a woman's perspective.

Some women began to argue that there should now be a third wave of feminism. Writers such as Jennifer Baumgardner and Amy Richards suggest that feminism should stop trying to drive every woman towards the white middle-class ideal of the 'super-mum'. Instead, it should embrace female identity in whatever shape or form it takes, challenging oppression of everyone from non-heterosexuals to sex workers. Feminist critics of the third wave protest that this is all a bit unfocused, but third-wavers insist they are simply adapting feminism for the women of today.

Thanks to feminism, the lives and prospects of most women in the Western world have advanced enormously over the last century. No longer is it acceptable, as it once was, for husbands to beat or rape their wives. No longer are women excluded from the vote or from pursuing careers in politics to the very highest level. And no longer are women's careers restricted to certain jobs and certain levels of pay.

But there is still plenty for feminists to do, even in the Western world, if they are to achieve the equality that they are striving for. The UK's Margaret Thatcher and Germany's Angela Merkel are still the only women to have become leaders of major Western powers. Women are still in a small minority as elected representatives at both local and national levels. Moreover, average pay levels for women remain significantly below those for men.

In other countries, including Iran, the challenge for feminism is far more extreme. In a world where women and girls endure anything from stoning for adultery and enforced marriage to sexual exploitation and barred access to education and careers, feminism remains very much a vital cause.

#18 Bread

There are few smells more enticing, more delicious than the aroma of freshly baked bread – as warm and comforting as a thick duvet on a winter's day and appetising enough for supermarkets to pump it into their stores in the knowledge that it will make people hungry enough to buy more food. There are few aromas, apparently, if any, which are so universally appealing and guaranteed to make people drool.

It's impossible to tell, of course, whether we humans liked the smell instantly when the very first loaf was baked long ago, or whether its attractiveness has gradually seeped into our subconscious over time, through its associations with security and sustenance. But the power of that smell wafting through the air is ample testament to the simple brilliance of bread as an idea. Even if it were nothing more than this matchless aroma, bread would be a great idea, but its real value is as a foodstuff.

It is quite simply one of the most nutritious and healthy foods there is, and it is hardly surprising that it is a staple for billions of people around the world. While it is true that man cannot live on bread alone, few other foods have bread's ability to provide day-to-day sustenance. It is above all a cheap source of the basic carbohydrate fuel we need to give us energy.

Yet bread is much more than just fuel for the body. It also contains fibre from the bran, the outside of the wheat, which helps digestion, and vitamins B1 and B3 which extract energy from food and keep the eyes, skin and nervous system healthy. A good supply of these vitamins is vital since the body cannot store them – and in poorer countries where bread is scarce, people often suffer from diseases like beriberi and pellagra due to lack of B vitamins.

Bread is also one of the most important sources of calcium in the diet – essential for healthy bones and teeth. Bread's calcium content may not be altogether natural. Because nearly everyone eats bread in the UK, millers are legally required to add a certain amount of calcium to white and brown flour to boost people's intake of the mineral. This has played a significant role in the virtual elimination of the childhood bone disease rickets from developed nations. When you learn that bread is also a major dietary source of iron (for healthy blood), folic acid (good for pregnant women) and minerals such as selenium, sodium, potassium, magnesium, copper, phosphorous and manganese, it's clear why bread is such a good food. There are downsides, though, as I'll come back to later.

Bread is one of the oldest recipes in the world, one of the first foods humankind ever ate that wasn't either eaten raw or cooked as it came. Maybe it was the very first. At heart, it's a very simple recipe, which just involves grinding grass seeds to a powder or flour, adding water to make a paste or dough, rolling it out, then baking it slowly. But if you think how many people cannot make their own bread today, you begin to realise what an achievement it was to come up with the idea in the first place, when no one had done anything remotely like this before.

Of course, we have no idea who those unsung innovators were, but they probably lived in the Middle East. In 2005, researchers found wild grain seeds, grinding stones and a stone oven at a 23,000-year-old site, Ohalo II, near the Sea of Galilee. Large ancient granaries in Jordan show that by at least 11,000 years ago, bread-making was well established. And there is ample evidence to show that bread was central to the diet of Ancient Egyptians. Archaeologists have even found (very stale) loaves of bread in Egypt dating back at least 5,000 years.

Remarkably, the earliest breads were not so very different from breads cooked around the world today. They were flat-breads, similar to Indian chapattis and naans, Middle Eastern pita breads, Arabic khubz and Mexican tortillas. The idea of leavening – raising bread to make it fluffier and lighter with gas bubbles from yeast – is fairly ancient too. It may have been discovered accidentally when a mix of flour meal and water was left standing for some time, allowing yeast grains, which occur naturally on wheat, a chance to ferment and create a lighter dough full of air. 'Legend has it,' report the European Confederation of Breadmakers, 'that a slave in a royal Egyptian household forgot about some dough he had set aside. When he returned, it had doubled in size. Trying to hide the mistake, the dough was punched down furiously and baked. The result was a lighter bread than anyone had ever tasted.' Nowadays, of course, yeast is added artificially, but for a long time, just adding this 'sour dough' to the next day's bake was the normal way of leavening bread. There are Egyptian hieroglyphs from over 5,000 years ago which show bake-houses with dough rising next to bread ovens.

In some parts of the world, bread is still made much as it was in those early days, and in countries like France, craft bakery is a fiercely protected tradition. But in places like the

UK most bread is made by an industrial process such as the Chorleywood bread process (CBP), which turns out a product that resembles and maybe even tastes like traditional bread, but is made in a very different way.

Instead of allowing the dough to ferment and rise for a few hours, the CBP gets air and water in almost instantly using high-speed mixers. So the whole process is much, much faster and can be entirely automated, which keeps the price of everyday bread very low. But it calls for extra yeast and chemical oxidants to get the air in, harder fat to maintain the structure, and also extra water.

In some industrially made breads, the hard fat is tough, hydrogenated trans-fats. But bad publicity about the health risks of trans-fats has persuaded some bread-makers to replace them with palm oils, which may turn out to be just as bad.

Although some traditional breads like ciabatta have a high moisture content anyway, industrial breads tend to contain much more water than comparable traditionally made loaves. Extra water means not only a significant saving in flour costs, but that the soft bread that people like can be achieved with tough lower-grade flour.

Getting the bread to hold together with all this extra water was easy with chlorinated 'bleached' flours, but these were banned in 1998 in the UK for health reasons. Now many bread-makers achieve the same with enzymes.

Moreover, the whole industrial bread-making process is so destructive of bread's natural vitamin and mineral content that they have to be 'restored' with artificial vitamins and minerals added to the flour. Add to that a range of bleaching chemicals such as benzoyl peroxide and chlorine dioxide, both skin and respiratory tract irritants, to make the bread look nice and white, and others to stop the flour sticking at high temperatures and you have quite a cocktail!

So the bread you buy in supermarkets may be just a bit less nutritious than traditional bread. In fact, in large quantities it could even be a health risk because of its high salt content. In the past, normal fermentation was quite enough to give bread a good flavour. The drastic cut in fermentation times in industrial processes means extra salt has to be added to stop the bread tasting like cardboard. According to some estimates, bread is now the biggest source of salt in the average diet – and that high salt intake brings attendant health risks.

All of this might take the sheen off the idea of bread being the greatest thing since, well, unsliced bread ... So, of course, maybe it is good, properly made bread that is a great idea, not all bread.

These caveats aside, bread has rightly been revered for its central role in much of the world's diet over many thousands of years. Bread's wonderful combination of simplicity, wholesomeness and food value mean that in many cultures it has come to symbolise our most basic need for sustenance, characterised in the Christian Lord's Prayer, 'Give us this day our daily bread' and by the naming of the family's basic provider as the 'breadwinner'. It is no coincidence that in Arabic, the words for 'bread' and 'life' are nearly the same. It is that essential.

#17 Vaccination

Vaccines are the greatest medical success story of all time. In the developed world, they have been so effective at eradicating many infectious diseases that it is easy to forget just how terrible these once were. Smallpox, diphtheria, polio, tetanus, measles, whooping cough, typhoid, rabies, anthrax and many other diseases were not distant and occasional threats. They were ever-present monsters that stalked people throughout their lives and kept them in a constant state of fear.

Today, we rightly feel it is a tragedy if any young child dies. Yet just six children out of every 1,000 born in the UK, for instance, die before the age of five. That is sad enough, but in 1750 only one child in three survived beyond the age of five. Every child would expect to witness most of his brothers or sisters dying, or at least see their lives permanently blighted by disfigurement or disablement. In the developed world, disease has been so far banished to the dark corners of an occasional threat that it is hard to imagine what it must have been like to live with this high level of mortality. Even in poor parts of the world, where disease is still rife, it is not the mass murderer it used to be.

Of course, there are other factors involved in the dramatic reduction in disease, such as better diet and hygiene, better living conditions, improved medicines and so on, but vaccination is far and away the most important – because it works to prevent disease no matter what all the other conditions are.

The statistics are astonishing. Smallpox, which once killed 2 million people a year and disfigured many more, has been wiped out entirely. Polio, which even twenty years ago was claiming 300,000 victims a year, now affects under 2,000. Deaths from measles around the world have dropped from 6 million a year to under 1 million. Tetanus, which once killed many babies, has been virtually eradicated in two-thirds of developed countries. The incidence of whooping cough has been reduced by 90 per cent. The reduction in diphtheria has been equally dramatic. Disease is in retreat around the world and it is largely thanks to vaccination.

It all began with smallpox. Smallpox was a highly contagious disease that spread rapidly. It affected people of all ages and races. In every year of the eighteenth century, nearly half a million people in Europe – and countless others elsewhere – died from the disease. It claimed the lives of one in every five Londoners. And those who caught the disease and were lucky enough to survive were often scarred for life with pockmarked faces.

In China, though, they had discovered a way to combat the disease. They noticed that once people had survived smallpox, they never caught it again, no matter how much they were exposed to the disease. So the Chinese scraped material from the scabs of victims of milder forms of smallpox and rubbed it into a scratch on healthy people who had yet to catch the disease. Some people died quickly from the infection, but most survived, and seemed to gain the same immunity to the disease as those who had been through it properly. The practice of 'variolation', as it has become known, spread across Asia to Turkey, where it was noticed by the British ambassador's wife, Lady Mary Wortley Montague. Lady Mary was so impressed that she had her own children inoculated[97] like this, and introduced the practice to the British upper classes.

It was a high-risk strategy, since many perfectly healthy people exposed themselves to smallpox and caught the disease, even if many more gained immunity. Then in the 1790s, a young country doctor named Edward Jenner was wondering why so many dairymaids had perfect complexions and seemed immune to smallpox. He guessed it might be because they had been through a similar, but much milder disease, known as cowpox, caught from the cows they milked. Medical ethics then were clearly not what they are now. Jenner decided to deliberately infect his gardener's young son, James Phipps, with material from the blisters of a dairymaid suffering from cowpox.[98] A few weeks later, he deliberately tried to infect young James with smallpox. James proved to be immune and remained so all his life.

After further trials, Jenner was able to persuade the British government of the effectiveness of his technique. Across Europe and North America, governments introduced compulsory programmes to vaccinate children and the incidence of smallpox dropped dramatically. The last case of smallpox in the United States was reported in 1949. In 1959, the World Health Organisation launched a programme to eradicate smallpox from the world entirely. It would have been impractical to vaccinate everybody. So instead, people were vaccinated in rings around any infection site to stop the disease

---

[97] Inoculation means deliberate exposure to the disease. Vaccination means deliberate exposure to a harmless version of the disease. Immunisation is when this process is applied to a group.
[98] The word 'vaccination' comes from the Latin word for cow, *vacca*.

spreading. It proved so effective that the last case of smallpox in the world was reported in Ethiopia in 1976 and in 1979, scientists announced that vaccines had eradicated smallpox from the world.

Vaccination works because the body has its own remarkable line of defence, the immune system. Whenever the body is exposed to a pathogen (a disease-causing germ), it reacts by producing floods of proteins called antibodies unique to that specific germ. It's important that the antibodies are unique because apart from attacking the germ directly, they act as beacons to trigger a massive attack by other aggressive body cells – and it's important that these fighting cells only target the enemy and don't expose the body to 'friendly fire'.

It takes a little while to produce the right antibodies, and the body may suffer the symptoms of disease before they are ready to mount their counter-attack. Eventually, if they are successful, the germs are beaten and the body recovers. The next time that the body encounters the germ, however, the antibodies are ready to target it quickly and eliminate it before the disease develops.

The aim with vaccination is to prime the immune system with the right antibodies by exposing it to dead, weakened or partial versions of the pathogen. These harmless pathogens trigger the production of antibodies, but don't cause the disease. With some vaccines, a single exposure is enough. With others, immunity needs to be built up gradually with a short series of vaccinations. Sometimes, the production of antibodies may drop off after a decade or so, and a 'booster' may be needed to restore immunity.

The challenge with vaccinations is to find the right vaccine. The vaccine has to trigger the production of the right antibodies, but it clearly should not make the patient ill. Medical scientists have no doubt that the best way of combating nearly every disease is to find a vaccine. With some diseases, one vaccine seems enough to provide long-term immunity. With 'flu, however, new variations of the virus are appearing all the time, and a new vaccine has to be developed to combat each one, so that those vulnerable to winter 'flu need to get a new vaccination every autumn to protect them against this year's version. Some diseases, like HIV, are very hard to create an effective vaccine for, since HIV actually turns the victim's immune system against him or her, but the rewards of success are so high that many researchers are devoting their entire lives to finding one.

Vaccinations, though, are becoming a victim of their own phenomenal success. They not only work to protect individuals; they also confer immunity on whole communities in what is called 'herd immunity'. Once a high proportion of people in the community have been successfully vaccinated, the germs are eradicated before they can spread. So even those who have not been vaccinated, and the few in whom the vaccine has not worked properly, are protected against the disease. This is why mass immunisation programmes are often compulsory. Herd immunity only works effectively if, typically, 95 per cent of people are vaccinated.[99]

---

[99] Herd immunity only works for diseases that are contagious. For diseases like tetanus, which is typically contracted when a wound comes into contact with contaminated soil, herd immunity offers no protection.

The problem is, though, that once herd immunity has built up to a certain level, the chances of catching the disease are very small. So people begin to wonder if the occasional side-effects of vaccinations are more of a risk than the disease itself. Individually that may sometimes be true. In recent years, there has been a well-organised anti-vaccine campaign to persuade parents not to immunise their children. The campaigners forget, of course, that the only reason why the side-effects of some vaccines are worth thinking about is because of the extraordinary success of immunisation programmes in eradicating the disease in the first place.

The campaigners seemed to have scored a major victory in 1998 when British doctor Andrew Wakefield published an article in the *Lancet* apparently demonstrating a clear link between the MMR (Measles, Mumps and Rubella) vaccine and autism. Wakefield's research was later discredited and he was struck off in 2010. But the damage was done. As the media spread alarm, take-up of the vaccine dropped dramatically. Uptake of the MMR, which at 92 per cent had been almost at the herd immunity level, plummeted to 80 per cent. Serious cases of measles rose from just 56 in 1998 to 1,348 in 2008, with two children dying from the disease, the first for a long time.

The point is that vaccination is extraordinarily effective at disease prevention even on an individual level. But its success leaps to another level when the whole community is vaccinated, creating herd immunity. That's how smallpox was eradicated. But this means that with some diseases people must be willing to accept a small personal risk of side-effects from the vaccination for the sake of massive benefits to the community as a whole.

The reality is that vaccinations have saved the lives of hundreds of millions of people already. We've already looked at the smallpox success, but it has been at least partially repeated with dozens of other once deadly or crippling diseases. In the USA, for instance, diphtheria declined from a high of 206,939 cases in 1921 to just one in 1998; whooping cough declined from 265,269 cases in 1934 to 6,279 in 1998; and measles has fallen from 894,134 cases in 1941 to just 89 in 1998. New diseases are being successfully fought all the time. Since the introduction of the haemophilus influenzae B (Hib) vaccine in the 1990s, for instance, the incidence of the distressing disease Hib meningitis, which once killed tens of thousands of children, has declined in Europe by 90 per cent and in the USA by 99 per cent.

All these diseases can now be prevented by vaccination:

Anthrax; Diphtheria; Haemophilus Influenzae Type B (Hib); Hepatitis A; Hepatitis B; Human Papillomavirus (HPV); Influenza; Japanese Encephalitis; Lyme Disease; Measles; Meningococcal Disease; Mumps; Pertussis (Whooping Cough); Pneumococcal Disease; Polio; Rabies; Rotavirus; Rubella; Shingles (Herpes Zoster); Smallpox; Tetanus; Tuberculosis; Typhoid Fever; Varicella (Chickenpox)

#16 The Telephone

In 1876, the Western Union Telegraph Company were deliberating on whether or not to take up Alexander Graham Bell's brand new invention. They were not very optimistic. 'This "telephone" has too many shortcomings,' an internal memo said, 'to be seriously considered as a means of communication. The device is inherently of no value to us.' US President Rutherford B. Hayes was only a little more enthusiastic after making the first phone call from the White House, commenting drily: 'An amazing invention – but who would ever want to use one?'

Of course, it's incredibly easy to laugh at their lack of foresight now, with the number of users of mobile phones alone hitting 5 billion in 2010. But back in the 1870s it wasn't so easy to see just why many people would want to use a telephone. By that time, the world was very up-to-speed, or so they thought, with instant communication. Telegraph wires were buzzing continuously with messages that seemed to deal instantly with every need from a business communication to a bit of personal news. Telegrams were brief, to the point and what's more provided a complete record of the message. The telegraph was reliable, professional and discreet. What could anyone want with a few snatched words, unrecorded chatter? The real demand in the 1870s was for a way of getting extra bandwidth, a way of sending multiple wires along the same cable so that telegraph traffic could be increased without laying thousands of miles of duplicate cables.[100]

---

[100] The astonishing take-up of emails when they launched in the 1990s shows that this assessment wasn't actually so wide of the mark.

This was the problem American electrical engineer Elisha Gray was working on when he came up with an idea for transmitting speech via electric cables. His idea was to use the effect of speech's varying sound vibrations on a liquid to vary electrical resistance and so create an electrical signal that reflected the pattern of the speech. The variations of that electrical signal could then be used to recreate the speech at the other end of the line.

Gray wasn't the first to think of the idea of electrical speech transmission. A young German inventor, John Philipp Reis, had created just such a device in 1860, which he called a 'telephon'. Thomas Edison, who had an axe to grind, later acknowledged that Reis had invented the first telephone, but claimed that it only transmitted music, not the fine detail of speech.[101] Of course, as with so many groundbreaking inventions, Reis could not get anyone in Germany interested, and only a few when his professor demonstrated it in New York in 1872. Maybe Gray, or maybe Alexander Graham Bell, the young Scotsman who arrived in Boston in 1871, both heard of, or even caught sight of, Reis's device. Maybe Bell also caught sight of Gray's patent application in the patent office, as author Seth Shulman claims. Whatever the truth – and there were powerful legal and financial reasons for bending

---

[101] Apparently, documents in London's Science Museum show that engineers from the Standard Telephones and Cables (STC) company conducted tests based on Reis's design in 1947, and found it could actually transmit speech quite well. They kept their findings quiet to avoid upsetting STC's negotiations at the time with the Bell Telephone Company created by Alexander Graham Bell, who is usually credited with inventing the telephone.

the truth – Bell is generally credited with the invention of the phone.

Recorded in Bell's notebook is a now-famous entry for 10 March 1876, the day when Bell made the world's first phone call, to Thomas Watson, the electrical engineer helping him with his experiments. Watson was in another room in Bell's Boston house, and the call was brief, with Bell saying merely: 'Mr Watson, come here. I want to see you.' A modest but historic start.

Judging from the Western Union's first response, Bell's telephone might have been forgotten just as quickly as Reis's. But Bell had wealthier connections, and he was also joined in the promotion of the new device by Edison, who made the telephone much more practical by replacing the liquid transmitter of Gray and Bell with a solid carbon transmitter.

Despite the gloomy predictions, people were instantly excited by the magic of the telephone. The idea of talking directly to someone across the city, or even in another city, seemed miraculous. Of course there were teething problems; the cumbersome first telephones were not like the neat little devices of today, and the sound quality was a little strained. But that didn't kill the thrill of hearing someone's voice from afar, and knowing that whatever you said could be heard instantaneously many miles away.

Within a couple of years, there were well over 100,000 phone users in the USA alone, and over 3 million by the turn of the century. Since then, the phone has gone from strength to strength. By 1950, by far the majority of people in developed countries had a phone, and half a century later, with the development of mobile phones, which obviated the need for extensive cabling and even a fixed address, telephone communication had swelled to include pretty much everybody in the world.

At first, the thrill of the phone was just a novelty. Yet it was quite some novelty. The coming of the train half a century earlier had astonished and frightened people in almost equal measure as it whisked passengers in a few hours between cities which for all of history had been a week or more's hard riding apart. Yet it was still physical and visible. You could see trains. You could touch them and examine the mighty pistons and cylinders that gave the locomotive its vast horsepower. But the telephone took you into the realm of the invisible. And communication by phone wasn't just fast; it was instant. The fact that your voice was recreated far away even as you spoke must have, for those experiencing it for the first time, created the same amazement that we'd experience now were someone to suddenly teleport us to another planet. That invisibility, that instantaneousness and that spreading of your personality across the world, must have made people feel that they really were entering a new age, an age of marvels like none before. In retrospect, the invention of the telephone does indeed mark the dawn of the modern age, the age of telecommunications.

Very soon, though, the telephone proved to be much more than just a marvellous new toy. Surprisingly quickly, it became a familiar and indispensable part of everyday life. It changed living patterns, too, forever. The impact was dramatic in once-isolated rural areas. Farmers and their families living on remote farms were no longer cut off from the world as they had been since time immemorial. They could call and chat to neighbours, order things without a long trip into town, call the vet or doctor in an emergency. The world must have seemed a friendlier, more secure place.

In town, too, though they no longer wrote the wonderfully crafted letters of the Victorian age, people could chat easily, briefly and in a more relaxed fashion. They could communicate with their friends, relatives and even lovers as never before. And, just as in the country, the phone must have made cities seem friendlier, more relaxed, more cohesive places. Migrants to the city, students off to university were no longer out of touch altogether, but could ring home to stave off homesickness or reassure worried mothers. And those waiting at home for someone late back from work or a trip no longer had to worry themselves sick, but receive a quick call.

There is no doubt that the telephone has shrunk the world, and made it a more comfortable, secure place (even if the news on the telephone is bad). People are no longer restricted to talking to people in their own close neighbourhood or in their place of work – but can conduct business, chat with friends, arrange meetings and so much more, with people across the city, across the country, across the world. The advent of the mobile phone has taken it one step further. It is so easy to be in touch with people, so easy to know where they are, what they are doing, and for humans who are essentially social animals this is immensely important – it may be the one thing which has made the move from small communities to vast cities not just bearable but even exciting and fruitful.

It is possible that the advent of the phone has hastened the break-up of traditional communities. It's so easy to chat to your friends; why talk to your neighbours? And maybe it has ghettoised social groups and made them less mixed. The sitcom cliché of the teenage daughter speaking on the phone[102] symbolised some of these new divisions. And of course there are the misanthropes like Ambrose Bierce, who defined a telephone so:

> Telephone, *n.*   An invention of the devil which abrogates some of the advantages of making a disagreeable person keep his distance.

Or those like Mark Twain who resent the phone's power to invade one's privacy, as the punch line to this Christmas greeting from 1890, just fourteen years after the phone's invention, makes so bitingly clear:

> It is my heart-warmed and world-embracing Christmas hope and aspiration that all of us, the high, the low, the rich, the poor, the admired, the despised, the loved, the hated, the civilized, the savage (every man and brother of us all throughout the whole earth), may eventually be gathered together in a heaven of everlasting rest and peace and bliss, except the inventor of the telephone.

But for all the Twains who want to cut us off, there are millions if not billions who cherish the miracle of being able to make contact with friends and family instantly, for a good laugh, sound advice or a word of comfort in times of trouble; the convenience of arranging a holiday, booking theatre

---

[102] 'Many a man wishes he were strong enough to tear a telephone book in half – especially if he has a teenage daughter.' – Canadian violinist Guy Lombardo

tickets, complaining about poor service; and the absolute necessity of getting instant help when there's been a terrible accident or crime, or a child is sick in the night. And I suspect that those tragic victims of the 9/11 attacks who called their loved ones, so poignantly, in their final moments would have no doubt of the phone's huge worth.

#15 Zero

Until quite recently, zero was not much thought of in the history of ideas. It is quite literally nothing and so doesn't draw attention to itself. It's almost asking to be ignored. 'Nothing will come of nothing', Shakespeare's King Lear warns his taciturn daughter, Cordelia. Moreover, zero seems to be so self-evident, as obvious as 1, 2, 3 and any other number, that it hardly qualifies as an idea. In fact, it's very far from obvious. Its discovery was slow and painful and science historians have just begun to acknowledge what a crucial breakthrough the finding of zero was.

When numbers were first developed in the ancient world, there was no need for zero. People needed numbers to know how many cattle they had, or how many bags of grain they owed to the tax collector. They didn't need a number to know they hadn't got any cattle and that they didn't have to pay any tax. And yet there is a problem with a number system that doesn't have zero.

Nowadays, we use zero in two ways. One is as the number zero: the number nothing or nought, the number exactly half way between −1 and +1. The other is as a 'place-holder'. It's the zero we put on the end of a number to indicate whether it's a ten, a hundred, a thousand or so on; it's how you tell the difference between 10, 100 and 1,000. Our system is called a base ten system, since the steps are marked in multiples of ten, and the number of zeros marks the number of multiples of ten in the absence of other digits. It was as a place-holder that zero made its first tentative appearance.

The Egyptians and Greeks didn't have a place holder. The Egyptians had different symbols for single digits (a vertical line), multiples of ten (an inverted U sign) and multiples of one hundred (a spiral). This was cumbersome even for quite small numbers. 999, for instance, would need 27 symbols – 9 spirals, 9 Us and 9 lines. The Greeks were marginally slicker, since they used different letters for each multiple, rather than simply repeating them. But this was still quite cumbersome and there was a limit to the biggest number they could have.[103] Moreover, it was hard doing arithmetic with them.

The Babylonians used a number system that worked, in some ways, like an abacus, making calculations easier. But instead of being based on ten like our numbers, their system was based on 60, which means the numbers went in multiples of 60. Initially, they could only tell which multiple it was – whether it was, say, 1, 60, or 3,600 – by the context, since they were all indicated by the same single mark. Then they started

---

[103] This was a myriad or 10,000. Archimedes, in trying to reckon how many sand grains there are in the world, found an ingenious way around this, by using multiples of myriads. His intention was to show that however many grains of sand there are in the world, it is a real number, not a limitless infinity.

adding little snicks to indicate which it was – in other words, place-holders.

It seems strange then that the Greeks, with all their mathematical skills, didn't adopt the zero. In his book *Zero: The Biography of a Dangerous Idea*, Charles Seife argues that the whole idea of zero was anathema to the Greeks because it indicated both the void and the infinite – which contradicted their world view in which the Earth, the planets and the stars are held together in near concentric circles, like the layers of an onion. 'The infinite and the void had powers that frightened the Greeks', claims Seife. 'The infinite threatened to make all motion impossible, while the void threatened to smash the nutshell universe into a thousand flinders.' Yet there was a more basic problem with zero. It would have upset the arithmetic logic which the Greek mathematicians were so brilliantly constructing.[104]

---

[104] It led Zeno in the fifth century to create the most famous of his paradoxes. In it Zeno proves that even running at his fastest, Achilles can never catch up with a tortoise. He does this by showing how far each runs in increments. Achilles runs at a foot per second and the tortoise at half that speed. The tortoise is given a foot's head start. In the first second, Achilles runs a foot, but the tortoise has moved ahead half a foot, too, so is still ahead. In the next half second, Achilles has run that half foot, but the tortoise has moved a quarter of a foot further on. In the next quarter of a second, Achilles runs a quarter of a foot, but the tortoise has moved on a further eighth of a foot. You can go on like this for smaller and smaller distances. Yet Achilles will, of course, never catch up. Of course, everyone knows Achilles would catch up quickly, but it was hard for the Greeks to find a flaw in Zeno's logic. The reason they couldn't is that they didn't have zero, and so no concept of a limit. Once we know the journey has a limit, and that the limit is zero, we don't have to go on dividing the fractions infinitesimally. So the paradox disappears.

Add any number to itself enough times, Archimedes reasoned, for instance, and it will exceed any other number. That's not so with zero. Similarly, if you multiply one number by another, you only have to reverse the process to get back to the originals. So 6 times 3 = 18 and 18 divided by 3 = 6. But zero throws this out too. 6 times 0 = 0, yet 0 divided by 6 is not 6, it is 0. And that's just the beginning of the problems with zero. It seems to imply that the whole logic of arithmetic is flawed. No wonder the Greeks chose to ignore it.

In India, however, they had no such problems, because, after working with the Greek numbering system, they switched to a system that was like that of the Babylonians, only based on the Greek 10 not the Babylonian 60. It's not clear exactly when it first appeared, but by the seventh century, if not earlier, the Indians were using a dot as a place holder, so 10 would be written '**1.**' and 100, '**1..**'. What was good about this system was that it allowed the Indians to make calculations very rapidly, in the same way in which we are taught to multiply and divide things at school.

It also freed the Indians to see numbers in abstract arithmetic terms rather than the geometric terms which the Greeks did. The Greeks would have had trouble taking 3 acres from a 2-acre field because that made no sense; but the Indian mathematicians were comfortable taking 3 from 2 and getting −1. With negative numbers in place, zero as a number was a logical arrival, slotting in between −1 and +1. Its earliest known appearance is in the astronomical treatise the *Brahmasphutasiddhanta* (*The Opening of the Universe*), written in the year 628 AD by one of the most brilliant mathematicians of the ancient world, Brahmagupta,[105] and it is he who is sometimes known as the Father of Zero. Brahmagupta noted some key properties of zero, such as: 'When zero is added to a number or subtracted from a number, the number remains unchanged; and a number multiplied by zero becomes zero.'

The Indian numbers, with their base ten and their zero place-holder, were so supple and effective for calculations that they were adopted across the Islamic empire after they were championed in Baghdad by al-Khwarizmi and al-Kindi in the ninth century. Fibonacci, also known as Leonardo of Pisa, promoted the system in Europe in his book *Liber Abaci* (the *Book of the Abacus or Calculation*), but it didn't come into widespread use here until the invention of printing in the fifteenth century.

It now seems so simple and obvious that we cannot imagine counting or calculating any other way, yet it was a remarkable step forward. The great eighteenth-century French mathematician Pierre Laplace wrote:

It is India that gave us the ingenious method of expressing all numbers by the means of ten symbols, each symbol receiving a value of position, as well as an absolute value; a profound and important idea which appears so simple to us now that we ignore its true merit, but

---

[105] Brahmagupta was born in Rajasthan in 598. He is known as an astronomer but there was at that time no real distinction between mathematics and astronomy, since the main purpose of maths was to better calculate the motions of the stars. Besides his pioneering of the number zero, Brahmagupta is famous for his work on quadratic equations and his method for finding square roots.

its very simplicity, the great ease which it has lent to all computations, puts our arithmetic in the first rank of useful inventions, and we shall appreciate the grandeur of this achievement when we remember that it escaped the genius of Archimedes and Apollonius, two of the greatest minds produced by antiquity.

By Laplace's time both 0 the number and 0 the place-holder were absolutely central to mathematics. None of the great achievements of mathematics would have been possible without it. And yet the logical problems of zero the number had not yet been resolved. It still embodied contradictions which threatened the amazing new mathematics of calculus, contradictions such as dividing by zero which mathematicians had to ignore, seeing only that calculus worked even if it was at heart illogical.

The problems with the zero – and its mysterious twin the infinite – seemed to have been solved in the nineteenth century, only for them to re-emerge in quantum mechanics and relativity, when scientists began to push mathematics about the atom and the universe – the infinitely small and the infinitely large – to its limits.

Quantum mechanics, in particular, seemed to indicate a breakdown in the logic that has been central to our drive to understand the universe in which we live. As Richard Feynman noted: 'The problem is, when we calculate all the way down to zero distance, the equation blows up in our face and gives us meaningless answers – things like infinity. This caused a lot of trouble when the theory of quantum electrodynamics first came out. People were getting infinity for every problem they tried to calculate.'

Meanwhile, there are other problems that crop up when the infinite universe is chased back to its beginning with a zero, at the Big Bang. These logical barriers that maths seems to come up with at the extremes seem to some to indicate that if we can solve the logical problems connected with zero, then maybe it will unlock some profound truth about our existence.

#14 Democracy

No words seem to endorse the thrilling power of the democratic ideal more resonantly than the closing sentence of US President Abraham Lincoln's brief speech in honour of the dead in the legendary American Civil War Battle of Gettysburg in 1863. 'We here highly resolve that these dead shall not have died in vain – that this nation, under God, shall have a new birth of freedom – and that government: of the people, by the people, for the people, shall not perish from the earth.'

Lincoln's ringing words seem so heroic and so simple that it is hard to see how anyone could deny the righteousness of democracy. Indeed, since Lincoln's day, democracy has become such a mantra for fair and enlightened government that, in the Western world at least, nations are thought of poorly if they do not live up to certain standards of democracy. And undemocratic behaviour by a politician or organisation tends to automatically be seen as wrong.[106]

The idea of democracy seems to have originated in the Ancient Greek city of Athens, reaching its height in the fifth century BC in the time of Pericles. But in Ancient Greece, democracy meant something different from what we think of as democracy today. Democracy today usually means *representative* democracy, in which government is delegated to a small number of people elected by the rest. The original Ancient Greek idea was *direct* democracy – that is, the passing of laws not by elected representatives but through a direct vote by the people.

Of course, in the Ancient Athens of Pericles, direct democracy was practical because only a tiny minority of Athenian citizens were actually considered eligible to join the Assembly of the People. Such a system might just work in small city states, but was totally impractical in large nation states. After the defeat of Athens by the Spartans, moreover, the Greek idea of democracy fell into disrepute, especially when attempts to

---

[106] Interestingly, when America's founders framed their Declaration of Independence, sometimes thought of as the starting point of modern democracy, not all of them focused on democratic ideals. They intended America to be primarily a republic that championed liberty and rights, not a democracy. 'A democracy,' wrote Thomas Jefferson, 'is nothing more than mob rule, where fifty-one percent of the people may take away the rights of the other forty-nine.' Another of America's founding fathers, John Adams, was if anything more damning: 'Democracy ... while it lasts is more bloody than either [aristocracy or monarchy]. Remember, democracy never lasts long. It soon wastes, exhausts, and murders itself. There is never a democracy that did not commit suicide.' For them, the purpose of elections was as the most reliable way of keeping the government 'more or less republican' in nature, not the embodiment of a great ideal.

restore democracy led to the persecution of the great philosopher Socrates. The treatment of Socrates turned his student Plato into a vehement critic of democracy. Democracy, for Plato, was the tyranny of the masses, in which minorities were abused by the mob majority, and Plato's student Aristotle echoed his views.[107]

For 2,000 years, democracy was largely abandoned as an intellectual idea. Enlightened thinkers championed instead the moral obligations of monarchs and oligarchs, and how people should be best ruled by the one or by the few. In the Middle Ages and beyond, however, an alternative route to democracy, the democracy of delegation, gradually emerged in the English notion of parliament, moved not by theoretical ideas but pragmatic demands. Parliaments had started in the Nordic world as assemblies of noblemen, but the English parliament in particular was forced to acquire a wider constituency under the pressure of broadening prosperity, as first lords and then prosperous farmers fought to rein in the power of the monarch, especially over taxes.

In the eighteenth century, two great English thinkers, John Locke and Thomas Hobbes, began to explore the intellectual and moral implications of this representative democracy. Locke argued that there must be a 'social contract' among

---

[107] Plato also argued that democracy tends to undermine the expertise needed to govern society well, encouraging only those who are expert at winning elections. Plato finds a remarkable modern echo in the criticism that the party leaders' debates on television reduced the 2010 British elections into a political *X Factor*, turning on presentation and a winning smile, not policies and expertise. The awkward-looking Gordon Brown, in particular, felt disadvantaged by this, trying to negate it by asserting: 'If it's all about style and PR, count me out.'

those who have 'consented to make one community or government ... wherein the majority have the right to act and conclude the rest'. These two ideas, the consent of the governed and majority rule, have become the central planks of democracy, although Locke did not use the word 'democracy' himself.

Locke didn't specify the form that consent would take, and it took a little while for the philosophers of the Enlightenment, radicals of the eighteenth century such as Thomas Paine, and the profound upheavals of the French and other revolutions to help the idea of representative democracy to clearly emerge. But in 1820, Scottish philosopher James Mill proclaimed 'the system of representation' to be 'the grand discovery of modern times', while his son John Stuart Mill later declared that representative democracy was the 'ideal type of a perfect government'. The gradual shift of Western governments towards democracy over the next century, though, was perhaps as much to do with the failure of other systems as with the perceived benefits of representative democracy.

With the victory of the Allies after the First World War, for instance, the time of kings and counts seemed finally to have passed. With the Second World War, the lure of fascism was extinguished. And in the 1990s, communism collapsed and economic failure drove many South American dictators from power. All the time, the spread of market economies drained power from centralised institutions, it seems, and delivered more into the hands of the middle and working classes.

In 1972, just 40 countries could be described as democracies. But a wave of liberalisations, from the Indonesian Revolution of 1998 to the Cedar Revolution in Lebanon in

2005, has dramatically boosted the number of democratic countries to 123. In the 1990s, American philosopher Francis Fukuyama predicted that liberal democracy will eventually take over the world, leading to what he described as the 'End of History'.

But the road to democracy is not proving quite as one-way and rapid as expected. Russia's leaders are developing their own brand of oligarchy, which they call 'sovereign' democracy. China is not moving as obviously towards democracy as people once thought. The Tulip Revolutions in Kyrgyzstan and the Orange Revolution in the Ukraine have not gone quite as expected and many African countries, such as Zimbabwe, have failed to develop the genuinely democratic institutions once hoped for.

What's more disturbing for champions of democracy is that democratic experiments often demonstrably fail to improve people's lives. 'Millions now believe that they run more risk of being killed or remaining poor under an electoral system than under a dictatorship,' writes Humphrey Hawksley in *Democracy Kills*. 'The average income in authoritarian China, for example, is now twice that of democratic India. In the same way, Haitians who are allowed to elect their government live twenty years less than those in dictatorial Cuba where average life expectancy is seventy-seven years.'

In Iraq and Afghanistan, American foreign policy seems to be predicated on the belief that if they can establish democracy there, these countries will become safe, stable and prosperous. That, they say, is what happened after the Second World War in Germany and Japan. But the historical evidence is not entirely on their side.

In both Japan and Germany, it seems that American policies were more punitive than encouraging, and the drive towards democracy in Germany came from the German people, not from their American conquerors. Political scientist James L. Payne suggests that democracy evolves when people are 'ready' for it, which means, essentially, that their leaders have given up employing force against each other, and democracy is the 'default' mode of settling disputes. That, perhaps, is why it may take a long time to achieve in Iran and Afghanistan.

So if countries arrive at democracy essentially by default, what's so great about it – and why shouldn't it be consciously replaced with other systems? John Stuart Mill put three key arguments in its favour. The first is that democracy forces the decision-makers to take notice of most people's interests and rights. Indian thinker Amartya Sen argues that 'no substantial famine has ever occurred in any independent country with a democratic form of government and a relatively free press'. The second is that democracy is more likely to lead to the right decisions, because instead of just a few people judging the effectiveness of policies, it is the maximum possible number. Mill's third argument is that democracy encourages people to think for themselves, and to think rationally and carefully about the consequences of their decisions.

For many people, though, the experience of democracy is not half as empowering as Mill hoped, bringing more a sense of powerlessness than empowerment. When cast against thousands or even millions of others, their single vote seems a futile gesture. Moreover, the political process seems to drive politicians towards similar ways of looking at things, leading Gore Vidal to say, cynically, that: 'Democracy is supposed to give you the feeling of choice, like Painkiller X and Painkiller Y. But they're both just aspirin.' Mahatma Gandhi argued that democracy was not even what really mattered. 'What difference does it make to the dead, the orphans, and the homeless, whether the mad destruction is wrought under the name of totalitarianism or the holy name of liberty or democracy?'

Yet whatever the flaws in democracy, and they are many, Lincoln's simple summation of its values still makes more sense of a way to run society than any other. It has proved the most capable of moving forward of any political system; the most capable of giving its citizens freedom and a sense of control over their lives; and the most capable of having the moral authority to create laws. It may not be able to save nations from war. It may not be able to save people who live under it from privation or ill health. It may not even be able to save people from injustice. But if nations and their people do suffer from any of these misfortunes, democracy maximises the chances of those responsible being held accountable.

#13 The Wheel

The wheel is the apocryphal starting point of civilisation – the breakthrough invention. Once the wheel was invented, mankind was on a roll and it was progress all the way to the modern age – and maybe, one suspects, towards the automobile which was seen as the pinnacle of human progress at the time when the invention of the wheel began to be heralded.

Because of the perceived importance of the wheel, many people telling the story of its invention have been tempted to fill in the gaps with pure speculation. The interest is especially in cartwheels. Experts describe in detail how the cartwheel must have been invented. Heavy loads, the scenario goes, were originally dragged on sledges with runners. This, modern experiments show (but no archaeological evidence does), was how the great stones were hauled to Stonehenge. Then some bright spark had the idea of laying down tree trunks as rollers beneath them. It would have been a laborious practice, since you'd have to continually carry the rollers round from the back to the front. Then maybe someone thought of trapping the rollers between two pegs. And then, finally, someone turned the trapped rollers into wheels and axles. The cart was invented.[108]

Yet there is almost no evidence that this is how it happened. The closest thing to it is an ancient pictogram from Uruk, in Iraq, the site of one of the earliest Sumerian civilisations. The pictograms date from about 5,500 years ago and clearly show a sledge. They also clearly show what looks like a sledge on wheels. And neither sledge, with or without wheels, looks much like what we'd call a cart. Interestingly, Sumerian cuneiform script also shows how the symbol for a 'sledge' did indeed look like a sledge – and this evolved into the symbol for a 'cart' which looked like a sledge on wheels. There is no evidence whatsoever for the rollers. Indeed, there just weren't the trees to make such rollers in Mesopotamia where the wheel is supposed to have been invented!

---

[108] Johnny Hart's *B.C.* cartoon strip brilliantly satirises this with his prehistoric wheel. A prehistoric inventor invents a stone wheel, but lacking any purpose, any roads, anything to transport, or any draught animals to pull him, he simply stands on the axles as if on a strange unicycle without pedals.

Interestingly, the thinking that links the invention of the cart and the rise of civilisation with Mesopotamia isn't actually quite backed up by archaeological evidence, either. There is actually evidence for carts in eastern Europe, far from 'civilisation', just as old as that in Mesopotamia. At Bronocice in Poland, for instance, a ceramic vase dating from 5100–5450 BC was found showing what looks like five four-wheeled carts, while clay models from Hungary up to 5,600 years old show clear pictures of four-wheel carts. Then there are some full-sized wooden wheels from around the same date that have been found in Switzerland and Slovenia. And most impressive of all, there are remains of complete wagons from the Novotitorovka culture in the Caucasus in Georgia, also dating from maybe 5,500 years ago.

The argument is that the technology of the cart was so marvellous that it spread rapidly across Europe and Eurasia, and later on to India and China. There is some evidence for this, interestingly, in the very word 'wheel', which is strikingly similar in languages across Eurasia. The Sumerian for wheel was *girgir*, the Hebrew *galgal*, the Georgian *gorgal* and the Proto-Indo-European $*k^wel- k^wel$. Even the Chinese bears some similarity, with the Mandarin being *gulu* and the Cantonese *gukluk*. All of this suggests at least a connection.

Yet the idea that the cartwheel was the breakthrough invention that kick-started technology doesn't seem to stand much scrutiny. Why, for instance, did places like Europe and Georgia remain firmly prehistoric long after the arrival of the cart? And why in Sumeria, the place where the wheel was apparently invented, do carts seem to have been used mainly as hearses? It took 1,000 years before carts were widely used for the transport of goods in Mesopotamia and equally long before they began to be used as moving platforms for javelin throwers in battle.

Perhaps there is a simple explanation for this delay. Carts are virtually useless without proper wide tracks, and even the best cart-tracks frequently become impassable in bad weather. Until suitable roads developed, pack animals were a much better way of carrying goods. Tellingly, while Roman roads ensured people in Europe carried on using carts, the use of carts for transport was almost entirely abandoned over much of the Middle East – including Mesopotamia – after the intro-duction of camels. Camels were much better for travelling through desert and drier areas. Oxcarts are very slow, and the oxen need lots of water and grass.

There is another aspect of the wheel story that is worth considering. The first wheel invented may not have been a cartwheel at all, but the potter's wheel. A stone potter's wheel found at the Mesopotamian city of Ur dates back at least 5,100 years, and there are even older fragments of pottery clearly thrown on a wheel. Some experts suggest that the pot-ter's wheel was in use up to 10,000 years ago. If so, that would make it twice as old as the cartwheel. The suggestion is that the cartwheel was created, eventually, when someone thought of turning the horizontal potter's wheel on its side. If so, it took them a very long time. It's more likely that the cartwheel was introduced only when there was a need for it.[109]

---

[109] A cartwheel is not simply a potter's wheel turned vertically. Scientifically, they are very different. A potter's wheel simply keeps the clay always at the same place relative to the potter's hand as it rotates. The cartwheel is essen-tially a lever. Imagine sticking a crowbar under a heavy box. You could lever

This is perhaps the crucial thing about the history of ideas, especially technology. There is a lot of truth to the old adage 'necessity is the mother of invention'. Ideas tend not to just pop up randomly from nothing; they are typically a response to a need. Or if they do emerge when they are not really needed, they are usually forgotten rather than setting a new agenda. Back in the first century AD, for instance, Hero of Alexander experimented with steam power, but it was another 1,800 years before its benefits were really appreciated and it turned from a vague idea into a solid technology.

The same is partially true of the wheel. Wheels were widely used in the Roman and Middle Ages, both in watermills and for carts, but they weren't necessarily key technologies. Civilisations could manage perfectly well without the wheel – a fact to which the early civilisations of the Americas bear witness. None of the great civilisations of the Americas used wheeled transport at all. It wasn't even as if they didn't know about the wheel. Charming little toy dogs and other animals on wheels have been found there dating back to 200 BC. But for the early Americans, wheels were just playthings. For real work, legs (both human and animal) were far more practical.

---

it forward bit by bit. A cartwheel works by allowing you to do this continuously. Moreover, it allows you to use the cart's own weight to help it along, because the wheel 'falls' forward once it is moving. It's sometimes said that a wheel reduces friction. That isn't true. A wheel relies on friction between the rim and the ground to keep turning. If there was no friction, it would simply skid. There is also friction between the wheel and the axle (hence the importance of greased bearings). But what it does is concentrate the friction into one small spot where the rim touches the ground, and use the full leverage of the wheel to overcome it. The bigger the wheel, the greater the leverage.

It's not that wheels are not a great idea. It's just that their true worth has really become apparent only in the last two centuries, some 5,000–10,000 years after they were invented. Wheels came into their own in the Industrial Age, and it is no coincidence, perhaps, that the beginning of this age is called the Industrial Revolution. People drew their image for this dramatic change from the whirring, turning wheels which suddenly seemed to be everywhere, in every factory and every machine, and carrying along the trains which whisked goods to the markets and people to the new cities of the age.

Wheels, crucially, enabled the shift from muscle power to machine power that marks out our modern industrial era, and with the present machine age, wheels have at last found their role. Wheels can be driven round by water, by steam power, by electric power, by petrol engines. In machines, their rotary motion means that an engine, which can push only in one or two directions, can go on and on pushing or pulling continuously, without moving from the spot. In transport, their rotary motion translates the push and pull of the engine into continuous movement along the ground.

There is barely a machine that does not have a wheel somewhere. It may be the tiny wheel that keeps the fan in your computer blowing. It may be the invisible roller that snatches your credit card when you withdraw money from the ATM. Or it may be something much bigger, like the giant wheels on the earth shifters in Alberta's tar sands pits, or the world's biggest tourist wheel in Singapore (165 metres high). Yet perhaps the most crucial of all, nowadays, are the rotors of electricity generators. Without these wheels, we'd have no electric power at all. The transport of the future might run on cushions of magnetic levitation, and not wheels, but the electric motors and generators that drive them and generate the levitation still need to turn.

#12 Logic

In the *Star Trek* TV series, all the human characters laughed at the Vulcan Spock indulgently because he was able to see things only from a logical point of view. The implication was that logic is a dull trap which humans with their illogical bent can escape with brilliant insight. It's nonsense, of course. Logic has been deeply involved in pretty much every advance in human knowledge. Logic and reason are also the soundest of all guides against folly.

As American jurist Oliver Wendell Holmes put it memorably: 'Reason means truth and those who are not governed by it take the chance that someday the sunken fact will rip the bottom out of their boat.' Actually he was wrong to say that reason means 'truth', since you can only arrive at the right answer by reason and logic, not the truth, but his thrust was memorably clear. Logic and reason are the best possible protection against mistakes. You might believe that you won't get run over if you stand in front of a speeding train because maybe the train will swerve around you ... but logic will tell you that it won't.

We actually use logic all the time, sometimes well, sometimes badly, to help us make decisions, to persuade people, to try to understand things. You might say, for instance, to chivvy along someone who believes they have all the time in the world to get ready: 'If we don't go in five minutes, we're going to miss the start of the show.' But there is a big difference between this kind of casual logic and the much more disciplined logic that philosophers and mathematicians aim for.

This disciplined or formal logic has rules that need to be followed carefully. Formal in this context doesn't mean the opposite of casual; it means that it follows forms, or rather patterns, that guard you against error. Logic is essentially the science of analysing forms of argument and finding principles on which inferences can be made.

An argument uses inference to move from accepted beginnings or 'premises' to a particular conclusion. If the premises are valid, then the validity of the conclusion depends on the strength of the inference. Logic's central task is to weed out the weak inference from the strong.

Over 2,000 years ago, Aristotle set out the basic rules that guided logic until the last century. The central model of Aristotle's logic was the syllogism. Syllogism is an argument containing three elements or 'propositions' – two premises and a conclusion. To cite the classic example: 'All men are mortal; the Greeks are men; therefore Greeks are mortal.' The content is irrelevant; it's the form that matters. It could just as easily be expressed as symbols: 'All Xs are Y; Zs are Xs; therefore Zs are Y.'

There is a crucial distinction between 'deductive' logic and 'inductive' logic, however. Deductive logic is concerned only with the form of an argument, never with the content. The idea is to find forms under which, if the premise is true, the conclusion is guaranteed to be, regardless of the subject matter. If it works, the argument is said to be valid and, if the premises are also true, the conclusion is said to be sound. Some logicians argue that this is the only kind of formal logic.

Inductive logic infers from things that have been observed in the world. You might infer, for instance, that because you had only ever observed white swans all swans are white. This seems a reasonable proposition, based on what you've seen, but it is not a valid inference because the conclusion is not inevitable. Of course, further observation would show that some swans are black. So there is always scope for error with inductive logic.

Inductive logic always seeks to extend premises, whereas deductive logic draws all its information from the premises alone, simply reforming the terms. If your train to work has arrived five minutes late every day for the last six years, for instance, it is logical (inductively) to infer that it will arrive five minutes late today – but of course it is not, as it should be with deductive logic, inevitable. Sod's Law will tell you that the one time in five years you are a few minutes late reaching the station, your train will actually be on time …

Despite its shortcomings, inductive reasoning is pretty much essential for science and most other intellectual disciplines. Indeed, the vast majority of scientific laws are derived inductively. The eighteenth-century Scottish philosopher David Hume argued that in fact the whole idea of scientific laws is inductive rather than deductive.[110] We don't know for

---

[110] There is a philosophical argument beyond this about even the validity of logic. In the seventeenth century, Descartes intended to set a bedrock, the ultimate irreducible logical statement about existence with his famous, *cogito ergo sum*, 'I think therefore I am'. But philosophers since have criticised his logic. They say that he infers too much from his statement. Descartes is,

certain, Hume pointed out, that nature is uniform and that things we've observed to be true will stay as they are. It's essentially about probabilities. Just because things fall to Earth with the acceleration due to gravity of 9.8 m/s, they may not always do so – but they probably will. The validity of reasoning inductively still provokes arguments among scientists and philosophers, but if theoretically it is flawed, in practice it is indispensable.

It's a mistake to think that because inductive logic doesn't have to be internally consistent like deductive logic, the rules are loose. In some ways, its demands are even more exacting, because there are so many more potential pitfalls. Science, for instance, may start with observations, but the inferences a scientist makes from those observations must be logical, or the process fails. A meteorologist might observe that the driest months of the year are June and July, but it would be wrong, of course, to infer that it was because both months begin with the letter J.

Logic can be used both to correct fallacies in scientific theories, when flaws in an argument are detected, and to create entirely new theories by logical extension. Even the most well-established and seemingly incontrovertible scientific truths can be adjusted like this. When Einstein spotted the

_____

for instance, not entitled logically to infer that it is he who is thinking; only that there is thinking going on. And could you be fooled into thinking that other people are thinking when in fact it's just you? Moreover, Descartes goes on from this to assert that the clarity of logic is evidence that it must be true, and that logic is true because God would not deceive us so fundamentally. This, many people have argued, is a circular argument, which is why Descartes' *cogito ergo sum* has in some ways become a symbol, ultimately, of uncertainty rather than the basic bedrock he intended.

limitations of Newton's laws of motion and gravitation and then devised his theories of relativity, for instance, he did so entirely on the basis of logical argument. Only later were his arguments vindicated by actual evidence.[111]

What makes logic so powerful and so crucial is that, if used well, it is an entirely objective teacher. The limitation is that we cannot always see the flaws in the logic. Indeed, many of us either consciously or subconsciously avoid looking for them if they seem to contradict our world view or make life difficult. That's why it took 1,800 years after the Greek thinker Aristarchus first suggested it for the world to catch up and accept that the Earth travels around the Sun.

It's not just in science, of course, that we use and misuse logic. Logic is the way we order our thoughts and make sense of the world. As we grow up, our eyes learn to interpret things we see, from recognising particular arrangements of lines and shadows as three-dimensional boxes to identifying faces as

---

[111] Interestingly, even the brilliant Einstein failed to follow through with his logic in his General Theory of 1915 when it seemed to contradict his 'common sense' view that the universe is unchanging, adding an abstract 'cosmological constant' to balance the inward pull of gravity in the universe. In 1922, the young Russian mathematician Alexander Friedmann did follow the logic of Einstein's theory through and rather than adding the illogical cosmological constant concluded that the reason that the universe is not collapsing under its own gravity is because it is being flung apart. By logical extension – classic inductive reasoning – Friedmann reasoned that the universe must have started as a tiny point, then expanded. Even Einstein pooh-poohed this at the time. But nine years later, observations by the astronomer Hubble showed that the universe really is expanding, just as Friedmann had argued, and the Big Bang theory is now well established. Einstein was the first to admit that he had been wrong. Sadly, Friedmann had died of typhoid six years earlier.

friendly or hostile. So logic helps us find our way through the world. Logical argument is, also, if our use of logic is good, an invaluable way of checking if our insights, however arrived at, are actually correct. And, of course, it can be a very effective way of justifying our ideas to other people. Indeed, logic can seem so powerfully persuasive that all of us bring it into our everyday conversation all the time.[112]

Immanuel Kant insisted that even casual reasoning should be considered logic. Logic, he argued, is simply the science of good judgement. Others, however, insist that only the formal discipline is real logic. Most people, in their everyday reasoning, are influenced by Aristotle's formal logic with its syllogisms. Over the last two centuries, however, formal logic has developed in new directions that are much less familiar to those outside academic circles, but have taken it into new and important areas.

One of the key breakthroughs was German mathematician Gottlob Frege's attempts to deal with the problem of 'multiple generality' in the 1870s. Classical logic can deal well with unambiguous quantities and connections such as *if*,

---

[112] This everyday logic is prone to fallacies which a trained logician would spot instantly, but most of us slip into (or get away with) all the time. There are false dilemmas: 'Either we put a cap on immigration or we'll all be out of jobs', which wrongly implies that there are only two alternatives. There are slippery slopes: 'If we legalise cannabis, youngsters will move on to hard drugs and the streets will soon be littered with drug addicts', which of course wrongly implies one as a logical extension of the other. There are straw men: 'Global warming cannot be happening because it is colder this summer than it has been for a century', which sets up a false target in order to knock it down. But if some of these pitfalls can be avoided, logic is one of the best ways of finding common ground and finding good, practical solutions to problems that work for all.

then, and and *not*, but it was not really understood just why it often broke down with generalities such as *some* and *every*. We can instantly see there's something wrong with the following proposition: If every boy loves games of football, then some games of football are loved by every boy. But classical logic finds it hard to say just why this doesn't work. The problem is partly with the language. Frege's solution was his idea of *Begriffsschrift* (concept writing) in which he developed a system of symbols that were entirely independent of language, such as 'quantifiers' (symbols for words such as *every, some, most* and so on).

At the same time, English mathematician George Boole was developing an entirely mathematical system of logic, now called Boolean logic, which was to form the basis of operations in all modern computers. Without this kind of logic, there would be no computers. The logic of Boole and Frege also had a profound influence on the direction of modern philosophy, and in particular the development of an approach to philosophy called analytic philosophy, with its emphasis on complete clarity and logic in arguments, that dominated the English-speaking world in the last century.

It's easy to see the limitations of logic. As Blaise Pascal said: 'The last function of reason is to recognize that there are an infinity of things which surpass it.' It is easy to see the absurdities, too, as Tweedledee demonstrates so eloquently in Lewis Carroll's *Through the Looking Glass*. '"Contrariwise," continued Tweedledee, "if it was so, it might be: and if it were so it would be; but as it isn't, it ain't. That's logic."' Yet it remains at the heart of human thought and progress, and the best possible corrective to some of the wilder follies of the imagination.

#11 Hope

In the myth of Pandora's box, the Ancient Greeks pinpointed Hope as the gods' one crucial gift to help us deal with all the evil and suffering that she had unwittingly unleashed on the world. But hope is a slippery customer. You might hope that it's going to be sunny this afternoon, only to be soaked to the skin when you go out without a coat. You might hope that the ring on the door means the postman is bringing your birthday present, only to find it's just a bill. You may hope that the financial crisis is going to end, only to discover that the stock market has plummeted and the currency is nose-diving.

Hope, then, is a deceiver. It fills you with false expectations and then fails to deliver. So why should we think hope a good thing? Surely it is better to be realistic, accept that things are as they are, and deal with the hard present rather than getting diverted by a fanciful future or, worse still, a sentimental past?

Many of the Ancient Greeks believed fate decreed that life is unchangeable. So hope must be an illusion, and evil. To the playwright Aeschylus, hope was 'the food of exiles'. To Euripides, it was 'man's curse'. Two and a half thousand years later, Friedrich Nietzsche infamously said with startling bleakness in *Human, All Too Human* (1878): 'In reality, hope is the worst of all evils, because it prolongs man's torments.'

Ever since, Nietzsche has been seen as a dismal black raven of despair – or a comic Cassandra croaking, 'Doomed, we're all doomed!' But actually, this is unfair to Nietzsche. He wasn't saying hope is pointless at all. What he was railing against was what he saw as the false hope played out by Paul in the Christian Bible; the Paul who says that the three great gifts given to mankind are faith, hope and love. That hope, Nietzsche said, was a delusion which prevented action in the present because of promises for the future – and actually hope simply masked a desire for revenge on those who had oppressed the Christians. Worse, it destroyed real hope by its deceit.

Whether you agree with Nietzsche or not, he alerts us to a key problem with hope. Pinning hopes on the wrong thing appears to be more damaging than no hope at all. At best, you can appear a misguided fantasist, or a foolish dreamer like Don Quixote, who hopes his vision of the world is a reality. At worst, it can make you into a Hitler.

The dilemma is how to tell what is good hope and what is bad. This may be a question of evaluation. Millions of people enter the lotteries around the world on a regular basis. Of course, when they buy their ticket, they hope to win. The odds vary from lottery to lottery, but typically if they buy one ticket a week they might expect to win the jackpot once every 250,000 years – after which time, they would have spent far, far more than the jackpot is worth (even if they had the gifts of immortality and staggering patience). It is possible to calculate these odds, and so evaluate how realistic the hope of winning is. You might know these odds, and still choose to go ahead, because you had no other hope of escaping poverty, or because the cost of a ticket is, for you, negligible.

However, it is not always easy to evaluate hope. In hindsight, Leonardo da Vinci with his fantastic drawings of machines such as his ornithopter (flying machine) seems like a prescient genius. But what if such machines had never come to pass? His contemporaries must have thought some of his ideas rather nutty, if they ever got to see them, and maybe they'd be right.

Perhaps, though, the crucial point about hope is not so much whether it's realistic or unrealistic, but its effect on motivation and confidence. A recent study showed that college students who were low in hope in their first year performed significantly worse in their degree exams three years later, even after controlling for intelligence, other personality traits and previous performance, than other students. It's no accident that the word 'hopeless' is also used to mean useless.

Similarly, a medical study of lung cancer patients reported in March 2010 seemed to confirm what many doctors had thought – that patients do better if they are hopeful. The study showed that over five years, optimistic patients diagnosed with lung cancer survived over six months longer than pessimistic patients. Other studies have shown that people who are low on hope tend to be anxious and depressed.

What this seems to show is that looking at things entirely pragmatically doesn't work for us. It makes us ill, or unable to perform. T.S. Eliot put it poignantly in *Burnt Norton*: '... human kind / Cannot bear very much reality.' But maybe it's simpler than that; we need to believe things can get better to motivate us to do anything different – to give us the will to act.

Sometimes, it's almost impossible to assess future possibilities accurately. Sometimes, the future possibilities seem to suggest no chance of change for the better. Sometimes a plan or idea seems too absurd to be realistic. But hope can at least provide the motivation to do something.

What hope does on a day-to-day level is give you a sense of a better time to come and thereby brings that better time into the present. It's very hard to be motivated by a plan, however logical and well worked out. We are driven by our emotions. What hope does is create the emotion in the present that makes us take the first step to realising that plan.

Interestingly, when Barack Obama was elected as US president in 2008, a key strand in his campaign was the banner of hope. His slogan, 'Yes We Can', was the embodiment of hope, and it was a great motivator. Millions of people in the USA who had never voted before went to the ballot box because Obama created a real sense of hope of change for the better. When the award of the Nobel Peace Prize to Obama quite early in his presidency was criticised, the *Minnesota Post* defended it like this: 'The spirit of hope is a powerful thing. To ridicule it is to diminish us as human beings. The Nobel Prize was awarded this year for a message of hope that essentially fed the world's commonality – its soul.'

As Martin Luther King said: 'Everything that is done in the world is done by hope.' He didn't mean everything, of course; he just meant the righting of wrongs. But that's quite a lot.

#10 Computer Programming

The computer was one of the great breakthrough inventions of the last century, and new ways in which its amazing power can be exploited are being found every day. Today we take for granted the kind of basic processing that gives our mobile phones the power to find a nearby restaurant in seconds, or create an image to send instantly to a friend on the far side of the world. Now computers are being built to completely model the flow of the world's oceans or create virtual avatars into which one day we may be able to download our entire personalities to bring us a weird electronic immortality.

The computer actually combines two different technologies: calculators and automation, and it is automation which has really given the computer wings, and automation which takes computer technology into fields far wider than simply desktop mathematics.

People have been using calculators for thousands of years. Counting with fingers or stones, tally sticks, abacuses and all kinds of things have all been used to aid calculation – and in the right hands an abacus could reckon complex sums much faster than early computers. In the seventeenth century, Blaise Pascal constructed the first mechanical calculator, called the Arithmetic Machine, to help his father do accounts, though it could only add and subtract. In 1671, Gottfried Leibniz created the *Staffelwalze* ('step-reckoner') so that 'excellent men [would not] lose hours like slaves in the labour of calculation, which could be safely relegated to anyone else if machines were used'.

Some of these early calculating devices were exquisite and ingenious but were limited in scope and prone to error, both because they could give a wrong reading and because human input was needed at every step. That's where the early nineteenth-century genius of Charles Babbage came in. Babbage's idea was to create a calculating machine that worked completely automatically, and so did away with human error. He wasn't necessarily the first to think of this, but he was the first to try to make it a practical reality with his Difference Engine – although even the Difference Engine never got further than a small-scale demonstration model.

Automation, too, had a long history before Babbage's day, as inventive minds used clever arrangements of wheels, cogs, levers and water pipes to make machines and toys perform tasks without any human intervention. Hero of Alexander was making automatic devices 1,800 years ago, while back in ninth-century Baghdad, the colourful Banu Musa brothers were creating amazing fountains that changed shape by the minute, clocks with all kinds of little gimmicks, trick jugs, flutes that played by themselves, water jugs that served drinks automatically, and even a full-size mechanical tea girl that actually served tea. By making clever use of one- or two-way self-closing and opening valves, devices for delaying action and responding to feedback, and simple mechanical memories, they created automatic control systems which are no different in essence from modern automatic machines. They used mainly water under pressure rather than electronics, but many of the operating principles are the same.

For a long while, though, automation seemed nothing more than a gimmick, creating clever toys to amuse the rich. It wasn't until the Industrial Revolution that it began to come into its own, with things like the punch card for the Jacquard loom, which had a pattern of holes to guide weaving machines to automatically weave particularly complex patterns in silk.

This is where Babbage comes in again. While the construction of Babbage's Difference Engine was proceeding in fits and starts in the 1830s, he was working on ideas for another machine, which he called the Analytic Engine. The Analytic

Engine, though never more than an idea on paper, was a huge conceptual leap from the Difference Engine.

The Difference Engine was essentially a sophisticated calculator with cogs and wheels to perform the operations; the Analytical Engine was a programmable 'mind' that could solve problems and learn from the solution how to solve them better in future. If it had ever been built, the Analytical Engine would have combined calculation with automation for the first time, and so created the first programmable computer. What Babbage needed was a way to programme his machine with instructions – and in the punch cards of the Jacquard loom, he realised in 1836, he had the answer. Punch cards could be used not only to control the working of his calculating machine, but to record results and calculation sequences permanently. In other words, it could be a memory.

Few people grasped the significance of Babbage's ideas. So it was with some gratitude that in 1843 he found a fan in Ada Lovelace, daughter of the poet Lord Byron. Ada was a self-proclaimed genius at maths and has been called the first computer programmer. It's hard to say just how much she actually contributed, but she clearly grasped the significance of Babbage's programmable 'mechanical brain' and its full possibilities, writing: 'Many persons ... imagine that because the Engine is to give its results in numerical notation, the nature of its processes must consequently be arithmetical and numerical ... This is an error. The engine can arrange and combine its numerical quantities exactly as if they were letters or any other general symbols.' She suggested it could ultimately be used for anything from playing chess to writing music.

In the end, both Babbage's and Ada Lovelace's ideas had to wait another century before they became anything like reality, both because there was no real demand for such a machine, since human 'computers' could be hired far more cheaply to do routine calculations, and because mechanical cogs and punch cards just didn't have the speed and accuracy needed, which was finally achieved with the electronic transistors and microprocessors that turned the computer into a reality in the mid-twentieth century.

It would be wrong to give sole credit to Babbage and Lovelace for the invention of computing, or even computer programming. There were many, many people who contributed, both before and since. But the nub of the central idea in computing – the idea embodied in Babbage's version of the punch card, the combination of automation and memory – is all there. It's this combination that gives the computer and its spin-offs such tremendous possibilities.

The idea can be summarised as the computer program, but that small term gives only a hint at the scope of the idea. Of course, programming has come a long way since Babbage's punch card, and now involves both pre-printed circuits and a slew of ever more sophisticated programming languages that direct a computer through binary code, the sequences of 0s and 1s, or ons and offs in its electronic circuitry.[113] But the principles are the same. On a very basic level,

---

[113] The binary code of the computer, with its 0s and 1s, is sometimes known as 'machine code', betraying its wider potential in all kinds of machines. A computer is, essentially, a machine that can respond only to very simple instructions – it can, ultimately, only be told to switch on or off in the right sequence. That's what machine code does.

programming means giving a machine instructions so that it can run itself. But if the program includes instructions for the machine to react to new input in particular ways, then it can learn and start to create its own instructions. Then the real potential of the computer and automated machines begins to be unleashed.

With the first programmable computers in the 1940s, the designers had to enter every 0 and every 1 laboriously in exactly the right order to programme the computer. Very soon, though, computer designers developed 'assembly codes' which allowed programmers to work with shorthand versions of the machine code that could be entered using text commands. But even assembly code meant the programmer had to spell out every procedure in exact and exhaustive detail, making the process very slow and prone to error, and every kind of computer had to be programmed individually.

The breakthrough was the development of 'higher level' languages which allow the programmer to write the program, known as the source, in more familiar, abstract terms. A 'compiler' program then translates the instructions into the machine code that the computer can understand. One of the first higher level languages was FORTRAN, created by John Backus in the late 1950s. FORTRAN stood for 'formula translation' because it allowed programmers to simply input mathematical formulae, rather than spelling them out in binary code. The beauty of these higher level languages is that they worked on many different computers, because they could be fed through the computer's compiler program. (Interestingly, these early programs were still fed into the computer using punch cards, just as instructions for Babbage's Analytical Engine would have been back in the 1840s.)

Since FORTRAN, computers have made giant leaps in their processing power, enabling programming languages to become more and more sophisticated, and more and more abstracted from machine code and the computer's basic hardware. Computers, of course, are now supplied with a huge range of 'software', programs that give their hardware particular instructions. Although advances in technology are crunching ever more processing power and speed into smaller units, and new developments such as 'quantum' and 'light' computing promise even more amazing capabilities, these still remain simple machines. It is up to the instructions – the programs and software – to realise these simple machines' staggering potential.

The scope of such programs is, in many ways, limited only by the imagination of the programmer, and the capabilities of the materials and operating systems involved. We already have robot vehicles that can explore distant planets and remote oceans. We have the internet that can instantly link up data from billions of computers around the world to act as a giant brain. Scientists are developing minute nano-machines that may be able to ferry drugs through the blood vessels to their target in the body, or carry out operations from the inside of the body.

In 2009, designers created a 'reconfigurable' supercomputer, the Novo-G, which can rearrange its internal circuitry to suit the task in hand, unlike the 'fixed logic' pattern of ordinary computers. That means it can turn its hand from controlling satellites to predicting the world's climate instantly, all at very high speed. Some computers are becoming so adept at language recognition that translators and secretaries may soon find themselves out of a job. Other computers are being programmed to write music or books or run rail networks or drive cars, or create imaginary worlds so convincing that we may soon find it hard to tell reality from the virtual.

Programs can create not just computers but machines of all kinds that can, in theory, do almost anything we want, and the true scope is only just beginning to be realised. Perhaps the big limitation, though, remains the programmers. Bill Bryson summed up the pitfalls perfectly in *Notes from a Big Country*: 'For a long time it puzzled me how something so expensive, so leading edge, could be so useless. And then it occurred to me that a computer is a stupid machine with the ability to do incredibly smart things, while computer programmers are smart people with the ability to do incredibly stupid things. They are, in short, a perfect match.' And maybe it is worth asking just what we really need, or want, from these stupid machines.

#9 Sewerage

No one who lived near the Thames in London in the baking summer of 1858 would have doubted that sewerage was the greatest idea ever. Thousands of newly installed flush toilets all over the city were spilling millions of gallons of ordure-filled water directly into the Thames, and cooked by the June heatwave, the river began to smell absolutely foul. So bad that the summer was remembered as the Great Stink. 'Gentility of speech is at an end – it stinks; and whoso once inhales the stink can never forget it and can count himself lucky if he lives to remember it', the newspapers reported.

People living near the river left for the country if they could or covered every window and door in perfume-soaked curtains. In the Houses of Parliament, right by the river, the stench was unbearable, despite the sheets soaked in chloride of lime covering the windows, and MPs contemplated moving the entire government to the country. As they held their noses and tried to debate, a new law to create a massive sewerage system to solve the problem was drafted and passed in just a little more than a fortnight. 'Parliament was all but compelled to legislate upon the great London nuisance by the force of sheer stench', *The Times* wrote.

The scheme they voted for was the groundbreaking work of Joseph Bazalgette. London's sewage had previously fed into ditches, some covered, some open, which slurped directly into the Thames. In places south of the river, these ditches were much lower than high tide, so the stinking soup backed up for several hours each day. Bazalgette's great scheme was to intercept these ditches before they got into the Thames with massive drains, including two running either side of the river under the newly built Victoria and Albert embankments, to carry the sewage far to the east of the city to discharge from vast tanks into the Thames estuary at low tide.

Building these great sewers was a vast undertaking, involving 318 million bricks, 880,000 cubic yards of concrete and mortar, and the excavation of 3.5 million cubic yards of earth. To them was added over 450 miles of smaller main sewers, each receiving the contents of 13,000 miles of local drains, flushing through half a million gallons of waste a day. It was an astonishing engineering feat, and worked remarkably well, removing entirely the incredible stench of ordure that had emanated through London's houses and streets for centuries, and it became a model for sewerage systems in cities around the world.

Living in modern cities today, where human waste is quickly flushed down the toilet apparently never to be seen or smelled again, it is astonishing to think just how much filth people literally lived with. It was bad enough back in the Middle Ages, when people walking through the city streets in the morning regularly had to duck to avoid the contents of night pots emptied from upstairs windows, and the streets were slippery with human and animal manure. But as cities like London grew, the problem got worse.

By Henry VIII's time, the open drains that ran down the streets, known as sewers because they ran seawards, were so smelly that the dumping of human waste into them was forbidden by law. Henceforth they were meant only for rainwater, and people were expected to deal with their own mess by building cesspits in their houses. And this of course brought its own problems. In 1660, Samuel Pepys wrote with masterly understatement that his neighbours' 'house of office' had overflowed into his cellar, 'which doth trouble me'.

By 1810, London had 200,000 cesspits and an army of euphemistically dubbed 'nightsoil men' whose job it was to empty them and sell the waste to farmers for manure. The space inside some cesspits and sewers was so cramped that the task was often delegated to young children – an occupation unimaginably more disgusting and dangerous than even shinning up and down a chimney. It must have been thoroughly unpleasant emptying chamber pots into these cesspits – a task left by many wealthier households to the unfortunate servants – and the smell emanating from the pits wafted through every house in the city.

No wonder then that the introduction of flush toilets in the early nineteenth century seemed like a godsend. No more chamber pots to empty, and the smell and the waste washed away cleanly in an instant. Every household that could afford it had a flush toilet installed as soon as possible. But there was a problem. Those flush toilets were emptying into the cesspits, and the massive amount of water they added soon filled the pits to overflowing. In some households, the foul soup simply bubbled up through the floorboards. From most it overflowed into the open drains, meant only for rainwater, and then on into the Thames.

It wasn't just the smell and the sight that became unbearable. All this sewage was flowing into the very rivers and streams that supplied the city's drinking water. Cholera and typhoid became rife. The link between cholera and contaminated drinking water was confirmed by the pioneering work of Dr John Snow after a terrible outbreak of cholera in the London district of Soho in 1854, which Snow traced to a water pump on Broad Street. After the completion of Bazalgette's sewerage system, cholera, once a major killer in London, virtually disappeared from the city. The tragic effects of this disease and typhoid elsewhere in the world today, all associated with sewage-contaminated water supplies, are perhaps the most powerful testaments to the benefits of a good sewerage system.

Bazalgette's scheme for London was not the first in the world, by any means. There is evidence of large-scale earthenware sewer pipes and brick-lined sewage drains in the Indus valley cities of 4,500–5,000 years ago. Harappa and Mohenjo-daro even had outdoor flush toilets linked to the sewage network. The Romans also had a complex sewage system designed for them by the Etruscans in the sixth century BC, which focused on the great underground drain, the Cloaca Maxima, which still exists today, and was flushed clean continually by seven rivers. The Roman historian Pliny writes that many Romans regarded the city's sewage system as its finest achievement.

Medieval Paris, too, had its own infamous underground drains, where Valjean hides so memorably in Victor Hugo's *Les Miserables*: 'Let the reader imagine Paris lifted off like a cover, the subterranean network of sewers, from a bird's eye view, will outline on the banks a species of large branch grafted on the river. On the right bank, the belt sewer will form the trunk of this branch, the secondary ducts will form the branches, and those without exit the twigs.'

But it is the combination of flush toilets and extensive networks of long, wide tunnels and branching networks of smaller drains pioneered by Bazalgette that finally took the ordure out of city life. Sewage systems like this make cities hugely more pleasant places to live. Pongs are fleeting, occasioning a laugh or a distasteful sniff – not a continuous and often overwhelming fact of life. The physical bulk of ordure has vanished too, flushed away almost the instant it appears into hidden spaces beneath the city and then floated invisibly away beyond the city confines. And all the diseases linked to living with excrement are largely things of the past.

Even with just a few hundred thousand people, excremental problems were thoroughly unpleasant without good sewage. Today's megalopolises would be unimaginable.

Of course, sewage systems haven't actually solved the sewage problems; they've simply moved them elsewhere. The mantra of sewage companies is 'the solution to ablutions is dilution' but it doesn't quite work. Some cities flush untreated sewage straight into the sea where they cause algal blooms that can suffocate marine life as well as putting swimmers and wildlife in danger of disease. But even those cities that treat sewage thoroughly before discharging it are left with the problem of how to dispose of the remaining moist 'sludge' which, unlike the nightsoil of the past, cannot be used as manure because it is so mixed in with industrial waste, chemicals from cleaning products, and much more. Some dump sludge far out to sea, but the detrimental effect on marine wildlife has led many countries to ban the practice. Sometimes it is put into landfill sites. No one yet has the perfect solution.

Despite these problems, good sewerage remains the blessing of modern cities, the thing which as much as anything distinguishes them from their filthy, smelly historic counterparts. As Forrest Gump fictitiously said, 'Shit happens' – but sewerage makes sure you're not stuck with it.

#8 The Scientific Method

At school, science students are often taught the Scientific Method as if there is a single, definitive way in which science can be approached – one which will guarantee the answer you find is scientifically valid. It's a four-step process:

1. *Make observations*
2. *Formulate a hypothesis*
3. *Test your hypothesis with experiments*
4. *Draw conclusions*

With luck you can move to a Theory, which is a hypothesis that's passed its experimental test a few times, and maybe you might even find a Law that can be proved by experiment again and again. It's presented as a foolproof system, and the only proper way to do science.

The great philosopher of science Karl Popper (1902–1994) refuted this approach entirely. Popper, who ironically was Professor of Scientific Method at the University of London, denied that there was such a thing as the scientific method – or rather a scientific method in this form.

Popper argued that we can never test a hypothesis to the point of proof. You might, for instance, notice that a few stars are hot and come up with a hypothesis that all stars are hot. You might even find that you observe thousands of stars, and that they all turn out to be hot. But you could never observe every star – or even if you could, you could never be certain that you had – so you can never prove anything. The best approach therefore is to *dis*prove ideas, not to try and prove them. Find one cold star, for instance, and your hot star hypothesis crashes down – so you have learned something: that not all stars are hot.

Popper asserted that this emphasis on falsifying a hypothesis is not only the most practical approach to science; it actually provides the test of whether a hypothesis is scientific or not. If a hypothesis cannot be refuted or proved false, Popper said, it is not scientific: '... science,' Popper wrote, 'is a history of corrected mistakes.'

A contemporary of Popper, American physicist Thomas Kuhn (1922–1996), had equally iconoclastic things to say about the authority of the scientific method and the accuracy of theories. Kuhn wasn't even as positive as Popper in suggesting that science moved forward by *correcting* mistakes. Science, Kuhn argued, is not a transition from error to truth, but a series of crises that lead to dramatic changes in assumptions, which he called paradigm shifts. The paradigm is the consensus on which questions to ask and how to answer them, and is determined at any one time by social and cultural factors which may have nothing to do with logic. These paradigms block any challenge to the consensus and take a real crisis to shift.

Criticisms like Popper's and Kuhn's might make you think the scientific method is fatally flawed – and some critics have assumed so, leaping on Kuhn's ideas in particular to discredit science. In fact, both men were deeply committed to science, and their scrupulous examination is part of the amazing strength of the scientific approach.[114] Science works because it is critical, self-questioning, systematic and continually tested. Only when it becomes complacent or careless does it really fail.

The scientific method really came into its own about four centuries ago, in what some people call the scientific revolution, and since then it has demonstrated again and again its power not only to explain the world around us in a convincing way but to use those explanations to both make accurate

---

[114] There was actually one more twentieth-century challenge to the scientific method which seems even more fundamentally damaging. That was Werner Heisenberg's Uncertainty Principle of 1927. Heisenberg demonstrated that the scientist's most basic method, observation, is deeply flawed. The very act of observing a subatomic particle changes it so that you can never be certain of two different properties, such as position and momentum, at the same time. Yet far from bringing down the science of subatomic particles, it proved to be the very cornerstone of the new science that became quantum mechanics, and has led to some fundamental insights into the nature of matter and energy.

predictions and open the way to some impressive technology, from antibiotic drugs to lasers. Every scientist might have his or her own particular way of working, but they are all working within the same basic scientific approach.

The origins of this approach date back to the time of the Ancient Greeks, as Aristotle emphasised the importance of observation – looking at the world as it actually is and trying to see what is going on, rather than relying on your imagination or divine inspiration. But the first clear exposition of a 'method' begins to emerge in the Islamic world between the eighth and eleventh centuries.

The alchemist Jabir ibn-Hayyan was the great pioneer of experiments, and in particular the importance of accurate measurements, devising sensitive scales to weigh chemicals before and after each stage in an experiment. The polymath ibn al-Haitham (also known as Alhazen) not only made important breakthroughs in the science of optics, among other things, but created the first clear outline of a system for finding scientific knowledge, going from observation to hypothesis to experiment to conclusion. The idea that our knowledge of the world could be developed by systematic investigation was a key breakthrough. It seems so self-evident now, but it was a revolutionary insight.

Gradually the Islamic ideas about science filtered through and inspired thinkers in Western Europe. Oxford University became a focus for new scientific thinking in the thirteenth century under the tutelage of Robert Grosseteste,[115] who

---

[115] Grosseteste developed the method of induction; reasoning from observation. Peter Watson describes how, anticipating Descartes, Grosseteste advised students to break the phenomenon being studied into its principal

emphasised how mathematics could be integrated into ibn al-Haitham's method. Grosseteste's student Roger Bacon pointed out how scientific study would not only provide insights into the natural world, but a way to master it, remarkably foreseeing submarines, cars and aircraft.

The great sea-change, though, seems to have occurred in the early seventeenth century. For the first time, thinkers began to question the wisdom of the Ancients such as Aristotle and Galen which had been rediscovered at the beginning of the Renaissance. They began to believe that they might find their own answers by using the power of their own rational brains to study the real world and learn from it.

The English philosopher Francis Bacon (1561–1626) was cited as an inspirational figure by most of the great scientific minds that followed, including Newton. Bacon was scornful of false knowledge arrived at without observation and introduced his own hugely influential version of the method, in which the scientist makes patient[116] and careful observations, forms a theory, then tests it by rigorous experiment. He also emphasised that scientists couldn't come up with the answers alone; they should form communities to share methods and

---

parts, then build up knowledge from there. He cited the example of a rainbow, and how it could be seen in many places, not just in the sky, but in the spray from a water wheel, the splashes from oars. From this observation, Theodoric of Freiburg theorised that rainbows were caused by light refracting through individual drops of water.

[116] Patience is key, Bacon argued, and is something the best scientists such as Newton and Darwin showed in spades. Progress is made in small steps, from small details to 'axioms': 'The understanding must not … be supplied with wings,' Bacon wrote, 'but rather hung with weights, to keep it from leaping and flying.'

research and subject their findings to scrutiny. This suggestion is perhaps Bacon's most important legacy, still seen today in scientific conferences, collaboration on projects and perhaps most crucially in the peer-review process to which findings are subject before they are published in scientific journals.

The second great contributor to the theory of the Method was René Descartes. Descartes' strength was never accepting things without question. In his *Discourse de la Méthode* (*Discourse on Method*) (1637), he emphasises how he arrived at answers: first by always taking care to begin only with things he knew for certain; second to divide the problem up into parts; third to proceed only in the smallest and simplest steps; and fourth to review everything to ensure nothing was in error or omitted.

While Bacon and Descartes supplied the theory, it was Galileo Galilei who put it all into practice with the first great series of scientific experiments. The famous story of his plummeting cannonballs at Pisa – when he dropped two different cannonballs from the Leaning Tower to show they were both equally affected by gravity – is apocryphal, though one of his students tried it. But more significantly, he conducted a crucial series of experiments rolling balls down slopes to show that gravity accelerates things, and at a constant rate.

From Galileo's time on, the scientific method was applied in various ways and with various degrees of diligence, but the real breakthrough was the change of attitude. Numerous people began to believe that they could learn by investigating the world, by thinking about their observations for themselves and by communicating their ideas with others to get feedback and suggestions. The scientific approach liberated men's and women's minds from thinking that they needed to be told answers – by revelation or by the scholars of old. They realised they had the power to find answers for themselves. It tapped directly into natural human curiosity and got many people tremendously excited.

It took a while for the full impact of this 'revolution' to sink in, which is why not everyone agrees that it was such a revolution – more an evolution. Throughout the seventeenth and eighteenth centuries, science remained the pastime of a few gentlemen 'natural philosophers'. But as the Industrial Revolution began to transform the world, so the true meaning of the scientific approach became clear. You didn't have to be a philosopher to study and learn about the world; you simply had to be a practical scientist who did practical research and pursued a career in science in academic and scientific institutions. The scientific method gave legitimacy to anyone who pursued it diligently. From the end of the eighteenth century onwards there was an explosion of scientific interest, a flood of a new breed of human beings called scientists and an accelerating avalanche of crucial scientific discoveries which have transformed both our world and our understanding of it.

#7 Evolution by Natural Selection

Charles Darwin's theory of evolution by natural selection is shockingly simple. No two organisms ever come into the world quite alike, Darwin suggested. Occasionally, a slight difference, a special trait, gives a particular organism a crucial edge in the prevailing conditions – a better chance of surviving longer and passing on their characteristics to their progeny. And as this well-endowed organism and its descendants produce more progeny, others less well adapted to the conditions die out – a process vividly dubbed by Darwin's contemporary Herbert Spencer as the 'survival of the fittest'.

This simple process, Darwin suggested, explains just how all the wonderful, teeming variety of life on Earth has descended from a common ancestor and how all the myriad different species that have ever lived evolved over time as natural variations became accentuated. In short, it explains the history of life on Earth entirely as a basic natural process.

Darwin was by no means the first to come up with the idea of evolution, or even the idea of evolution by natural selection. Over 2,500 years ago, for instance, the Ancient Greek thinker Empedocles suggested that the life we see on Earth today came about because the most fit survived while the others perished. And in ninth-century Baghdad, the Islamic thinker al-Jahiz wrote: 'Animals engage in a struggle for existence [and] for resources, to avoid being eaten and to breed … Environmental factors influence organisms to develop new characteristics to ensure survival, thus transforming into new species. Animals that survive to breed can pass on their successful characteristics to [their] offspring.'

Indeed, during the late eighteenth and early nineteenth centuries, the discovery of fossil after fossil of dinosaurs and other long-extinct animals built up a weight of evidence that life on Earth had a long history, and that many species had come and gone through time. French natural historians such as Étienne Geoffroy St-Hilaire, George Cuvier and the Chevalier de Lamarck all developed their own ideas on evolution half a century before Darwin. Even Darwin's grandfather, Erasmus Darwin, had a theory of evolution.

What made Darwin's work so groundbreaking was that he provided a comprehensive, well-worked-out theory of how it all happened and, crucially, put the mechanism of natural selection at its heart. Alfred Russel Wallace, working in the Far East, came up with a similar idea, and both men's theories were introduced to the scientific community at the same meeting in 1858. But by that time Darwin had spent two decades diligently building up a huge weight of evidence and developed his theory so much more completely than Wallace that it is rightly Darwin, not Wallace, to whom most of the credit goes.

The year following that first public outing of the idea, Darwin published his book *On the Origin of Species* which amply bears out just how fully developed his ideas were. It is one of the greatest science books of all time – beautifully written and easy to understand, yet completely solid and immensely detailed in its science. And what is remarkable is just how complete the ideas have proved to be in the century and a half since it was written.

Despite the legendary furore provoked by Darwin's books, the rows over evolution actually died down quite quickly at the time and the concept was soon widely accepted, not just among the scientific community but by all but the most dyed-in-the-wool among the clergy, too. In fact, it was scientific criticism of Darwin's mechanism for evolution – natural selection – that threatened to undermine his work most severely. The physicist Lord Kelvin's worryingly short estimate of the age of the Earth – far too short for Darwin's evolutionary process to have taken place – proved, in the end, to be mistaken. But for a long time there seemed to be a hole in the heart of Darwin's work – just how were traits passed distinctly on and on through the generations rather than simply fading away?

This problem bedevilled Darwin for the rest of his life. Yet, unbeknown to Darwin – and unbeknown to most of the scientists working on evolutionary ideas – the problem had been solved by Austrian monk Gregor Mendel even as Darwin published the *Origin*. Mendel's work with plants showed how traits can be preserved from generation to generation through the combination of factors, later known as genes, inherited from both parents.

By the time Mendel's work was rediscovered in the early twentieth century, Darwin's reputation was fading. Even Mendel's genes didn't entirely revive it, because genes didn't seem to work in the gradual way needed for Darwinian evolution, but were simply 'on' or 'off' – genes, in Richard Dawkins' neat metaphor, seemed to be digital while evolution looked 'analogue'. Then in the 1920s, a mathematical approach by geneticists such as Ronald Aylmer Fisher showed how the 'digital' nature of gene variations (mutations) was smoothed out over large populations. With this reconciliation, biologists could at last dovetail genetics and evolution by natural selection into what came to be called by some the 'modern synthesis' and by others, the 'neo-Darwinian synthesis'. Since then, Darwin's ideas have gone from strength to strength.

Interestingly, in the 1960s, Darwin's ideas were given a new twist, when Richard Dawkins suggested in his famous book, *The Selfish Gene*, that the real battle for survival that drives evolution is not between individual organisms, but between their genes – the organism is simply a vehicle for the genes. This startling idea gave Darwin's theories a real shot in the arm. They were already so widely accepted by then that they seemed almost dull. But Dawkins' suggestion gave them a whole exciting new dimension and opened up many rich avenues of research.

They also seemed to wake up the religious opposition, maybe because they seemed so chillingly mechanistic and because they placed 'selfishness' at the heart of life. Right from the day the *Origin* was published, Darwin's ideas, of course, upset many people of particular religious views, because they entirely banish God from any role in the creation of species – and in particular go against the Biblical story of the Creation. But criticism from religious groups, rather than diminishing as the scientific evidence mounts, has begun to heat up.

Recent surveys, for instance, suggest that more than half of all Americans entirely reject the idea that life evolves – despite the overwhelming scientific consensus on the evidence. And when it comes to the acceptance of Darwin's theory of natural selection, in which evolution progresses in an entirely automatic (entirely God-free) way, the numbers shrink further – with only 14 per cent of Americans agreeing with it. One challenge to evolutionary theory has come from a notion labelled 'Intelligent Design'. It sounds scientific and is often presented in a pseudo-scientific way, but its argument is that the astonishing complexity and aptness for their circumstances of most life forms on Earth must indicate that they were designed intelligently, that is by God. This idea is an old one, convincingly demolished by the philosopher

David Hume two centuries ago, and more recently by Richard Dawkins in his book *The Blind Watchmaker*.[117]

Despite these challenges, the scientific consensus is overwhelming. The evidence that species do evolve by natural selection has mounted up so powerfully that very few scientists doubt that it provides a remarkable and astonishingly complete explanation of the nature of life. It seems to work right from the microscopic, where it shows very clearly how things like antibiotic resistance develop, to the macroscopic, where it shows how whales and hippos are actually very close relatives. It shows how dinosaurs morphed gradually into birds. It shows how butterflies acquired particular wing patterns. It explains why cheetahs are so fast. It gives us a way of exploring why humans are naked and other apes are hairy. Indeed, it touches every aspect of life. Life is the most amazing, varied, rich and interesting phenomenon in the universe – and yet Darwin's idea shows us to a very large degree how it has come to be as it is … and how it may change in the future.

#6 Abolition of Slavery

There is no more hideous stain on the history of the Western world than the transatlantic slave trade. It is deeply to our shame that our ancestors treated anyone, let alone so many, with such brutality. There is no escaping such shame. Twelve

---

[117] The title of the book comes from the early nineteenth-century theologian William Paley's assertion that if you found an object as complex as a watch, then you would rightly assume it to be the creation of a watchmaker – and so you must assume that a beautiful and complex organism must be the creation of a divine watchmaker.

million people were shipped from Africa to the Americas between the sixteenth and nineteenth centuries and the lives of these people and their offspring born into slavery were utterly blighted. The sufferings of most of the slaves were largely silent, but whenever you read a solitary witness voice from that time it brings home the true misery with enough force to make you weep or rage that this vile trade ever happened.

Indeed, it is so natural at this distance in time to dismiss the slave trade as an aberration of the past that it is easy to forget just how important an idea it was to abolish it. If you can't imagine something happening now (wrongly as it happens, as I'll return to later), it doesn't seem such a great idea to abolish it. Yet the fact is that enough people believed slavery was acceptable to sustain it for nearly three centuries. Perhaps most Europeans and Americans, benefiting from the fruits of slave labours, simply turned a blind eye rather than actively condoning it. It ended only when the voices raised in protest became loud and effective enough (helped no doubt by changing economic circumstances).

It matters to remember that abolition was a great idea because there are abuses in the world today that in the future may seem just as unimaginable as the slave trade does to us now. We live with the fact that a third of the world's people are living in abject poverty, for instance, because we feel powerless to change it. Maybe it was not so different for ordinary people thinking about slavery a few hundred years ago. Ultimately, the slave trade didn't disappear because most people didn't approve of it but because it was actively abolished. 'All that is necessary for the triumph of evil,' the eighteenth-century Irish statesman Edmund Burke is believed to have said, 'is for good men to do nothing.'

Of course, it is the transatlantic slave trade that looms largest whenever the issue of slavery is mentioned, but slaves have existed throughout history – and so have moves to free them. Ancient Rome, for instance, had a slave trade every bit as extensive as the transatlantic trade, with entire nations brought into slavery. Indeed, it is thought that a quarter of Ancient Rome's population were slaves. Interestingly, there were those who protested against their slavery then, such as the famous gladiator slave Spartacus, who led a slaves' revolt, and those among the slave-owning class who acknowledged that slavery was wrong. Stoics protested against the ill-treatment of slaves and some early Christians such as John Chrysostom condemned the very idea of slavery. Indeed, the idea of manumission – freeing one's slaves – became so popular that the Emperor Augustus was forced to make laws limiting the practice.

Slavery didn't end with the collapse of the Roman Empire, though. It is not just that slaves became serfs, peasants bound for life to a particular feudal lord; more than 1 in 10 people were fully enslaved in Medieval Europe, including many Slavic people who gave their very name to the practice. A thousand years ago, the port of Bristol was thriving on the slave trade just as it did in the eighteenth century, only at this time the traders were Vikings and the slaves were English. Christians, although urged to treat slaves well, felt that justice need only be done in the next world, not this. But many English Christians felt uncomfortable about their own people being enslaved overseas, especially by heathen races like the Vikings.

Just a few years before the Norman conquest, the Saxon bishop Wulfstan, an early abolitionist, put a stop to Bristol's slave trade, writing: 'They used to buy men from all over England and carry them to Ireland in the hope of gain; nay they even set forth for sale women whom they had themselves gotten with child. You might well groan to see the long rows of young men and maidens whose beauty and youth might move the pity of a savage, bound together with cords, and brought to market to be sold.'

Not long after, William the Conqueror, long thought of as the oppressor of the English, issued what may be the first national ban on trading slaves, in 1102, stopping 'that shameful trading whereby heretofore men used in England to be sold like brute beasts'.

Gradually, over the next half-millennium, slavery dwindled in Europe, until only Russia had slaves, and in 1723 Peter the Great turned Russian slaves into serfs. But slavery had not disappeared; it was simply focused elsewhere – in the Arab nations where slaves brought from Europe as well as elsewhere were often kept, and of course in the Americas where slaves were brought by European traders from Africa.

The history of the transatlantic slave trade began when the first African slaves arrived on the Spanish-colonised island of Hispaniola (modern Dominica and Haiti) in 1501. By the end of the century, the infamous 'slave triangle' was well under way, with European ships carrying cargoes of textiles, rum and manufactured goods to Africa, taking on a new consignment of slaves and sailing to the Americas before taking sugar, tobacco and cotton back to Europe. British ships alone carried over 3 million African slaves to the Americas.

The Enlightenment brought a change in attitudes, and an anti-slavery movement led by Quakers began to grow among the British public. Although the Evangelist politician William Wilberforce is the best-known figure, it was a surprisingly widespread movement, with dissenting religious groups finding rich support among the factory workers of the Midlands and North, and even among women and children who ran their own anti-slavery campaigns. Another side that has come to light in recent years is the significant role played by black people, such as the freed slave Olaudah Equiano, whose autobiography was widely read, and Quobna Ottobah Cugoano.

Through the 1780s the movement gained such momentum that in 1787 the Parliamentary Committee for the Abolition of the Slave Trade was set up under the leadership of Wilberforce to enquire into the possibility of abolishing the slave trade. The extensive and committed research compiled by committee members such as Thomas Clarkson, which threw the suffering of slaves into the spotlight, built up an eventually unanswerable case. On 25 March 1807, the British Parliament passed the Slave Trade Act, making the slave trade illegal throughout the British Empire.

Getting the slave trade banned was just the first battle, however, and in the 1820s the abolitionists were active again, campaigning to set existing slaves free – finally succeeding with the Slavery Abolition Act of 1833, under which all slaves in the British Empire were liberated after 1 August 1834. It took a long, long time, though, to finally remove the chains from the black slaves of the Americas. In the United States, the African-Americans were not really freed until the end of the segregation laws in 1965.

It is unimaginable that there should still be slaves in the Americas now, but the emancipation of slaves didn't happen by chance. It was achieved through the idea of abolition and the courageous, dedicated efforts of campaigners from Moses Brown to Rosa Parks over nearly two centuries. There is no other idea among our list of great ideas that is quite so necessary, quite so vital in correcting a great wrong as abolition, and no idea, perhaps, that has done quite so much to directly alleviate human suffering. Abolition is the one absolutely essential idea, the one we cannot do without if we are to live with any degree of comfort in the world.

And the battle is not yet over. Appallingly, abolition is not a great idea of the past that no longer matters. The enslavement of Africans in the Americas may be history, but there are now more slaves around the world than ever before. The slavery is not legal as it was for the African-Americans but it is just as real, and the sufferings of those enslaved just as terrible. According to Anti-Slavery International there are now 27 million people in slavery around the world – men, women and children forced to work through violence or the threat of it, under the complete control of their 'employers', and sometimes even bought and sold. This slavery takes many forms, from domestic slavery in northern Sudan to child camel jockeys in the United Arab Emirates.

Perhaps the largest group of modern slaves, though, are the victims of 'human trafficking', the trading of young women and children who are then sexually exploited, as well as coerced into other kinds of forced labour. Sickeningly, this is apparently the fastest growing criminal industry in the world, and only a little way behind the drugs trade as a target for the world's nastiest crime syndicates. According to the Council of Europe: 'People trafficking has reached epidemic proportions over the past decade, with a global annual market of about $42.5 billion', while the United Nations estimates that nearly 2.5 million people from 127 different countries are being trafficked around the world each year. These bald statistics hide ghastly individual tales of exploitation, as young girls are abducted into prostitution abroad. Although the trade is so far underground that it is hard to be sure of numbers, child protection agencies believe there are thousands of child sex slaves, many from Eastern Europe, in the UK alone.

The numbers involved in slave trading around the world today are, shockingly, greater than the transatlantic slave trade at its worst, yet because so many of the victims are traded singly and clandestinely the trade slips under the radar. Abolition, of course, was targeted against the legal institution of slavery, not against this modern criminal enslavement. But the need to end it is just as imperative. The victims are isolated and traumatised minors, with no courageous spokesmen, no Toussaint l'Ouverture[118] to lead the fight against the slave-bosses. That's why the drive behind abolition is needed more than ever. Abolition is not an idea of the past; it is the idea that all slavery must end and is the most urgent, most crucial idea of all.

---

[118] The rebel slave leader who won Haiti independence from Napoleon's France.

#5 Use of Fire

In itself, of course, fire is not an idea but a natural phenomenon. The big idea with fire is *using* fire, of deliberately starting a fire – not simply to revel in its destructive power but to
use it in a controlled way.

It's hard to be certain just when humans first thought of
doing so. Ancient signs of burning, such as charred wood,
may well be the marks of natural wildfires, not campfires.
Fire-hardened shards of clay at East African sites such as
Chesowanja and Koobi Fora may be telltale signs of campfires
dating back 1.4 million years, while bear bones in a cave at
Swartkrans in South Africa may have been charred by equally
ancient cooking fires. But they could be just the scorch marks
of a blaze ignited by the heat of the sun or a flash of lightning.
Some palaeontologists suggest the world's oldest manmade
fire is actually a 790,000-year-old site at Bnot Ya'akov Bridge
in Israel, where a fire seems to have been lit repeatedly on the
same site over a period of up to 100,000 years.

What seems likely, though there is no conclusive proof,
is that the first bright sparks to think of lighting fires were
human ancestors such as *Homo erectus* who lived in Africa a
million or more years ago. The flame was then carried around
the world by their descendants as they walked out of Africa.

Anyone who has tried lighting a fire in the open without the
aid of matches or firelighters of any kind will know just how
tricky it is. Even in bone-dry conditions with perfect kindling
it can take a lot of effort – with energetically rubbed sticks or
struck stones needed to get a proper fire going. So those first
fire-starters must have been not only ingenious enough to get

their flames lit; they must have been thoroughly convinced that the effort was worth it. Indeed, if one takes the 'proof of the pudding is in the eating' line of argument, then fire must surely win the battle of the greatest ideas hands-down. Think of all the countless trillions of fires that have been ignited all around the world since that first flicker in Africa. What other idea has consumed so much sustained and repeated effort over such a long time? And considering the risks of injury or worse when lighting fires, it's clear that the benefits of lighting fires must be substantial.

So just what is it that's so great about lighting fires? It's pretty likely that for the earliest of our ancestors protection came close to the top of the list. Fire not only provides a light to see predators and enemies through the dangerous hours of darkness; it also provides a powerful and handy weapon to drive them away. Think of Indiana Jones with his flaming torch in the snake pit, or any other resourceful adventure film hero trapped in a perilous place, and you get the picture. Fire uniquely provides powerful protection against almost any kind of attacker, even for those with neither skill nor powerful physique.

Fire's warmth was no doubt just as attractive. Even in the tropics of Africa, nights can get cool enough to have made life uncomfortable for our naked or only slightly hairy hominid ancestors. It might well have been impossible for humans to have spread beyond Africa into cooler parts of the world without fires to keep them warm through winter. Indeed, it is difficult to imagine how most of the places humans have lived throughout history could have been permanently settled at all without the warmth of fires. Just think how miserable life becomes on the chillier nights of winter in the temperate parts of the world where billions of us now live if the heating fails even for a while. Now think of life without any form of heating at all and the crucial importance of fire in simply keeping us warm is plain.

Still, although it seems almost blindingly self-evident that our earliest human ancestors lit fires for light, protection and warmth, there is no evidence from this distance in time that they actually did so. What there is evidence for, in the charred animal bones found in ancient fire sites, is that they used fire for cooking. There are not only burned bones at the Swartkrans site in South Africa that hint at a little early roasting, but at a handful of other sites around the world dating from 200,000 years ago or more. There are burned rhino bones alongside a 400,000-year-old hearth near Menez-Dragan in France, while the charred animal skulls at the equally ancient Zhoukoudian cave site in China indicate that baked brains were a favourite dish some 400,000 years ago.

It is hard to overstate the crucial influence of cooking in human evolution and diet. Cooking enables us, above all, to eat more meat and some otherwise inedible vegetables and roots. Like other apes, humans simply cannot eat much raw meat, so the discovery of fire and cooking perhaps represents a massive turning point in human evolutionary history. Palaeontologists debate fiercely over what the impact of turning at least partly carnivore was. Some argue that the sudden availability of a high-protein diet was what helped the human brain take a giant step forward. Others believe that the true benefit of meat and cooked vegetables is to give a high-energy diet, crucial to the unusually high energy demands of the human brain.

It is of course hard to say conclusively which came first – whether the human brain developed with the change in diet or the diet changed with the development of the brain. Either way, the change had a profound impact on the human ape's place in the world. Although humans may have hunted for raw meat long before they began to cook it, cooking surely gave them the incentive to hunt more. Either way, no longer were humans simply ambling plant browsers like other apes; they were now active hunters, able to range far and wide into all kinds of habitats, where familiar plants might be scarce but where they could still find the high-energy meat they needed to fuel their activity.

Hunting and cooking also had a profound effect on human social interaction – perhaps the key changes that brought us to where we are today. No longer would humans tend to browse alone. They would work together in groups when hunting, then sit around the fire to cook their food and share it among their fellows. And maybe it was around those early campfires that so many of our basic human interactions developed, including language. It is no wonder that fires have such a powerful place in the human psyche and the ability to stir the deepest emotions.

As if this weren't enough, there is one other early use of fire for which there is tangible evidence; that's the use of its heat to alter materials. Discoveries in the southern tip of Africa in 2009 revealed that as long as 164,000 years ago, humans were using fires to heat-treat stones to make sharper, tougher weapons. Later, of course, humans learned how fire could give them the gift of metals. Fire enabled rock ore to be melted to extract the pure metal, and also made the metal soft or even liquid enough to be shaped. The discovery of metals and their role in human development is another story, but it is a simple fact that without fire we would have no metal at all.

Of course, our relationship with fire has changed profoundly since those very first campfire sparks. Yet it still plays an absolutely pivotal role in our lives. In metaphor, if not in fact, our whole modern society is a vast campfire. Every city in the world, the vast majority of economic activities and most of our means of transport roar along to the burning of fuel, whether it is wood or coal, oil or gas. When we talk about energy, we are talking, essentially, about heat energy, since wind and water power still play such a small part. Indeed, the very concept of energy came from nineteenth-century efforts to understand how fire, in steam engines, produced power.

And this of course brings us right to the heart of whether fire use is a great idea. It is a powerful idea certainly, maybe the mightiest idea of all time. Fire continues to awe with its power and we continue to be mesmerised by our ability to control it. Fire gives us power over the natural world, power over the elements, power to travel beyond our world driven by rockets.

Indeed, in some ways, fire has turned each and every human into a god. When the Titan Prometheus of Ancient Greek legend stole fire from the gods, he was not simply giving a great gift, he was equipping mankind with godlike power. No wonder the gods bound him in chains. If we have been seduced by such power, it is hardly surprising.

With it, we can lighten the darkest night; we can stay warm through the iciest winter; we can drive away the most dangerous foes; we can turn inedible food edible; we can shape metal to make bridges and aeroplanes; we can fire bricks to erect cities; and so much more.

But, of course, the power of fire has its dark side. There are not simply the tangible dangers of fire: stand too close to a fire and it will burn you; let it get out of control and it may destroy your homes and your cities; misuse it in bombs and other heat-based weapons and its terrible destructive power is inescapable. There are, too, the less tangible dangers created by the pivotal role of heat energy in our global culture. The fires of our society are now heating the air so avidly that the whole world, it seems, is getting steadily warmer. Although there are plenty of noisy sceptics who insist that the evidence for global warming is shaky, the consensus among scientists is that we may be putting a few too many logs on the fire for our own good.

#4 Music

'Music,' wrote the German poet Berthold Auerbach (1812–82) in his *Music Talks with Children*, 'washes away from the soul the dust of everyday life.' Friedrich Nietzsche was even more emphatic: 'Without music life would be a mistake.'

Now, more than ever, music is the soundtrack to our lives. Sometimes it is unwanted, like the piped music that irritates in the supermarket or the jingle that is there in lieu of an actual answer when you call some faceless corporation. But most of the time it is wanted, and portable music players and all kinds of other sound systems can now set your ears vibrating with it whenever there is silence to fill.

Music is such an integral part of our lives that is perhaps wrong to call it an idea. Yet some scientists insist it has no evolutionary value. It's an accident of evolution, or it's an invention that was gradually developed. 'Music is auditory cheesecake,' psychologist Steven Pinker argues. 'It just happens to tickle several important parts of the brain in a highly pleasurable way, as cheesecake tickles the palate.'

In other words, the pleasure triggers were there in the brain already – and music just turned out to be a good way to trigger them. Music is useless in evolutionary terms, it seems, and simply taps into the same response set off by human cooing and crying. '... [M]usic could vanish from our lifestyle,' Pinker declares in *The Language Instinct*, 'and the rest of our lifestyle would be virtually unchanged.' He's not saying, of course, that music is a waste of time – simply that it exists only for the pleasure it brings; it has no survival value, and so cannot be regarded as an evolutionary trait like language or vision.

Not everyone agrees with this line. Some music psychologists such as Daniel Levitin argue that it *is* an evolutionary trait. Levitin argues that the length of time music has been around suggests that it must have more value than simply pleasure. Pleasures, however great, would be more ephemeral. A bone flute, made from the wing bone of a vulture, was found in Hohle Fels cavern in south-west Germany in 2009, and estimated to date from well over 30,000 years ago. It was one of eight ancient flutes found in the area, four made from bird bones and four from mammoth tusks. It all suggests a

prehistoric band, and that music was already fairly sophisticated this long ago. It's quite something to imagine these
ancient people listening to a lively concert in their cavern at
night tens of thousands of years ago.

Levitin cites three possible evolutionary benefits of music.
The first is the one Darwin suggested 150 years ago – that it
aids sexual selection, with musical and dancing ability attract-
ing a mate, because it creates pleasure. Another is the idea that
it helps social bonding and so promotes a group's survival.
The third is that it helps to promote cognitive development.

Whatever the truth, there is no doubt that now and through
the centuries, music has had the capacity to strike such a deep
emotional chord, to use the obvious metaphor, that it seems
to touch the very meaning of life. 'All deep things are song,'
wrote Thomas Carlyle. 'It seems somehow the very central
essence of us, song; as if all the rest were but wrappages and
hulls!'

Music's resonance is so powerful that in times of extreme
emotion it can seem even more important than food. Deep
into the terrible Nazi siege of Leningrad in 1942 when the
city's starving people were reduced to gnawing on leather
belts to gain a tiny scrap of sustenance, an orchestra gathered
to play, for the first time in the city, Dmitri Shostakovich's
new symphony No. 7, dedicated to Leningrad. Loudspeakers
broadcast the symphony through the stricken city and tens of
thousands of people wept together.

A year before, the young French composer Olivier
Messiaen, after being captured by the Germans, was in the
Stalag VIII-A concentration camp near Görlitz in Poland.
There he met three other musicians, and instead of giving into

the despair of the situation, obtained some paper from a sympathetic guard and wrote for them all the astounding '*Quatuor pour la fin du temps*' ('Quartet for the End of Time'), which was premiered in the icy camp in front of a vast audience of freezing prisoners and their guards.

Both these stories suggest that there is something far more powerful at work with music than pure pleasure. Music has the capacity to tap into, indeed shape, our emotions to a remarkable degree – not just the lineaments of tragedy, but pride, joy, frivolity, anger, longing and just about every emotion, subtle or strong. Advertisers and filmmakers know this, and use it to deliberately provoke particular feelings. Advertisers use the power of association, choosing music for commercials that stirs particular feelings such as pleasure or pride, so that you link these feelings with the product. And filmmakers guide your emotions through a film, helping you to weep at the climactic reunion, or shiver with anticipation as the hero descends into the darkened basement. It would be hard to imagine films like *Brief Encounter* or *Lord of the Rings* with dialogue only.

Music heightens the emotions at key events, such as weddings, religious festivals, parades, anniversaries. And the music so often coincides with the peak of the event. Even at a simple birthday party, the singing of 'Happy Birthday' is the focus of emotions, while a piper's lament can bring a lump to the throat at a funeral. Such events would seem hollow, even impossible, without music.

But simply listening to music, or playing it, entirely in isolation can seduce our emotions even more powerfully, whether it's the sheer pleasure of the fragile, elegant beauty of a Mozart concerto, the excitement of a terrific dance track or the profound sadness of a true song of love lost. Music draws emotions out of us in such a true way that some people insist it is a spiritual quality. Beethoven averred: 'Music is the mediator between the spiritual and the sensual life.'

Pianist Karl Paulnack believes, rather, that it serves a vital psychological need to help us get through life intact, like a miraculous psychotherapist.[119] When he addressed parents of incoming students at the Boston Conservatory of Music in 2004, he said: 'Music is a basic need of human survival. Music is one of the ways we make sense of our lives, one of the ways in which we express feelings when we have no words, a way for us to understand things with our hearts when we cannot with our minds.' As the essayist Leigh Hunt, partner of the great Victorian novelist George Eliot, put it simply but beautifully: 'Music is the medicine of the breaking heart.' But it is also the food of love, the champagne of carnivals, and so much more. Indeed, there is music everywhere:

> There's music in the sighing of a reed;
> There's music in the gushing of a rill;
> There's music in all things, if men had ears:
> Their earth is but an echo of the spheres.
> – Lord Byron, *Don Juan*, Canto XV. St. 5

---

[119] Music therapy is an increasingly popular treatment for people with emotional problems.

#3 Contraception

Sex without consequences. Hmm. For some it sounds like bliss. For others it sounds deeply immoral. For others still it sounds simply unrealistic. And that's the problem with contraception. While some think it's great; others think it's a great sin. (Spike Milligan believed it should be used on every conceivable occasion ...)

When the American social reformer Mary Sanger campaigned for what she termed 'birth control'[120] in the early twentieth century, she was in no doubt about how crucial contraception was. Unwanted pregnancy, Sanger believed, was the greatest curse women faced, especially working-class women. Unwanted pregnancy entirely ruined women in a way men couldn't imagine. Social revolution was nonsense, she felt, while women were still at risk of pregnancy from every sexual act.

It wasn't simply the trials of pregnancy, becoming a social outcast and the burden of raising an unwanted child, though

---

[120] Contraception has, typically, just a single meaning which is essentially personal. Contraception is the measures a woman or a man take to prevent the woman conceiving a child after sex. Mary Sanger's term 'birth control' has a public aspect, too. Governments such as the Chinese have practised birth control, limiting couples to just a single child, in order to slow population growth. The policy has undoubtedly restricted the growth of China's population. But the costs have been severe, with many girl children sent away or even murdered to allow the single child to be a boy, and many Chinese men are now facing the prospect of a life without a partner because of the shortage of girls. The philosopher Bertrand Russell was fairly adamant about the public side of birth control, however, saying that 'those who in principle oppose birth control are either incapable of arithmetic or else in favor of war, pestilence and famine as permanent features of human life'.

all these were tragic enough; Sanger also witnessed the desperate efforts of pregnant girls to get rid of their babies. 'Suggestions as to what to do for a girl who was "in trouble", or a married woman who was "caught",' she wrote, 'passed from mouth to mouth – herb teas, turpentine, steaming, rolling downstairs, inserting slippery elm, knitting needles, shoehooks.' And she personally nursed girls who were in terrible pain or bleeding to death from botched abortions. No wonder, then, that Mary Sanger was so adamant that educating the world about methods of birth control was the greatest service she could do for women. 'I would strike out – I would scream from the housetops. I would tell the world what was going on in the lives of these poor women. I would be heard. No matter what the cost. I would be heard.'

She spent her life campaigning for birth control education, and was deeply gratified to hear of the introduction of the contraceptive pill in 1960 before she died. H.G. Wells regarded her life's work as of the utmost importance, and one of the great marks of progress in the twentieth century, saying in 1935: 'When the history of civilization is written, it will be a biological history and Mary Sanger will be its heroine.'

Yet her work was always controversial. Although she might have expected natural allies in the women's movement, she actually found many feminists and suffragists deeply opposed to her. Some of them believed that sex subjugated women and should be avoided altogether. Others thought that motherhood was the highest calling and that birth control was an insult to womanhood. And the fact that Mary Sanger, lacking support from feminists, found allies among the eugenicists, who believed that racial supremacy could be enhanced by discouraging reproduction among the lower classes, only seemed to play into the hands of those who found contraception a rather dubious aim.

When the contraceptive pill was launched in 1960, though, many women hailed it as a great breakthrough. US Congresswoman Claire Booth Luce proclaimed: 'Modern woman is at last free as a man is free, to dispose of her own body, to earn her living, to pursue the improvement of her mind, to try a successful career.' And Congresswoman Luce's hopes seemed to be borne out in the 1960s. Although many other social changes also played a part, women did begin to go to university in unprecedented numbers, did start to pursue careers and did seem to take charge of their bodies and experience an amazing sexual liberation. But then in the 1970s, medical research began to hint that there might be some side effects to the pill, including an increased risk of breast cancer and heart disease. Some feminists immediately asserted that the pill was a male invention to allow men to have sex with women without the consequences – at the risk of women's health. In fact, studies since have suggested that the link with breast cancer is ambiguous, and that the health risks of pregnancy are much greater.

More significantly, the pill, and all kinds of contraception, became associated with promiscuity and premarital sex. Many traditional religious and conservatively minded people began to condemn any artificial methods of contraception. The Catholic Church in particular confirmed its view that artificial contraception was contrary to the true purpose of sex. Irish Catholics, famously, urged the 'rhythm method' as the only way to have sex and avoid conception. Cambridge Catholic mother Victoria Gillick, equally famously, tried to prevent doctors prescribing the pill to her five underage daughters without her consent, claiming that: 'Doctors encourage children to be promiscuous.' Mrs Gillick lost her case, but the issue of doctors prescribing the pill, or even giving confidential medical advice on sexual matters, to young teenagers has remained a thorny one ever since. In 2002, Mrs Gillick won £5,000 damages against a sexual health charity, which alleged she was responsible for a rise in teenage pregnancies by encouraging promiscuity.

In fact, the widespread availability of contraception – pills, condoms and other methods – and even the introduction of the morning-after pill, has not stopped the UK racking up one of the highest teenage pregnancy rates in Europe, or the USA becoming the country with the highest teenage pregnancy rate in the developed world. In many countries around the world, people marry young and teenage pregnancy is a normal part of married life, but in Europe and North America, where teen pregnancies are mostly extra-marital, it has become a social issue, with tabloid newspapers proclaiming each example of the 'youngest teen mum' as evidence of a damaged society and the sexualisation of children, with sex education and the all-too-free availability of contraception as the major culprits.

Each faction in the debate uses the evidence to support its own standpoint, but the evidence is ambiguous. In Europe, the Netherlands, where contraception and sex education is freely available, has the lowest teenage pregnancy rate of all. But teenage pregnancy rates are also low in Spain and Italy, and many attribute this to traditional values. In the USA, the high teenage pregnancy rate became the justification for the moral backlash in the 1990s which fuelled 'abstinence-only' programmes.

In 2004, the Bush administration allocated $131 million dollars to urge schoolchildren to abstain from sex, and virginity pledges became popular among certain groups of American teenagers. The abstinence programme diverted attention from the fact that teenage pregnancy declined steadily between 1991 and 2004. One study attributed 75 per cent of this decline to better use and knowledge of contraception. Another said it was half due to better contraception and half due to abstinence. Ironically, since 2004, teen pregnancy rates have risen again. Interestingly, some research suggests that teenagers who pledge abstinence are much more likely to indulge in higher risk (of disease transmission) sexual activities such as oral and anal sex.

Sexually transmitted diseases are, of course, another issue that feeds the controversy over contraception. Notoriously, Pope John Paul II decried the use of condoms even to prevent AIDS, let alone prevent conception, and called industrialised nations' focus on contraception and abortion part of 'a culture of death'. Many AIDS campaigners, anxious for people to use condoms to prevent the transmission of AIDS, were of course horrified. Recent research shows that condoms actually reduce transmission of the HIV virus by 80 per cent. It was with some dismay, therefore, that they found Pope Benedict XVI reiterating a similar view when he travelled to Africa for the first time as Pope in 2009. Benedict erroneously claimed that the distribution of condoms would 'aggravate' the spread of AIDS.

Now that effective contraception is now widely available in the developed world – not just in pill form, but also as condoms and coils – it is easy to forget what a difference it has made to people's lives, especially to those of women. The picture that Mary Sanger painted of the burden pregnancy placed on women was real and debilitating. It wasn't just the tragedy of unmarried girls who got 'in trouble'; it was the continuous and exhausting trial of repeated pregnancies even for women who were safely married and adequately supported. Improved hygiene and medical care has meant that the number of women who die in childbirth, or from complications in pregnancy, is now thankfully small. But in the not so distant past, without effective contraception, pregnancy was the norm for many married women. Very few women today would ever want to go through the emotional and physical exhaustion Dickens' wife Catherine must have felt after her tenth successful pregnancy and twelve miscarriages in just fifteen years between 1837 and 1852.

There are, of course, profound moral issues involved, and many people have expressed concern about the emotional impact on women of delaying motherhood too long.[121] Aldous Huxley's *Brave New World* also created what turns out to be a nightmare, dehumanising vision of sex without consequences. Nonetheless for most women, and for most men, the

---

[121] Research by scientists at Liverpool University in 2008 suggests that the contraceptive pill may lead women to choose the 'wrong' partner. The scientists suggested that while on the pill, women choose men who have a similar immune system to themselves, responding to their scent. That combination can lead to unhealthy babies. Moreover, the scientists said, if a woman stops taking the pill – perhaps to get pregnant – she may suddenly find her chosen man less attractive.

availability of effective contraception has been hugely liberating. The real problems are perhaps more prosaic. 'I want to tell you a terrific story about oral contraception,' tells Woody Allen. 'I asked this girl to sleep with me and she said "No".'

#2 Writing

There is a simple reason why the story of humankind is divided into prehistory and history. In prehistory, there was no writing to record the story; in history there was. The discovery of writing was the most significant watershed in human history. It made history possible.

Of course, people could pass on thoughts in the prehistoric age. Stories and valuable information could even be learned and transmitted verbally from person to person and generation to generation. Everything from myths and epic poems to practical ideas such as how to skin a bear could be spread across the world and remembered through the years like this. But the story was only as reliable as the teller. For all kinds of reasons, stories passed on verbally would shift, getting further from the original like the famous game of Chinese whispers.[122]

Writing changed all that. It preserved the original message exactly as it was expressed. That was vital for legal agreements, laws and government decrees, and meant that nobody could argue about what was said and what wasn't (in theory!).

---

[122] There's an apocryphal example of the errors that can creep in from the First World War, when the message was passed down the trench: 'Send reinforcements; we're going to advance,' which reached the far end as: 'Send three and four pence; we're going to a dance.'

More significantly, stories and information could be read by anyone at any time – whether it was the next day in the next street, or far away and many years later (as long as the writing was preserved). That meant that you didn't have to be face-to-face to give someone a message. You didn't even have to be living in the same era. In other words, writing allowed accurate communication at a distance.

It also meant that a store of stories, ideas and information could be accumulated over time, so that each generation built on the learning of those that had gone before. Instead of continuously fragmenting and becoming corrupted over time, information could become increasingly ordered, increasingly reliable, as each generation added its own contribution. Without this, the great storehouse of ideas bequeathed to us by history would have been largely lost. The thousands of years of progress in science and other areas would have been much, much slower if not impossible. And we'd never have the wonderful treasury of literature from Shakespeare and Tolstoy to *Alice in Wonderland* and Harry Potter.

The creation of writing was an astoundingly powerful, world-changing event. Yet it is something we take a little for granted. We learn it, slowly, when we are so young that the memory of our struggle with words and sounds is soon forgotten. As adults we rarely stop to think of the incredible mental process which turns thoughts in our head instantly into letters on a page or on screen. And we read those letters then, mostly, translate them into ideas almost as fast as the eye can scan them. It's probably the most astonishing of all common feats of the human brain. Yet it didn't evolve; we weren't born with this skill. It had to be invented in the first place, and every human being has to learn it afresh when he or she enters the world. Remarkably, most do.

The origins of writing are shrouded in mystery. The oldest proper writing was traditionally thought to be the cuneiform of Mesopotamia, the wedge-shaped marks on clay, dating from around 3000 BC. But in the last few decades, other scholars have been putting the case for other scripts.

Some argue that Egyptian hieroglyphs came before cunei-form, for instance, while Chinese scholars put the case for the first writing appearing in China. Then, in 2009, a team from America and Pakistan used computers to analyse ancient marks on clay tablets and amulets and other artefacts found in the Indus valley in Pakistan. The language of the ancient civilisations which flourished in the Indus valley from around 3,200 to 1,700 years ago has been lost, so it is hard to interpret whether symbols found on artefacts are proper writing or just signs, such as road signs and loading marks. But computer analysis of the marks suggested that symbols recurred in particular sequences that suggest they might be letters. More controversially, Indian doctors Rha and Rajaram claimed in 1999 to have deciphered the inscription on a tablet dating from 3500 BC, as reading 'It irrigates the sacred land'. If con-firmed, this would be the oldest writing, but they were accused of faking the data.

Almost equally controversial are interpretations of mysteri-ous marks found on tablets, figurines and pottery belonging to the Vinca culture in south-east Europe. Lithuanian-American archaeologist Marija Gimbutas (1921–94) believed these marks, which date back 7,000 years or more, were a form of writing in a script which she called Old European. Finnish linguist Harald Haarman believes the Old Europeans were driven out of Europe by the invasion of Indo-Europeans (from who most people in Europe and southern Asia are now descended) and ended up on Crete where they became the Minoan civilisation. Haarman notes remarkable correspondences between 'Old European' and the mysterious Linear A script on the famous Rosetta stone.

At the moment, the consensus is still that cuneiform came first, but that could easily change. What's clear, though, is that writing didn't suddenly appear. It gradually developed over a very long time. The consensus is that the immediate precursor was marks made for trade and administration, such as the cuneiform-like marks on clay tokens found across the Middle East, which seem to be receipts for particular numbers of cattle, sheep or bags of corn. But marks and symbols date back much earlier. In 2010, for instance, palaeontologists found that certain symbols seemed to be repeated in cave paintings found across France dating from 10,000 to 40,000 years ago, such as spirals, zig-zags, arrowheads, crosses and so on. They may not be writing, but they seem to be attempts to record or communicate through particular marks.

The theory is that full-blown writing evolved through pictograms – iconic drawings of particular objects, such as a fish, a reindeer or a spear. Pictograms like these have been found in Mesopotamia and Egypt as well as the Indus valley and China. At first they were identifiable little drawings, but over time they became reduced to just a few symbolic strokes. This kind of development is clear in cuneiform.

The limitation of pictograms is that they cannot express anything but abstract ideas. That's why the discovery of the 'rebus' principle was such a massive breakthrough. It seems like a child's game to us, but it was ingenious. The idea is that pictograms can be combined for their sounds alone to make other words. Thus, in an English system, the pictogram for 'bee' might be put next to the symbol for '4' to create the word 'before'. The Egyptian spelling of the name of the pharaoh Ramesses, for instance, begins with the sign for 'sun', Ra. Similar correspondences can be seen in cuneiform.

In time, these rebuses probably developed into entirely phonetic symbols – that is, letters with a particular sound from which any word at all can be built up. Egyptian hieroglyphs and Chinese characters are a mixture of pictograms and phonetic symbols. But in Europe and the Middle East, at some time around the second millennium BC, the pictograms were abandoned altogether when it was discovered that every known word, and any that could be invented, could be built up just from a simple 'alphabet' of phonetic symbols, with the key addition of sounds for vowels as well as consonants. There is an argument that this was an even more radical breakthrough than the rebus principle, and maybe it was one of the key factors that allowed cultures in the Middle East and the West to overtake China, which had once seemed so advanced.

It's well known how the Western alphabet was inherited from the Greeks, with even the name coming from the first two letters of the Greek alphabet, alpha and beta. But just how the Greek alphabet evolved is a mystery. There are alphabetic signs in later Egyptian hieroglyphs and in later cuneiform, but there is a suggestion that it was traders such as the Phoenicians who may have found it a convenient shorthand way to write down the Babel of languages they encountered as they moved around the Mediterranean. Pictograms and rebuses only work in one language – alphabets can build up a word in any language, letter by letter.

However it came about, the alphabet unleashed the power of writing by allowing the writer to construct and even coin anew any conceivable word. Indeed, it is quite possible that the scope of the alphabet allowed writers and scholars to think in new abstract ways as well. It would have been hard to develop a complex, abstract idea through conversation alone. Writing opened the way for really elaborate, and rigorous, trains of thought to develop. Indeed, it may have been the key factor behind the astonishing flowering of thought in Ancient Greece. Either way, the Greeks certainly took advantage of it, and scholars such as Socrates, Plato and Aristotle showed just what you could do with writing to move human thought on to another plane entirely – and we still have their written words to prove it.

Writing is now so integral to our lives that it is impossible to imagine life without it. Whether it's used for brief text messages to friends or great literary masterpieces, cooking instructions or scientific treatises, it is absolutely indispensable. And you have that in writing ...

#1 The Internet

No technology has ever had such a profound and instant impact on so many people as the internet. Some 2 billion people, a third of the world's population, already use the internet, and the numbers are growing every day. More significantly, perhaps, the number of hours that people spend online is growing, so that the internet is filling a huge proportion of our waking lives.

It's all been so rapid that it's hard to assess just how it will change the world, but there's no doubting the excitement of people who say it's the most significant development in human communication since the invention of writing. Some say it will change the way people interact forever, as they meet, communicate and even live in virtual worlds. Others say that it is altering our brains, as the constant clicking and stimulus of new information prevents the laying down of long-term memories and keeps the brain in a constant state of agitation.

It's opened up a cornucopia of information, of course, yet its sprawling, untamed nature means that the information is not always easy to find. Nor are there the same checks on the authority and accuracy of material that you might find in traditionally published works and books. But the sheer quantity and range of data dwarfs any library that has ever been seen in the world by a long way, and it is there pretty much instantly in your home or office, night and day. The internet has democratised information. It's not that the information wasn't available before, but the time it took to access it, perhaps by going to specialist libraries, limited much of it to the privileged few.

What's more, although there is plenty of material that's now quite old, much is being updated continuously. Information of all kinds, from the latest research on distant galaxies to changes in local bus times, can be spread instantly to everyone who is interested, right round the world. This kind of immediacy is both exciting and frightening.

The internet is not just about information, however. By far the majority of traffic, in terms of bits of data, is the uploading and downloading of media – films, TV programmes, music and so on. It doesn't necessarily involve a lot of people but these media are so data-heavy that they create a lot of traffic. This kind of use of the internet is growing by the day. The internet has made a staggering range of entertainment available freely on demand.

Yet some people feel that its most significant impact of all has been on the way people communicate. In 2009, more than half a billion people, for instance, communicated by Skype, allowing friends and relatives half a world apart to see and talk to each other so casually and so easily that the distance between them melts. In July 2010, half a billion people, too, were using the social networking site Facebook. That was twice as many as in 2009.

The proliferation of such sites and other ways of communicating online, such as chat rooms and online gaming forums, has made some people suggest in doom-laden tones that the whole basis of human interaction is being altered by the internet. People are forming numerous virtual 'fantasy' friendships online, the argument goes, and becoming less able to form real relationships. This is probably a misplaced fear, and may actually prove no more harmful than the escapism of reading books.

It's all very far removed from the origins of the internet, which emerged from the era of Cold War fear. Back in the 1960s, the US military depended heavily on its computer network to provide advance warning and response to nuclear attacks. The worry was how to ensure the network kept working in the event of a pre-emptive nuclear strike by the Russians. The answer was to cross-connect the computers with a series of links called the Advanced Research Projects Agency Network, or Arpanet. Arpanet split data travelling between computers into 'packets' which could be directed by a router to particular computers. If any part of the network was damaged, the router could redirect the packets to undamaged parts.

Packet switching created a fast network, and as universities and other organisations joined Arpanet, people realised what an effective way it was of swapping information. Eventually, the US military disconnected itself from the network, leaving it open for a huge number of organisations around the world to join in. As it went international, it became known as the internet.

At the end of the 1980s, the internet was well established, but it was for specialists only. And there were so many different computers and kinds of data that access was effectively limited to a few terminals, severely limiting the potential for data exchange. Then, in 1990, Tim Berners-Lee, a scientist at CERN, came up with the idea of the World Wide Web. This was the breakthrough the internet needed to really go global.

At the heart of the web are its sites, the places where computers connected to the internet put the data that others are meant to see, divided into electronic pages. Usually this is uploaded to a server, a junction computer linked into many other users. For home users, the server is typically provided by their Internet Service Provider or ISP; large business users often have their own. This separation between the web pages and the computer means that other computer users do not have direct access to the data on your computer.

To avoid problems with different formats and computers, all web pages are translated into a standard form or 'protocol'. Originally, when the web carried just text, this was called HyperText Transfer Protocol, which is why most website addresses begin with the letters 'http'. Now, however, all kinds of media are exchanged across the web, including video and sound, and hypertext is just one of a range of hypermedia links or hyperlinks.

What was amazing about this system is that it meant anybody could access information on any open website anywhere in the world without any specialist knowledge. The only problem was finding the page you wanted, which was solved by computer programmes called browsers which searched the net for particular pieces of data.[123]

---

[123] Back in 2004, two young American journalists made a spoof *Twilight Zone*-style documentary in which they imagined the world's internet and media entirely in the hands of the sinister Googlezon corporation, an amalgamation of Google and Amazon. People smiled at the time, but could it have been disturbingly prescient? Google seems harmless. You just type a word or two into the search box and up pops a list of relevant websites. Nothing could be simpler – it's so simple that people do it 70–80 billion times a month. That's the number of searches conducted using Google – over two-thirds of all web searches. Yahoo!, by contrast, carries a paltry 9 billion.

For the average internet user, Google delivers, and its friendly cartoons and famous motto, 'Don't Be Evil', portray it as a friend that you can trust. But just how does it work? The secret to Google's success is ranking. In other words, it decides the sites most relevant to your search by ranking them. Just how Google ranks them is a secret, but people like using Google because it works amazingly well. It depends not only on the appearance of

The coming of the World Wide Web coincided with the introduction of inexpensive personal computers for the home and the office, and the combination initiated a growth of the internet more explosive than even its most ardent advocates could have foreseen. By the end of 2009, there were almost quarter of a billion separate websites, each with numerous pages, and a million new ones are being added each week. Moreover, the growth is accelerating.

All kinds of things are now predicted for the internet, some sane, some merely fanciful. One of the more down-to-earth is the airily named 'cloud computing'. Cloud computing could make personal computers a thing of the past by harnessing a 'cloud' of servers linked over the internet. That way, the internet can provide all the computing power and software you ever need via a simple access device. It's like turning on the tap to get water rather than storing your own – which is why some people call it, less glamorously, 'utility' computing. IT companies are all racing to develop it and Google is among the leaders, with its own online business software, Google Apps, already widely used.

---

keywords on the site, but things such as backlinks, the number of links the site makes to other sites.

Every webpage owner wants their site to come up top on Google, and that's where problems arise. Google claims its system is entirely neutral, but if you know how to play the system, you can slew results to ensure certain sites soar up the rankings. This has massive implications for both commercial interests and for the spread of particular ideas. Search the words 'Global warming', say, and near the top you get not a neutral site explaining the facts but a pseudo-science site portraying global warming as a myth. Google also gives its advertisers advice on how to exploit ranking to ensure their ads get seen. Could this mean that those who pay most get the most exposure while others are left out in the cold?

One of the concerns about cloud computing is just how happy people are to put so much personal data online. Security on the internet is already a major issue. Some people believe the vast, ramshackle open, free-for-all nature of the net is its greatest strength. By making information freely and widely available, it's breaking down the power of hierarchies and making the world a better place, they say. Governments and global corporations find it harder to get away with cover-ups when their actions can be broadcast on the web by just a single witness. In 2009, for instance, people began to talk of a 'Twitter revolution' in Iran, as dissidents kept the world informed of developments, although in the end it seems the story turned out to be hyped (another effect of the internet, which is to blow molehills in mountains in moments).

The flow of information on the internet is a worry for some governments, sometimes for good reasons, sometimes for bad. It's well known that government organisations monitor internet traffic continuously. Indeed, the United Arab Emirates and India threatened to ban the encrypted Blackberry exchange system because their monitors couldn't read it. Their motive was concern about terrorists, but China has been accused of monitoring the internet to target dissidents and of blocking access for its people to certain information.

Some people wonder if the days of entirely open internet use are numbered, as experts raise fears about 'cyberwars' in which enemy governments or terrorists exploit the internet to cause havoc by interfering with all the systems connected to it.[124] Viruses can already cause havoc, but the potential for interference is much greater with so much of the world's everyday business, from the restocking of supermarket food stores to the running of trains, now dependent on the internet.

This is the extraordinary thing about the internet. Its power and reach have already become so great that it makes many people nervous. On the other hand, it's that very same power and reach that others find reassuring and exciting, because it connects the world as never before. With so much information and so many experiences shared, we might be able to understand each other better, and realise how interdependent we all are. Some people talk about the internet turning humanity into a single giant brain, a single organism with billions of different cells.[125] That's probably rather fanciful, but there's no doubt that the internet has got everyone thinking.

---

[124] Experts talk about cyberwars being fought by dropping 'logic bombs'. Apparently, these have already been used, well before the internet. In 1982, at the height of the Cold War, American spy satellites detected a gigantic explosion in Siberia. It turned out to be a gas pipeline which exploded because of a malfunction in the computer control system that Soviet spies had stolen from Canada. What the spies didn't know was that the CIA had tampered with the software so that it would break down after a certain time and wrongly reset the pipeline's pump and valve settings.

[125] In August 2010, Arecibo observatory astronomers announced a new pulsar star in space, discovered by the combined power of 50,000 home computers acting in concert via the internet.

The Panel

The publisher would like to acknowledge the help provided by the panel that helped to determine the world's 50 greatest ideas that formed the basis for this book. The illustrious panellists were:

Philip Ball is a freelance science writer and the author of many popular books on science and its intersections with the arts. Philip has a BA in Chemistry from the University of Oxford and a PhD in Physics from the University of Bristol.

Merryl Wyn Davies is a writer and anthropologist. She is the bestselling co-author of *Why Do People Hate America?*, and *Introducing Anthropology*.

Fern Elsdon-Baker is an expert on Darwinian evolutionary theory and head of the British Council's Darwin Now project.

Dylan Evans is an author and academic at University College Cork, Ireland. He is an expert in behavioural science and the author of numerous books including *Emotion* and *Placebo*.

Patricia Fara is the Senior Tutor of Clare College at the University of Cambridge, UK. Her latest book is *Science: A Four Thousand Year History*.

Cordelia Fine is an academic psychologist and writer at Macquarie University, Australia. She is the author of the critically acclaimed *A Mind of Its Own* and *Delusions of Gender*.

Steve Fuller is Professor of Sociology at the University of Warwick, UK. His latest book is *Science: The Art of Living*; his next book is *Socrates vs. Jesus: The Struggle for the Meaning of Life*.

Nick Groom is a Professor of English Literature at the University of Exeter (Cornwall Campus), UK, and Director of the research centre ECLIPSE.

Chris Horrocks is an author and principal lecturer in History of Art based at Kingston University in Surrey, UK.

Manjit Kumar is a scientist and bestselling writer. He was the founding editor of the *Prometheus* journal and his most recent book, *Quantum*, was shortlisted for the BBC Samuel Johnson Prize for Non-Fiction 2009.

Anthony O'Hear is Professor of Philosophy at the University of Buckingham, UK, Director of the Royal Institute of Philosophy, and Editor of the journal *Philosophy*. He is also a prolific author and journalist.

David Orrell is a renowned mathematician and bestselling author. His work has been featured in the *New Scientist*, the *Financial Times* and by the BBC. His most recent book is *Economyths*.

Nick Powdthavee is an academic at the Department of Economics at York University, UK. His specialist area of study is the economics of human happiness and he is the author of *The Happiness Equation*.

Ziauddin Sardar is a writer, broadcaster, academic and cultural critic. Described by the *Independent* as 'Britain's own Muslim polymath', he has written and lectured widely upon Islam, the sciences, literary criticism, art criticism and critical theory.

John Sutherland is Lord Northcliffe Emeritus Professor at UCL, a visiting professor at Caltech, newspaper columnist and former Chair of the Man-Booker Fiction Prize panel. He is the co-author of *Love, Sex, Death & Words: Surprising Tales from a Year in Literature*.

John Waller is an historian of science and medicine at Michigan State University, US. He is an author and expert on the history of modern medicine and life science.

Maryanne Wolf is the Director of the Centre of Reading and Language Research at TUFTS University in the US. She is an expert in the development of language and the brain and author of *Proust and the Squid: The Story and Science of the Reading Brain*.